WHEN THE WORLD CALLS

ALSO BY STANLEY MEISLER

United Nations: The First Fifty Years

Kofi Annan: A Man of Peace in a World of War

When the World Calls

The Inside Story of the Peace Corps and Its First Fifty Years

STANLEY MEISLER

Beacon Press, Boston

Beacon Press
25 Beacon Street
Boston, Massachusetts 02108-2892
www.beacon.org

Beacon Press books
are published under the auspices of
the Unitarian Universalist Association of Congregations.

14 13 12 11   8 7 6 5 4 3 2

This book is printed on acid-free paper that meets the uncoated paper ANSI/
NISO specifications for permanence as revised in 1992.

Text design by Wilsted & Taylor Publishing Services

Library of Congress Cataloging-in-Publication Data
Meisler, Stanley.
  When the world calls : the inside story of the Peace Corps and its first fifty
years / Stanley Meisler.
    p. cm.
  Includes bibliographical references and index.
  ISBN 978-0-8070-5049-1 (hbk. : alk. paper)
  1. Peace Corps (U.S.)   2. Economic assistance, American—Developing
countries. 3. United States—Foreign relations—Developing countries. I. Title.
HC60.5.M45 2010
361.6—dc22   2010033723

To Sam, Mike, Michèle, Joshua, Gabriel, and Jenaro

Contents

The Peace Corps was only an afterthought during John F. Kennedy's election campaign in 1960. But it was an afterthought that excited the imagination of thousands of college students. The enthusiasm swelled with the admonition of President Kennedy's inaugural address, "And so, my fellow Americans, ask not what your country can do for you; ask what you can do for your country." The outpouring of letters from college students was so great that Kennedy feared he could not set up the Peace Corps in time to accommodate the first wave of graduates. The Peace Corps, now celebrating its fiftieth anniversary, is surely Kennedy's most enduring legacy.

I was not there at the madcap, exciting, glorious beginning. I started my work at Peace Corps headquarters just after the election of Lyndon B. Johnson to a full term as president, a year after the assassination of President Kennedy. Accepting a job offer from the Peace Corps was not an easy decision to make. I was in the Washington bureau of the Associated Press then, and I looked on the federal government as our antagonist. The federal government hid information from the American people, and it was the job of the Washington correspondent to ferret it out. Joining the federal government was sort of like joining the enemy.

But the Peace Corps was different. It was an oasis of idealism and goodness in the vast Washington bureaucracy. Everyone, even Washington correspondents, loved the Peace Corps. The Volunteers were heroic figures. And since I had spent a year studying and traveling in Africa as a Ford Foundation fellow, I had the kind of background that might help them out. After a couple of weeks of reflection, I pushed aside my misgivings and accepted the offer to work in the evaluation division.

I soon found out how different the Peace Corps was. On my first day of work, I walked out of my office at the scheduled closing hour and noticed that no one else was leaving. So I slipped into the office of one of my colleagues, Richard Richter, the future ABC television news producer, and asked him what was going on. He laughed and explained that everyone liked to show their commitment by working well past closing time and coming in on Saturdays. Since he had already finished his work for the day, he agreed with me that it seemed pointless to hang around, and we headed to the bank of elevators. As we did so, our boss, Charles Peters, spotted us from afar. "What do you two guys think this is?" he bellowed. "The Department of Agriculture?"

I took lengthy trips, usually a month or longer, for the Peace Corps. I went to Ethiopia twice, to Cameroon twice, and once each to Tanzania, Senegal, Gambia, Ghana, India, and Iran, interviewing Volunteers about their experience and hearing their comments and complaints. In Washington, especially after Peters named me his deputy, I followed the machinations of the staff, for even an agency as unbureaucratic as the Peace Corps had its share of bureaucratic infighting.

After I left the Peace Corps and joined the Los Angeles Times, I still watched the Peace Corps, most closely when I was based in Africa. I called on Peace Corps staff and Volunteers whenever I could. Sometimes old friends on the staff treated me as if I still worked for the Peace Corps. These contacts proved vital in Ethiopia when the authoritarian regime of Emperor Haile Selassie was unraveling because of student fury—a phenomenon that was ignored by almost all Americans on the scene except for the Peace Corps Volunteers and staff. I have devoted a chapter in this book to the little-known but remarkable story of the Peace Corps in Ethiopia.

Any history of the Peace Corps must follow two threads—the work of the Volunteers overseas and the tensions of the policymaking in Washington. I have tried to move from one to another as smoothly as possible. They are, of course, interconnected. The incessant campaign to increase the size of the Peace Corps in the early days, for example, sometimes led to fraternity-like clusters of Volunteers in the main cities.

I have also tried to be selective. Any attempt at an exhaustive history would bog down and become meaningless. By September 30, 2009, the end of the 2009 fiscal year, a total of 198,809 Volunteers had served in 139 countries. The varieties of the interplay of lives and experiences are enormous. The ups and downs in Washington have also been too numerous to understand easily. During the first fifty years of the Peace Corps, there have been nine U.S. presidents and eighteen Peace Corps directors. The Washington part of my narrative deals mainly with those who left important imprints on the Peace Corps and on those involved in controversies that tell us a great deal about the meaning of the Peace Corps.

The Peace Corps has sometimes bent its programs to meet the whims of the White House. In the 1980s, Honduras received the largest Peace Corps program in the world as a reward for letting the United States use the country as a base for the contras attacking the Sandinista government in Nicaragua. When the Cold War ended, the Peace Corps foolishly rushed volunteers to Eastern Europe as agents of capitalism. During both the Vietnam and the Iraq wars, many volunteers wondered if they were serving overseas as the smile on the face of the imperial American tiger.

A good deal of my narrative explores this tension between the independence of the Peace Corps and the demands of U.S. foreign policy. This tension reflects a great danger, for the Peace Corps would lose its credibility and its acceptance if it lost its independence.

The Peace Corps has one great inner resource. The strength of the Peace Corps has always depended on the energy and commitment of the Volunteers. No matter how asinine the director in Washington, no matter how much the U.S. president despises the agency, no matter how faulty and lackluster the program in their countries, most volunteers have persevered, determined to do the best they can. That quality has persuaded many countries to ask for more Volunteers, year after year.

One aspect of the story astounded me as I studied the Peace Corps after so many years away: the impressive array of talent among former Volunteers. The alumni roster includes two U.S. senators, nine members of the House of Representatives, two governors, three mayors, twenty ambassadors, a host of university presidents, the board chairs of Levi Strauss and the Chicago Bears, and the founders of the Nature Company and Netflix. Novelist Paul Theroux, television news anchor Chris Matthews, and New Yorker writer George Packer are also former Volunteers. It is obvious that the United States itself has benefitted a great deal from the Peace Corps.

I have tried throughout this history to set down a narrative. I have not shied away from adding analysis to illuminate the story, but it is the story that interests me most. It has been an exciting, even astonishing, and yet sometimes combative fifty years, and I have tried to capture the narrative that fueled that mood.

CHAPTER ONE

The Challenge from JFK

Senator John F. Kennedy, now revered as a president, was not a figure of great stature when he was nominated by the Democratic Party in 1960. He was young, only forty-three, handsome, kind of dashing, brimming with energy, full of smiles, but also short of experience—perhaps, many thought, even shallow. The Democrats had made the mistake of scheduling a special session of Congress after their nominating convention. The session accomplished little, and even worse, it made obvious the fact that the Senate was dominated by the party's vice-presidential candidate, Senate Majority Leader Lyndon B. Johnson, not the party's presidential candidate. Kennedy looked like no more than a hanger-on.

While they intended to vote for him, many party liberals found Kennedy troubling. His Republican opponent, Vice President Richard M. Nixon, was a contemptible figure in their eyes, riding to the House and Senate—and even the vice presidency—on shameless campaigns that slimed his opponents as soft on communism. Nixon had to be defeated for sure, but liberals were uncertain about the man they hoped would smash Nixon down.

Kennedy's record on Senator Joseph P. McCarthy of Wisconsin was ambiguous at best. With his wild exaggerations of the numbers of communists lurking in U.S. government offices and his willful slandering of the reputations of innocent men and women, McCarthy, the self-appointed scourge of reds and pinkos, had bequeathed the vile word *McCarthyism* to the English language. But Kennedy had never denounced him.

It would have been difficult for Kennedy to do so. After all, his father, Ambassador Joseph P. Kennedy, was McCarthy's friend and financial supporter. Furthermore, his younger brother, Robert F. Kennedy, worked for the investigations subcommittee that McCarthy used for his witch hunts. McCarthy had even dated two of his sisters, Eunice and Patricia. Kennedy had angered McCarthy by voting against some of his proposed legislation, but when the Senate finally censured McCarthy in 1954 and rendered him powerless, Kennedy did not vote at all. He was in the hospital recovering from back surgery. Kennedy said later that he would have voted for censure had he been able to go to the Senate. But no such statement came from the hospital at the time. His closest aide, Ted Sorensen, concluded in his memoirs published more than a half-century later, "JFK showed no courage on that vote."

Some liberals were troubled as well by his Catholicism, although they preferred not to think so; priding themselves on being tolerant, they did not want to be identified as bigots. But the hierarchy of the Catholic Church had now become an obvious conservative force in the United States, with bishops, priests, and Catholic organizations trying to censor American cultural life. Liberals began to object, in the words of Kennedy biographer James MacGregor Burns, to "the imposition on Catholics and non-Catholics alike of Catholic standards, through legislation and economic and political pressure, on education, censorship, marriage, and divorce, on medical practices of contraception, legal abortion, and in other matters." Church leaders even tried to prevent theaters from showing Vittorio De Sica's great movie *The Bicycle Thief* because, as one priest said, it "glorifies a thief." No one thought Kennedy harbored a view so foolish and ignorant, but the influence of the hierarchy on his thinking was still a nagging question.

The election campaign erased (or at least set aside) these doubts for a majority of American voters. Kennedy took the Catholic issue head on in a remarkable speech to an assembly of Protestant ministers in Houston on September 12. "I believe in an America," he said, "where the separation of Church and State is absolute—where no Catholic prelate would tell the president (should he be a Catholic) how to act, and no Protestant minister would tell his parishioners for whom to vote—where no church or church school is granted any public funds or political preference—and where no man is denied public office merely because his religion differs from the president who might appoint him or the people who might elect him."

As the campaign intensified, voters began to realize that Kennedy was special, not an ordinary politician. He mastered the issues, memorized an array of data, and delivered his ideas with economy, clarity, and wonderful rhythm. He was self-confident, poised, energetic, and bold. He did not share all the views of Democratic leftists, but he won their admiration anyway, for he was intellectual and pragmatic, prepared to tackle problems with intelligence, not cant. His youth ceased to rankle and began instead to reinforce his promise of a dynamic presidency. Young voters in particular felt swept up in a tide of excitement for him.

The television debates, the first in U.S. history, made his particular appeal clear. Kennedy and Nixon took part in four weekly debates that ended eighteen days before the election. Much has been written about how Nixon, who regarded himself as a formidable debater, misunderstood the intensity of the television camera and came across as haggard, unshaven, and dark during the first debate. But even more important, Kennedy, who was at ease with himself and with television, established himself as a politician of wit, style, and agility, and Nixon could not match him in any of these qualities.

The differences between the two were etched during the third debate, when Kennedy was asked about a Republican demand that he apologize for a speech by former president Harry S. Truman in which Truman had warned voters, "If you vote for Nixon, you ought to go to hell." While noting that his own way of speaking differed from that of Truman, Kennedy replied with a smile, "But I really don't think there's anything that I could say to President Truman that's going to cause him, at the age of seventy-six, to change his particular speaking manner. Perhaps Mrs. Truman can, but I don't think I can."

Nixon felt compelled then to deliver some lengthy humbug. He insisted that "whoever is president is going to be a man that all the children of America will either look up to or will look down to." He noted that Truman's successor, President Dwight D. Eisenhower, had "restored dignity and decency and, frankly, good language to the conduct of the presidency of the United States." If elected president, Nixon concluded, he hoped that "whenever any mother or father talks to his child, he can look at the man in the White House and, whatever he may think of his policies, he will say, 'Well, there is a man who maintains the kind of standards personally that I would want my child to follow.'" This oration came from a man who would be exposed by tape recordings years later as one of the most foul-mouthed presidents in the history of the republic.

The third debate felt surreal, for the two candidates did not argue face to face. Instead, Kennedy spoke from a studio in New York, Nixon from a studio in Los Angeles. As Kennedy hurried from the studio to fly to Michigan, he was clearly still annoyed by a remark that his distant opponent had made. "I would remind Senator Kennedy of the past fifty years," Nixon said. "I would ask him to name one Republican president who led this nation into war. There were three Democratic presidents who led us into war." The accusation that President Woodrow Wilson "led us" into World War I, President Franklin D. Roosevelt "led us" into World War II, and President Truman "led us" into the Korean War struck Kennedy and his aides as an unseemly low blow, even for Nixon.

It is not clear why, but in the next few hours, Kennedy would surprise his staff and publicly embrace a new idea—the most novel idea of his entire campaign for the presidency. His plane arrived at Willow Run Airport in Ypsilanti shortly before two o'clock in the morning of Friday, October 14. A motorcade then took him fifteen miles to the campus of the University of Michigan in Ann Arbor. Kennedy had not planned to speak there. The schedule called for him to grab a few hours of sleep in a room at the Michigan Union building before boarding a train for a daylong whistle-stop tour through the state. There were limited votes at a college campus in any case in those days, for the U.S. Constitution had not yet been amended to lower the voting age to eighteen.

A large crowd of students, perhaps as many as ten thousand, had been waiting several hours for a chance to glimpse the handsome and dynamic candidate. Deborah Bacon, the dean of women, had lifted the 11:00 p.m. curfew for women so they could take part. Freshman Eleanor Segal and her sister Sara, who was in high school, managed to make their way to a second-story window of the Union building so they could sit on the ledge, their feet dangling, and watch the candidate below. Joel Sherman, another freshman, and some classmates climbed an old tree alongside the building and perched on a massive branch. The morning was unusually warm and dry for Michigan in October, making the long wait tolerable, even pleasant.

Kennedy could not ignore the crowd or the microphone set up in front of the doors of the Michigan Union. Sorensen told his fellow speechwriter, Richard Goodwin, "He won't just let them stand there. He's going to speak. Maybe that'll give us a chance to get something to eat. I'm starved." The two aides slipped into the student cafeteria, knowing that Kennedy would not need them while talking to the students. In just a few moments, according to Goodwin, a campaign worker rushed into the cafeteria and announced, "You know what he just did? He proposed a peace corps." That was an exaggeration.

In his talk, Kennedy had won immediate cheers of approval by introducing himself as "a graduate of the Michigan of the East, Harvard University." He said that he would take the opportunity "to say one or two words about this campaign that is coming into the last three weeks." Due to the problems pressing on the United States, he called this campaign the most important since the election of Franklin Roosevelt during the Great Depression. Then, without any warning, Kennedy issued a challenge.

"How many of you who are going to be doctors," he demanded, "are willing to spend your days in Ghana? Technicians or engineers, how many of you are willing to work in the Foreign Service and spend your lives traveling around the world? On your willingness to do that, not merely to serve one year or two years in the service, but on your willingness to contribute part of your life to this country, I think will depend the answer whether a free society can compete."

Joking that "this is the longest short speech I have ever made," Kennedy concluded by asking their support for the election campaign and "for this country over the next decade." The speech lasted barely three minutes. Before he reached his room for the night, he told his aide Dave Powers that he thought "he had hit a winning number."

Kennedy had not proposed a peace corps, but he did plant its seed in that brief encounter at the University of Michigan. A plaque on the Michigan Union building now proclaims, "Here at 2:00 a.m. on October 14, 1960, John Fitzgerald Kennedy first defined the Peace Corps." The definition, however, was rather vague and tentative. Kennedy's words, moreover, had no national impact. Russell Baker of the *New York Times,* one of America's most illustrious journalists, was among the reporters covering the Kennedy campaign. Kennedy's little speech had come too late to make the Friday edition of the *Times.* For the Saturday paper, Baker wrote a delightful, front-page piece about Kennedy's revival of old-fashioned whistle-stop campaigning. Describing the candidate's brief speeches as the train stopped in towns throughout Michigan on Friday, Baker wrote, "Mr. Kennedy, to be sure, said nothing that was new . . ."

The idea of a kind of peace corps was not original with Kennedy.

Representative Henry Reuss, a Democrat from Wisconsin, had introduced a bill earlier in the year calling for the study of a possible youth
corps. Congress approved the bill and appropriated $10,000 for the proj-
ect. Senator Hubert Humphrey of Minnesota, using the term "Peace
Corps" for the first time, introduced a bill later in the year establishing
such an agency. That bill languished, but Humphrey campaigned for a
peace corps during the presidential primaries, which he lost to Kennedy.
Kennedy had asked Goodwin to look into these proposals, and several
academicians prepared studies for the campaign. Kennedy supporters
like Gen. James Gavin included calls for a youth or peace corps in their
campaign speeches. The youth wing of the party had even distributed
a mimeographed leaflet promising that the candidate was exploring the
possibility of a youth peace corps. Businessman Milton J. Shapp lobbied
for one in a meeting with Sorensen. Later, when he campaigned successfully as the Democratic candidate for governor of Pennsylvania, Shapp
claimed he had put the idea of the Peace Corps in Kennedy's head.

But Kennedy and some of his staff, though sympathetic, were also
wary of the idea. It had the potential for ridicule. Coming from a young
candidate, it could be dismissed as the foolish and fuzzy project of a
starry-eyed amateur. Yet, as the campaign drew closer to the end, Kennedy clearly warmed to the proposal.

Harris Wofford, the future senator from Pennsylvania who worked
on the campaign, tried years later to analyze why Kennedy raised the issue during his brief speech at the university. Wofford wrote that "the best
guess anyone on the staff could give" was that Kennedy, still angered by
Nixon's insinuation during the debate that the Democrats were a war
party, wanted to counter with a Democratic peace proposal. Kennedy
may also have been troubled by rumors, later proven false, that Nixon was
contemplating a peace corps proposal of his own. In any case, Kennedy
made no proposal that night. Faced with thousands of enthusiastic young
men and women, he simply decided to test an idea.

Although it attracted no notice beyond the Michigan campus, many
students eagerly accepted the test and its challenge. The challenge came
at the right time. The 1930s had been the years of economic hardship
and leftist militancy for many young Americans. The 1940s had been the
years of war and the G.I. Bill of Rights. But the 1950s, with few serious
veterans left on campus, had been the bland years. "The message during the fifties," said Alan Guskin, a Michigan graduate student in social

psychology, "was 'Don't sign anything. Keep quiet and get your Ph.D.'" Now, as the 1960s dawned, a new mood was stirring, a need to take an active part in life outside campus, a need to enlist in causes. The new nations of Africa were in the news. Ghana, in fact, had attracted attention and admiration as the first black African colony to win independence, and Kennedy's challenge to help Ghana and other developing countries fit the new mood.

A few nights later, Representative Chester Bowles of Connecticut, a Kennedy foreign policy adviser, talked to the students in the Michigan Union ballroom. During the question-and-answer session afterwards, Bowles was asked about the Kennedy speech. To explain what Kennedy had in mind, Bowles described the work of his son and daughter-in-law, Sam and Nancy Bowles, who were teaching in the British colony of Nigeria as part of a program sponsored by a private organization, the African-American Institute.

Inspired by both Kennedy and Bowles, Guskin and his wife, Judy, a Michigan graduate student in comparative literature, sat down in a nearby restaurant after the Bowles speech and, setting their thoughts down on paper napkins, began writing a letter to the *Michigan Daily,* the student newspaper. Their letter, which was published, noted that both Kennedy and Bowles had "emphasized that disarmament and peace lie to a very great extent in our hands and requested our participation throughout the world as necessary for the realization of these goals." The Guskins then pledged, "We both hereby state that we would devote a number of years to work in countries where our help is needed."

After the letter was published, Samuel Hayes, a professor of economics who had written a paper on a possible youth corps for Kennedy, joined the Guskins in forming a committee to drum up support for a peace corps. They convened a meeting and persuaded 250 students to sign a pledge that they would volunteer. Hundreds more signed the pledge later. The word spread to other college campuses, and letters from would-be volunteers in many schools began to reach the mailboxes of Democratic headquarters in Washington, D.C., astounding party officials.

As letters from young people mounted and reports came in about hundreds of signatures collected at the University of Michigan, Kennedy and his aides lost their caution about a peace corps. They decided to adopt the idea as their own and make a campaign promise that Kennedy, as president, would launch a peace corps. They figured that, at the very least, that kind of dramatic proposal would enhance Kennedy's dynamic image during the last days before the election.

Sorensen, Goodwin, and Archibald Cox wrote the draft for what they called the "peace speech." Kennedy delivered it before 20,000 enthusiastic supporters at the Cow Palace in San Francisco on Wednesday, November 2, six days before election day. Although the speech was steeped in the rhetoric of the Cold War, Kennedy said, "The generation which I speak for has seen enough of warmongers. Let our great role in history be that of peacemongers."

After ridiculing Vice President Nixon for enlisting President Eisenhower to campaign alongside him [Kennedy likened Nixon to a circus elephant hanging on to the tail of another], Kennedy said he wanted to discuss "two areas where peace can be won"—disarmament and "our representations abroad." He dealt with the issue of disarmament swiftly, promising that his administration would produce enhanced research to enable U.S. disarmament negotiators to work in an informed and innovative way.

The bulk of his speech, however, was devoted to the problem of representation abroad. First, he warned that the communists were doing a far better job of training their young people to work for communism outside their own countries. "For the fact of the matter is," he said, "that out of Moscow and Peiping and Czechoslovakia and Eastern Germany are hundreds of men and women, scientists, physicists, teachers, engineers, doctors, nurses, studying in those institutes, prepared to spend their lives abroad in the service of world communism."

Against this impressive communist commitment, according to Kennedy, the United States could muster only an inept foreign service with lackluster overseas missions. The United States had chosen too many ambassadors who were "ill-equipped and ill-briefed" and whose "campaign contributions have been regarded as a substitute for experience." He insisted that "men who lack compassion for the needy here in the United States were sent abroad to represent us in countries which were marked by disease and poverty and illiteracy and ignorance . . ."

He was scathing in his accounting of the foreign service's lack of fluency in foreign languages. He said that 70 percent of the new foreign service officers could not speak any language besides English. In Athens, he said, only six of the seventy-nine Americans in the embassy spoke Greek. In Belgrade, only three of the forty-four Americans spoke Serbo-

Croatian. And no one in the New Delhi embassy could speak Hindi or any other Indian language.

After completing this litany of U.S. failure, Kennedy said, "I therefore propose that our inadequate efforts in this area be supplemented by a peace corps of talented young men and women, willing and able to serve their country in this fashion for three years as an alternative or as a supplement to peacetime selective service, well-qualified through rigorous standards, well-trained in the languages, skills, and customs they will need to know." He said that these workers would be directed and paid by the U.S. foreign aid agencies. Summing up the proposal, he said, "We cannot discontinue training as soldiers of war, but we also want them to be ambassadors of peace."

Unlike his remarks in Michigan, this speech attracted nationwide notice. The double-decker headline on the front page of the *New York Times* proclaimed, "Kennedy Favors U.S. 'Peace Corps' to Work Abroad; Calls for Volunteer Service as Alternative to Draft—Taunts Nixon on Coast."

The speech, of course, drew barbs from Nixon. He denounced the proposed Peace Corps as "a cult of escapism" and "a haven for draft dodgers." But it was impossible to dampen the youthful fervor for the new idea.

On the Sunday after the San Francisco speech, two days before the election, a convoy of cars with University of Michigan students drove the sixty miles from Ann Arbor to the Toledo, Ohio, airport to meet Senator Kennedy in the midst of a hectic campaign swing. The meeting had been arranged by Mildred Jeffrey, a Michigan Democratic Party committeewoman whose daughter, a student at Michigan, had kept her informed about all the signing on campus. The Guskins presented their statement, with eight hundred signatures, to a pleased Kennedy.

"Are you really serious about the Peace Corps?" Alan Guskin asked the candidate.

"Until Tuesday, we'll worry about this nation," Kennedy joked. "After Tuesday, the world."

After Kennedy left to speak in Toledo, the Guskins joined Sorensen and Goodwin in the airport coffee shop. "Is this the first platoon of the Peace Corps?" Sorensen asked with a smile. In fact, within a year, the Guskins would be Peace Corps Volunteers assigned to Thailand.

The Kennedy campaign team was in a confident mood as Election

Day approached—more confident, in fact, than they should have been. Although the polls promised a substantial victory, the margins, as it turned out, were inflated. Kennedy did defeat Nixon to become the thirty-fifth U.S. president, by a margin of 303 to 219 electoral votes; but in the popular vote, Kennedy led by fewer than 200,000 votes out of a total of more than 68 million cast. A few shifts of sentiment could have completely reversed the results.

A few years later, in his biography of Kennedy, Sorensen described the 1960 campaign as devoid of any "clear-cut, decisive issue." "Kennedy did not attempt to create any single specific issue," Sorensen wrote. "Instead, he jammed his speeches with a whole series of facts and figures to express his dissatisfaction with standing still, his contention that America could do better." In fact, Sorensen said, Kennedy made only one new proposal during the entire campaign: the creation of the Peace Corps.

This uniqueness makes it easy to exaggerate the importance of the Peace Corps, both to the campaign and to Kennedy himself. In a news analysis published by the *New York Times* on the Sunday after the election, reporter Peter Kihss listed the four foreign policy campaign pledges that President-elect Kennedy "considers . . . the most important." They were a nuclear test ban treaty, the evacuation of Nationalist Chinese troops from the islands of Quemoy and Matsu, the unleashing of anti-Castro Cuban exiles, and a Middle East peace conference. The Peace Corps was listed in the story but was not included among the most important promises.

In Theodore H. White's *The Making of the President 1960,* long regarded as the model for a narrative of a presidential campaign, the account of the closing weeks of Kennedy's election campaign does not include any mention at all of the impromptu challenge to the students at the University of Michigan, the peace speech at the Cow Palace in San Francisco, or any call for a Peace Corps. White obviously did not regard the idea of the Peace Corps as a significant vote-getter.

The Kennedy proposal, in any case, was only lightly sketched. The few details suggested that Kennedy envisioned a junior U.S. government corps of foreign aid workers, smarter and better trained than their seniors but still taking orders from them. If the Peace Corps had started out that way, it probably would not have endured. Someone else, as we will see in the next chapter, was needed to create the Peace Corps in the guise that we know it.

Yet there would not have been a Peace Corps at all had Kennedy not taken hold of the idea and challenged many thousands of young people anxious to make their lives useful and meaningful. Many came forward simply because he called them. This was even more true after he delivered those famous lines in his inaugural address that still serve as a mantra for the Peace Corps, "And so, my fellow Americans, ask not what your country can do for you; ask what you can do for your country." For many years, even after he was assassinated, the Peace Corps Volunteers were known in some Latin American countries as *los hijos de Kennedy*—"the Children of Kennedy." It may sound somewhat corny, but it was an apt description.

CHAPTER TWO

Sarge's Peace Corps

R. Sargent Shriver, the first director of the Peace Corps, was a brother-in-law of the new president. The Kennedys prided themselves on their closeness and their hierarchy, however, and in-laws had no rights to the highest rung of family power. On vital family matters, such as the election of a Kennedy, assignments came down from on high, and Shriver carried them out with great enthusiasm and competence.

Shriver was handsome, gregarious, smart, thoughtful, and full of curiosity, but not full of himself, and the Kennedys did not always know what to make of him. Shriver's embrace of liberal causes and his work as head of the Chicago Interracial Council led some Kennedys to joke he was the House Communist. Bobby Kennedy liked calling him a Boy Scout.

The family made it clear that Shriver's own ambitions were secondary. Perhaps unrealistically, he had once harbored hopes of running for the Democratic nomination for governor of Illinois in 1960. But when the family patriarch, Ambassador Joseph Kennedy, heard a rumor about this in 1959, he told Shriver, "Under no circumstances are you to run for governor next year." 1960 was going to be Jack Kennedy's year, and everyone in the family, including Shriver, was obligated to work for Jack's election as president.

The Kennedys were descended from an impoverished Irish Catholic farmer who had sailed for the United States and settled in Boston after the potato crop failed in 1848. Shriver's American roots were deeper.

The first Shriver family, German Protestants known as the Schreibers then, had arrived in the New World long before the American

Revolution. The Shrivers, working as tanners in the German-speaking region of southern Pennsylvania, soon moved to the Catholic colony of Maryland and converted to Catholicism early in the nineteenth century. By now, Shriver regarded himself as part of the Maryland Catholic aristocracy. "We're nicer than the Kennedys," Shriver's mother once told *Time* magazine. "We've been here since the 1600s. We're rooted in the land in Maryland."

Shriver was adamant about his religious observance, and this piety must have reinforced his Boy Scout image among the Kennedys. His moral strictures were so strong that he threw up when a girlfriend, whom he intended to marry, confessed that she had once slept with a suitor. The Kennedy brothers were bemused by his long, frustrating courtship of their sister Eunice. It took five years before the reluctant Eunice agreed to marry Shriver, and, according to biographer Scott Stossel, he was still a virgin on his wedding day at the age of 37. That kind of morality was dissonant from the lifestyle of the Kennedys. After all, Ambassador Kennedy and his son, the president, were notorious womanizers.

Shriver owed his livelihood, and perhaps his marriage, to the elder Kennedy. The fortune of Joseph P. Kennedy, known as one of the wealthiest and ruthless men in the United States, was grounded in banking, Wall Street, Hollywood, the liquor industry, and real estate. He had achieved more celebrity by serving President Franklin D. Roosevelt as chairman of the Securities and Exchange Commission and ambassador to Britain. When Shriver started dating Eunice, the ambassador showed more enthusiasm than his daughter and offered the young man a job.

Shriver did not grow up in poverty, but his father's investment company was bankrupted by the Depression. His father then supported the family on low-level, poor-paying Wall Street positions. Sarge managed to work his way through Yale on a scholarship and odd jobs and went on to Yale Law School only when the father of a friend decided to pay the tuition. After combat duty as a naval officer in the Pacific during World War II, he found himself dissatisfied by work in a law office and then worked as an assistant to the editor of *Newsweek* magazine. When his future father-in-law offered him a job, he asked the advice of a *Newsweek* editor, Raymond Moley, who had been one of Roosevelt's closest counselors in the early days of the New Deal. "Don't go anywhere near the bastard," Moley told him. ". . . He'll eat you alive." Despite the advice, Shriver accepted the job.

Ambassador Kennedy assigned Shriver to help manage the Merchandise Mart in Chicago. The building, one of the largest in the world, sorely needed high-paying tenants. Using his persuasive charm, the young and energetic Shriver succeeded in attracting a host of well-known clients such as NBC and Eastern Air Lines into the building. The Mart became one of the most lucrative sources of the Kennedy family fortune. Shriver was soon regarded as an obvious favorite of the ambassador, and when Eunice agreed to marry him, it may have been as much because of her father's pressure as Shriver's entreaties.

Bobby Kennedy, who did not have a high regard for his brother-in-law, had to find a role for him in the successful campaign. Shriver was an effective salesman, a president of the Chicago School Board, a civil-rights enthusiast, and an active socialite, yet Bobby perceived him as little more than a dilettante. "Bobby always spat on Sarge," Charles Peters, who worked with the campaign and later with the Peace Corps, told biographer Stossel. "His people considered Sarge weak, a nonplayer." Bobby put Shriver in charge of generating ideas about civil rights and urban affairs and of setting up farmers', businessmen's, and professional organizations for Kennedy—in short, all the Boy Scout stuff that the Kennedys did not regard as vital.

Yet Shriver took part in one of the most vital moments of the campaign. His civil-rights coordinator, Harris Wofford, a young Notre Dame law professor, received a panic-stricken phone call from Coretta King one night two weeks before the election. Her husband, Martin Luther King Jr., had been sentenced to serve six months in jail on the ridiculous charge of driving in Georgia with an Alabama driver's license. "They are going to kill him, I know they are going to kill him," a sobbing Mrs. King told Wofford.

Wofford, a friend of the Kings, thought it would help Coretta if Jack Kennedy took a few minutes to phone and offer his sympathy and concern. Wofford knew that the Kennedys, out of fear of losing several southern states, did not want Jack to ally himself publicly with King, but a demonstration of kindness to King's pregnant wife would surely not hurt Kennedy. In fact, Wofford was sure, a symbolic act like that would swell the black vote for Kennedy.

Wofford failed to reach anyone in the Kennedy entourage that night but finally phoned Shriver in Chicago the next morning. When Shriver heard Wofford's idea, he did not hesitate. "Jack doesn't leave O'Hare for another forty minutes," he told Wofford. "I'm going to get it to him. Give me her number and get me out of jail if I'm arrested for speeding."

When Shriver reached Kennedy's room at the O'Hare International Inn, he found the nominee with Ted Sorensen, press secretary Pierre Salinger, and aide Kenneth O'Donnell. He was sure the three would rail against the idea, so he kept it to himself. But he got his chance when Sorensen soon left to work on a speech, Salinger rushed off to meet reporters, and O'Donnell went into the bathroom.

"Why don't you telephone Mrs. King and give her your sympathy?" Shriver asked his brother-in-law. "Negroes don't expect everything will change tomorrow, no matter who's elected. But they do want to know whether you care. If you telephone Mrs. King, they will know you understand and will help. You will reach their hearts and give support to a pregnant woman who is afraid her husband will be killed."

"That's a good idea," said Kennedy. "Why not? Do you have her number? Get her on the phone."

According to a grateful Mrs. King, Kennedy then told her, "I want to express to you my concern about your husband. I know this must be very hard for you. I understand you are expecting a baby, and I just wanted you to know that I was thinking about you and Dr. King. If there is anything I can do to help, please feel free to call on me."

When Bobby Kennedy found out about the call, he was furious. At campaign headquarters in Washington, he chastised both Shriver and Wofford, shouting, "Do you know that three southern governors told us that if Jack supported Jimmy Hoffa, Nikita Khrushchev, or Martin Luther King, they would throw their states to Nixon? Do you know that this election may be razor close and you have probably lost it for us?"

Yet Bobby made a surprising and injudicious phone call to the Georgia judge, urging him to let King go. Feeling mounting pressure from others as well, including prominent Georgia officials, the judge released King the next day. After his release, King told reporters, "I am deeply indebted to Senator Kennedy, who served as a great force in making my release possible. For him to be that courageous shows that he is really acting upon principle and not expediency."

King's father, an influential Atlanta pastor who had supported Nixon, announced, "I had expected to vote against Senator Kennedy because of his religion. But now he can be my president, Catholic or whatever he is. It took courage to call my daughter-in-law at a time like this.

He has the moral courage to stand up for what is right. I've got all my votes and I've got a suitcase and I'm going to take them up there and dump them in his lap."

Shriver then arranged for the publication and distribution in black churches of more than a half-million copies of a pamphlet that told the story of the Jack Kennedy phone call and the release of King. The difference between candidates was clear. Nixon had made no symbolic gesture to the Kings. President Eisenhower, who had the authority to do even more, had done nothing as well.

It is fanciful, of course, to attribute victory in a close election to one campaign incident rather than a myriad of others. But Theodore White, noting that the black vote for Kennedy was many times his margin of victory in Illinois, Michigan, and South Carolina, wrote that "the candidate's instinctive decision [to phone Mrs. King] must be ranked among the most crucial of the last few weeks." That "instinctive decision" would not have been made if Shriver had not embraced Wofford's idea with boundless enthusiasm and then deftly figured out a way to carry it out. The ability to embrace and enact the ideas of others with wonderful verve would prove one of Shriver's most valued traits as leader of the Peace Corps.

As soon as Kennedy was elected, he entrusted Shriver with the job of chief talent scout. The president-elect wanted his brother-in-law to head a task force that would "find the most dedicated, bright, tough-minded, experienced guys in the country" to fill the cabinet and other perches of the new administration. Kennedy wanted Shriver to scour the academic, business, political, diplomatic, labor, and foundation worlds in the search for what the president-elect called "the brightest and the best." Writer David Halberstam described Shriver as a "big game hunter," as he brought in the likes of Ford Motor Company president Robert McNamara (who took the job of Secretary of Defense) and Harvard dean McGeorge Bundy (who would serve as National Security Adviser).

But there was no job for the hunter. Nothing had been offered after his discussions with the president-elect about senior positions for himself in the Justice, State, and Health, Education and Welfare departments. Sarge and Eunice returned to Chicago the day after the inauguration with vague thoughts about Illinois politics in his mind. But the new president phoned a few hours after their arrival.

At least 25,000 letters had been posted to Kennedy asking for a chance to serve in the Peace Corps. Shriver and his talent scouts had also been bombarded with inquiries about it—but, of course, it didn't exist. As a result, Kennedy wanted Shriver to head a task force creating the new Peace Corps. Shriver would joke later that Kennedy wanted him in charge because the president and his aides were sure his campaign proposal was too fanciful to get off the ground. "It would be easier to fire a relative than a friend," Shriver wryly noted.

Kennedy wanted Shriver to follow the model set down in a paper written by Professor Max Millikan of the Massachusetts Institute of Technology after the election. Millikan had proposed a pilot program of a few hundred volunteers with the milquetoast name "International Youth Service." The volunteers would work under the supervision of the U.S. foreign aid agency. His approach was cautious, experimental, and small, and Kennedy agreed with it.

"Because of the experimental nature of the program, and the limited information now available about needs," Kennedy said in a press release accompanying the Millikan report, "it should certainly be started on a small scale."

But all Shriver's public relations and sales instincts rebelled against the Millikan report. As Wofford, a member of the task force put it, the report was "contrary to every bone in Shriver's body and every cell in his brain." That kind of caution, Shriver believed, crippled America's foreign aid program. Moreover, the polls showed that 70 percent of Americans favored the creation of the Peace Corps. How could you offer them something slow, piddling, and tentative? Shriver did not even invite Millikan to the first meeting of the task force on Monday, February 6, soon after the inauguration.

Until the eve of that meeting, however, Shriver did not have a comprehensive, well-reasoned alternative to propose. But then he found a report titled "A Towering Task" among his papers in his room at the Mayflower Hotel. The report was written by Warren Wiggins, the thirty-four-year-old deputy director of Far East operations for the International Cooperation Administration (ICA; soon to be renamed the Agency for International Development, or AID), and William Josephson, a twenty-six-year-old lawyer in the agency. They took the title of the paper from a line in Kennedy's first State of the Union address. Talking about the need to expand the economy of the entire non-communist world, Kennedy had said, "The problems in achieving this goal are towering and unprecedented—the response must be towering and unprecedented as well."

According to Peace Corps lore, Shriver's excitement after reading the report led to what was known as "the midnight ride of Warren Wiggins." In a flash of drama, Shiver dispatched a telegram to Wiggins at 3:00 a.m., asking him to show up at the meeting that morning. Shriver has always maintained he sent that telegram. But in an interview more than thirty-five years later, Wiggins said he never received any telegram, but, hearing rumors about the meeting, he managed to persuade someone on Shriver's staff to let him in as a high official of the foreign aid agency. Josephson was out of town that week.

When Wiggins arrived at a conference room in the Mayflower, he was startled to see copies of the report at the place of every task force member. Shriver opened the meeting. "Now I've never met this man before this morning," he said. "But before we begin today's meeting, I want you all to read his report because it comes closest to representing what I think should happen."

"My heart was pounding," Wiggins recalled. "I thought then that I had made my connection with the new administration. That was what I wanted. I had hooked myself into the administration with that sentence by Shriver, and that is what I wanted."

Wiggins's feelings reflected the new mood in Washington. In just a few weeks, Kennedy had made young people feel that his administration, his New Frontier, would be active, smart, stylish, and caring and would sweep away the crust and creakiness of the old Eisenhower administration. Young bureaucrats such as Wiggins and Josephson wanted to take part in the changes. They had written a couple of papers, one warning that the political situation in Vietnam was deteriorating, the second proposing reforms in foreign aid, but the papers made no impact. Instead, Josephson recalled, "Everybody wanted our views about the Peace Corps." Wiggins finally persuaded Josephson that "if we were to have any input into the Kennedy Administration, we had to write about the Peace Corps, because that is what it wanted to hear from us." Wiggins and Josephson then set down their ideas about the new Peace Corps and sent the paper to their bosses, to Shriver, and to people close to him like Wofford.

What attracted Shriver the most in "A Towering Task" was Wiggins and Josephson's insistence that the Peace Corps must be large enough to make an impact on the developing world, to satisfy the aspirations of tens of thousands of young Americans, and to swell the American public's pride in the accomplishments of its government. Wiggins had worked on the Marshall Plan, and he believed that this program for European economic recovery after World War II would have failed if it had started too small to make an impact.

"In other words, it is here postulated," Wiggins and Josephson wrote, "that a 'small,' 'cautious' National Peace Corps may be worse than no Peace Corps at all. It may not receive the attention and talent it will require even for preventing trouble. A slow, cautious start may maximize the chance of failure."

The paper stressed speed as well as size. In a section evidently suggested by Josephson, the paper proposed that President Kennedy launch the Peace Corps even before it was authorized by Congress. This could be done by executive order, Josephson believed, and it would be the only way to speedily accommodate the thousands of college applicants who would graduate in a few months.

All this was exactly what Shriver wanted to hear. "Anyone who knows Shriver," said Peace Corps information officer Donovan McClure in an interview years later, "is aware that convincing him to start big wasn't the hardest sell that Wiggins would ever have to make. Indeed, if Wiggins hadn't come through with 'A Towering Task,' Shriver doubtless would have sent out for it through room service."

The paper, however, had a major flaw. Wiggins and Josephson's sense of big was, to say the least, grandiose. If "A Towering Task" had been an exercise in art criticism, it would have deemed Michelangelo's *David* a failure for not being as immense as Mount Rushmore. Wiggins and Josephson talked of sending "a few thousand" volunteers to Mexico, 5,000 to 10,000 to Nigeria, and "it is not impossible to imagine a 50,000 Peace Corps teacher force in India." The paper devoted fifteen of its thirty-one pages to a proposed model program that would send 17,000 English teachers to the Philippines over a five-year period, with no more than 5,000 serving in a single year. Even Wiggins admitted years later, "In most ways, I didn't know what the hell I was talking about."

The Wiggins-Josephson paper gave Shriver the intellectual rationale for starting boldly and for rejecting all the admonitions about the need to take only halting, experimental steps. The American public would have lost interest in an experiment comprising a few hundred volunteers. Eager young college graduates would have lost patience and enthusiasm and moved on to other pursuits. The new agency needed the acclaim and celebrity that would greet its well-publicized early missions to the Third World.

But Shriver's embrace of the paper spawned a major problem as well. All the lore about midnight rides and towering tasks encouraged the future bureaucrats of the Peace Corps to think too big. No one ever talked about 17,000 volunteers in the Philippines or 50,000 in India again. The realities of programming would soon make such figures laughable. But officials would easily fall in love with numbers, trying to make their programs bigger than anyone else's. An overzealous Peace Corps official in the field, for example, might not look too closely at a ministry's request for a hundred volunteers and then discover to his dismay, when the volunteers showed up, that there were only jobs for eighty or even fewer.

This problem was enhanced by Shriver's decision to name Wiggins director of program development and operations, and later deputy director, of the Peace Corps. During the first five years, in fact, Wiggins was surely the most influential figure in the Peace Corps aside from Shriver. Wiggins proved an able and intelligent administrator, but he never lost his love of size. Neither did Shriver.

The task force completed its report to the president in a little more than two weeks. Several members of the team contributed to the writing, with Wofford handling the final draft. Shriver pored over every line. The report laid down their vision. The Peace Corps must not be tentative and insignificant. It must be independent, not an appendage of the ICA. "This new wine should not be poured into the old ICA bottle," the report said. In a concession to universities and nongovernmental organizations, the report promised that the Peace Corps would contract these groups to run most of the programs overseas. (This concept was dropped quickly; the Peace Corps, with rare exceptions, decided to run all its overseas programs.) The president also was urged to ensure "that the Peace Corps be advanced not as an arm of the Cold War but as a contribution to the world community."

Finally, speed was of utmost importance. The report was sent to Kennedy on Friday, February 24. "If you decide to go ahead," Shriver wrote in a memo accompanying the report, "we can be in business Monday morning." Kennedy did not move that fast, but fast enough. On Wednesday, President Kennedy signed Executive Order 10924, creating the temporary agency of the Peace Corps. Although Congress did not pass legislation authorizing the permanent Peace Corps until more than six months later, the date of the executive order—March 1, 1961—is regarded as the official birthday of the Peace Corps.

Shriver sent President Kennedy a list of several leading academics who might serve as director of the Peace Corps. But the president wisely threw the list away and selected Shriver. Shriver protested and came up with excuses: the stigma of nepotism, his suitability for other jobs in the administration, his hopes for a political career in Illinois. But Kennedy rejected all these arguments, and in the end, Shriver gave in to his brother-in-law.

Sarge now led the newest agency in government, the first outpost of Kennedy's New Frontier. But what was the Peace Corps? It was a name, a concept, and little more. Shriver didn't have a building in Washington to hang the Peace Corps's shingle. He had no staff beyond his tiny task force. He had no requests from any country in the world for help. And, of course, he did not have a single Peace Corps Volunteer.

But he had his unquenchable enthusiasm, his extraordinary energy, and his good sense. "To get an agency going takes others two or more years," said Peter Braestrup, who covered the beginnings of the Peace Corps for the *New York Times*. "Shriver did it in six weeks." There was a madcap air to all the excitement and hysteria at the start, and, as Scott Stossel would point out later, it resembled a Frank Capra movie or a screwball Hollywood comedy.

One annoying doubt hung over the beginnings. Although Kennedy had immediately signed an executive order creating the Peace Corps, he had not yet agreed to accept it as an independent agency. His aides were not pleased with the image of the Peace Corps envisioned by the task force's report. When he read it, Sorensen was disappointed and told Shriver he had expected them to propose something different. Wofford ran into presidential assistant Ralph Dungan in the White House restaurant and was surprised to hear that the White House wanted the Peace Corps to serve as a component of the new Agency for International Development (AID); the Volunteers would work as junior staffers in overseas AID projects run by AID senior officers. "Not if Sarge has anything to say about it," Wofford told him.

Influential advisors, like the economist John Kenneth Galbraith, agreed with AID director Henry Labouisse that it made most sense to put all U.S. foreign assistance programs under a single umbrella and a single chief. It was difficult to argue with the logic of such a neat organizational chart. But Shriver was sure it would emasculate the Peace Corps. In a letter to Labouisse, Shriver tried a more political argument. "I believe it would be a grave political error," he wrote, "to tie the Peace Corps so closely to foreign aid as to compromise its new wide base of support." In short, the Peace Corps was too popular to let it be tarred by the unpopular foreign aid program. Shriver said that Vice President Lyndon Johnson and the leaders of Congress agreed with him.

Shriver lamented to Wofford that there were only "about twenty people in Washington who have our concept of an autonomous Peace Corps." But he believed his brother-in-law was among the twenty, and that was all that mattered. Shriver felt confident enough before the issue was settled to depart on an overseas trip to persuade presidents and prime ministers to invite Peace Corps Volunteers into their countries.

In late April, while Shriver was overseas, the White House held a meeting to decide the matter. President Kennedy was too busy with the aftermath of the Bay of Pigs fiasco to chair the session. Dungan did so instead. He rejected the arguments of Wiggins and Josephson, the Peace Corps representatives, and told them that the Peace Corps "could not be favored or given extraordinary treatment at the expense of overall government considerations." Shriver had prepared a special memorandum for Kennedy on the question, but Wiggins and Josephson were not sure Dungan had passed it on to the president. Wiggins cabled Shriver in New Delhi, "Peace Corps not repeat not to have autonomy. Dungan describes himself as acting on behalf of the President."

The cable shocked Shriver. "I can remember sitting on the bed out there, dripping with sweat—it was hotter than Hades— . . . and saying to myself, 'Oh, boy, that's the end,'" he recalled twenty years later. Shriver paced up and down the room. Then some colorful and vehement words of Lyndon Johnson echoed in his head. The vice president was chair of the Peace Corps Advisory Council and a strong advocate of independence for the agency.

"This town is full of folks who believe the only way to do something is their way," Johnson had lectured Shriver and others in a recent meeting. "That's especially true in diplomacy and things like that . . . . You put the Peace Corps into the Foreign Service and they'll put striped pants on your people when all you'll want them to have is a knapsack and a tool kit and a lot of imagination. And they'll give you a hundred and one reasons why it won't work every time you want to do something different . . . . If you want the Peace Corps to work, friends, you'll keep it away from the folks downtown who want it to be just another box in an organizational chart."

Shriver phoned Bill Moyers in Washington. The twenty-six-year-old Moyers had been a high-ranking assistant to Johnson, and the vice president had agreed with great reluctance recently to accept his resignation so he could join the Peace Corps staff. Shriver asked Moyers to persuade Johnson to make the case for independence in a private meeting with Kennedy. Johnson agreed with his usual gusto. He cornered Kennedy, linking the practical case for independence with the political admonition that it made no sense to cloak the wildly popular Peace Corps with the widely unpopular foreign aid program.

Faced with pressure from both his brother-in-law and his vice president, Kennedy gave in and overruled Dungan. The Peace Corps would be an independent agency of the federal government. The White House staff chafed at Johnson's end run past them. When Dungan passed Moyers in a hallway, he said, "Well, you sons of bitches won." Wofford called Kennedy's change of policy "the biggest early decision" in the history of the Peace Corps. Shriver proclaimed Johnson "a founding father of the Peace Corps."

The trip to solicit invitations for volunteers from Third World leaders fulfilled all Shriver's hopes. The traveling team comprised Sarge, Wofford, Franklin Williams, a lawyer who had just left the staff of the California attorney general, and Ed Bayley, a former Wisconsin newspaperman. The pace was frantic. In three weeks, they rushed to nine countries: Ghana, Nigeria, Turkey, Pakistan, Burma, Malaya (now Malaysia), Thailand, the Philippines, and Singapore. Bayley muttered more than once, "Why does Sarge insist upon running the Peace Corps as if it was the last stage of a presidential campaign?" The most important stops were in Ghana and India.

Ghana came to independence in 1957, the first black African colony to do so, and its leader, President Kwame Nkrumah, regarded himself as a prophet of pan-Africanism and a natural chieftain of emerging Africa. He also became infatuated with his own power, encouraging a worshipful atmosphere where people hailed him as Osagyefo (the Victorious Leader). Nkrumah also knew the United States well, for he was a graduate of Lincoln University in Pennsylvania, a college long regarded as the black Princeton. Williams was a classmate of Nkrumah, one reason Shriver took him on this trip.

When the team arrived in Accra, the capital of Ghana, Shriver had a rare attack of laryngitis, either from strain or a cold, and he told an airport news conference in a hoarse voice, "We've come to listen and learn." The embassy was in a nervous mood. The *Ghanian Times,* an influential newspaper, had just denounced the Peace Corps as an "agency of neo-colonialism" and an "instrument for subversion." "We reject all twaddle about its humanitarianism," the editorial said.

But Nkrumah agreed to receive Shriver and his aides, and when they met, Nkrumah, in a philosophical mood, did most of the talking. "Powerful radiation is going out from America to all the world, much of it harmful, some of it innocuous, some beneficial," he said. "Africans have to be careful and make the right distinctions, so as to refuse the bad rays and welcome the good." Citing the disastrous recent attempt by the Central Intelligence Agency to overthrow Cuban leader Fidel Castro with an invasion by Cuban exiles at the Bay of Pigs, Nkrumah said that the CIA was a dangerous ray that must be resisted.

"From what you have said, Mr. Shriver," Nkrumah went on, "the Peace Corps sounds good. We are ready to try it and will invite a small number of teachers. We could use some plumbers and electricians, too. Can you get them here by August?"

Nkrumah then elaborated. He wanted volunteers who would teach, "but not propagandize or spy or try to subvert the Ghanian system." For that reason, he suspected teachers of social science and didn't want any of them. But teachers of science, mathematics, and English were welcome. Shriver agreed to all conditions, knowing that this blessing by Nkrumah would encourage invitations from the rest of Africa.

India was an even bigger prize, for Prime Minister Jawaharlal Nehru was regarded as the leader of the non-aligned nations, the countries that refused to ally themselves with either the United States or the Soviet Union in the Cold War. John Kenneth Galbraith, the new ambassador, warned the team that it would be difficult to persuade Nehru to accept the Peace Corps.

When they met, Nehru, wearing the trademark red rose in his tunic, leaned back in his chair, displaying a fatigue that made him seem to doze off during Shriver's spiel about the Peace Corps. When Shriver finished, Nehru spoke in a languid, condescending way. "In matters of the spirit," he said, "I am sure young Americans would learn a good deal in this country and it could be an important experience for them. The government of the Punjab and the Minister for Community Development apparently want some of your volunteers, and we will be happy to receive a few of them—perhaps twenty to twenty-five. But I hope you and they will not be too disappointed if the Punjab, when they leave, is more or less the same as it was before they came."

Shriver's team members did not realize it at the time, but Nehru's words, though overstated, were prescient about some of the future problems the Peace Corps would face. What mattered far more at the time was that Nehru, despite his annoying, patronizing tone, had offered them an official invitation. Shriver was elated. With both Nkrumah and Nehru accepting volunteers, very few of the other Third World leaders would reject them.

An incredible amount of work had to be done in a very short period of time before the Peace Corps could dispatch a volunteer to Ghana, India, or anywhere else. Shriver needed talented staff, and he was continually on the prowl for anyone who seemed imaginative, different, energetic, and down to earth, and when he found such people, he lost no time hiring them. When Shriver had decided to hire Franklin Williams, for example, Williams told him he couldn't leave his job in the California Attorney General's office immediately, Shriver replied, "Yes you can" and phoned Mosk right then. "Stanley," he said, "we got to have your assistant, Williams." And he got his way.

Shriver offered Jack Hood Vaughn, who was the chief of AID operations in Senegal, Mali, and Mauritania, the job of director of Latin American operations, but then he reneged because he thought he had too many former AID officials in top Peace Corps positions already. He was afraid that he would tarnish the Peace Corps with the slow, inflexible reputation of the foreign aid program. When Wiggins heard about the withdrawal of the offer, he rushed to Shriver. Did he realize that Vaughn had boxed for many years? He had won the amateur featherweight championship of Michigan, fought professionally in Mexico under the name Johnny Hood, coached the University of Michigan boxing team, and sparred with Sugar Ray Robinson in Detroit. "My God, how did I miss that?" said Shriver. He immediately renewed the offer. Recalling the story long afterwards, Vaughn, who would succeed Shriver as director of the Peace Corps, explained, "Shriver always loved jocks."

Shriver could not resist hiring a well-known mountain climber, Robert Bates, president of the American Alpine Club, to head the Peace Corps program in Nepal. After months of flattering phone calls, he finally persuaded the renowned cardiologist Charles Houston, Bates's partner in climbing K-2 in Pakistan, to head the program in India.

Assessing the pioneer Peace Corps staff decades later, Moyers wrote,

"Not since the early days of FDR's New Deal had such a critical mass of unconventional talent descended on Washington." The work exhilarated them. "We walked to the office each morning," Charles Peters recalled, "alive with the sense that we had important business to attend to, serving a country and a president we believed in." No one was intent on making the Peace Corps his or her career. Since Shriver intended to keep the Peace Corps free of bureaucracy, he insisted that no member of the staff could remain longer than five years. This would be enshrined by Congress in its Peace Corps legislation.

Shriver and his staff moved into the Maiatico Building at 806 Connecticut Avenue, across Lafayette Park from the White House. The building had once housed the U.S. officials who managed the Marshall Plan, so it seemed like a fitting home for this new enterprise. The Peace Corps faced an enormous number of tasks in those early months.

The growing staff had to sift applications, test applicants, select potential volunteers, and reject others. Officials had to travel overseas, confer with foreign officials, and set up jobs for the volunteers. Universities had to be contracted to train volunteers. The volunteers, mostly BA graduates without any notable specialty, would need two to three months of training in language, history, culture, and the skills that they would impart to others. Staff had to move overseas to supervise the volunteers. The host governments would house volunteers, but the Peace Corps would have to rent homes for its overseas staff and their families.

The Peace Corps could not forget Congress. Legislation creating the Peace Corps had to be passed, and Congress had to confirm Shriver as director and appropriate funds for the organization. The wooing of Congress was largely left to Shriver. He was a master at this because it was difficult to resist his energy, charm, and dazzling grasp of detail. He met almost four hundred senators and representatives one by one during 1961, usually over breakfast at the Congressional Hotel. An admiring President Kennedy later called his brother-in-law "the most effective lobbyist on the Washington scene."

Some members of Congress did resist. Rep. Frances P. Bolton called the Peace Corps "a terrifying thing" because she feared Americans would go overseas "without an understanding of the places they are going and without any certain knowledge of what they are doing." Rep. H. R. Gross, echoing Richard Nixon during the campaign, denounced the Peace Corps as "a haven for draft dodgers."

This kind of rejection was echoed outside Congress by the Daughters of the American Revolution. At the 80th Continental Congress of the DAR in April 1961, the 2,500 delegates passed a resolution that warned of dire consequences once the Peace Corps Volunteers were "separated from the moral and disciplinary influences of their homeland." The DAR also fretted that the "brains and brawn" of Americans would be drained "for the benefit of backward, underdeveloped countries." CBS commentator Eric Sevareid dismissed the Peace Corps as "pure intentions supported by pure publicity."

But the idea of the Peace Corps had excited the imagination of many more Americans. The Peace Corps had become a phenomenon, the most popular new enterprise of the Kennedy administration. It was different and modern and full of style. The Peace Corps was so fashionable that the *New Yorker* devoted five cartoons to it during 1961. The magazine also ran a hilarious Thomas Meehan story about a fifty-two-year-old self-pitying advertising man who bungles a suicide and decides to join the Peace Corps instead.

Almost anything the Peace Corps did was newsworthy. The *New York Times* ran announcements of new staff appointments, no matter how low-ranking, as if they were the new chiefs of staff for the Army, Navy, Air Force, and Marine Corps. The first applicants selected for Peace Corps training were listed in the *Times* as if they were Guggenheim fellows. Hometown newspapers eagerly ran stories and photos of their native sons and daughters whenever they were accepted by the Peace Corps. The ex-journalists hired by Shriver to spread the word about the accomplishments of the budding agency had an easy time.

The atmosphere was frenetic, sometimes frantic, and enervating. The *Washington Post* published a photograph of the lights glowing in the Peace Corps building at a time late at night when all the other government buildings were dark. Everyone worked late, no matter what job they had. Alyce Ostrow, a young administrator assigned to test and select applicants, recalls leaving the building exhausted near midnight one evening and finding an exhausted Shriver in the same elevator. One member of the staff told Peter Braestrup of the *New York Times,* "Shriver mercilessly drains people. He won't take 'tomorrow' for an answer."

Shriver liked to make policy decisions after collegial meetings. "My style was to get bright, informative, creative people and then pick their brains," he said. Everyone at the meetings called him "Sarge." He met often with his senior staff and encouraged them to speak their minds and argue with each other. He had hired people who were unafraid to contradict him. He was unafraid to answer back. "The way I most like to resolve a matter in my own head is to get conflicting points of view argued in front of me," he said.

There is no doubt that the final decisions were always his. Some aides, like Wiggins, were more influential than others. But no one was an éminence grise. The Peace Corps that emerged in the summer of 1961 was Sarge's Peace Corps. The Kennedy in-law usually charged with secondary assignments had done so well he was now a national celebrity. The Peace Corps was a wonderful achievement, but it still felt a little hollow. Not a single volunteer had yet set foot in a foreign land.

CHAPTER THREE

The Pioneer Volunteers
and the Postcard

The historic first contingent of Peace Corps Volunteers—twenty-nine men and twenty-one women, all teachers—arrived in Accra, Ghana, on August 30, 1961, after a twenty-three-hour Pan Am charter flight from Washington. U.S. Ambassador Francis Russell arranged what he called a "high-level reception" of Radio Ghana reporters and Ghanian dignitaries for the first Peace Corps Volunteers to reach their host country anywhere in the world. In a cable to Washington, the ambassador had proposed that the debarking Volunteers sing a traditional Ghanian song that they had learned in training. Fortunately, the group boasted several fine singers, including Alice O'Grady, who performed in Gilbert and Sullivan's *The Mikado* on weekends in San Francisco, and the singers practiced during the flight. When the fifty young Americans descended and grouped, they began to sing "Yen Ara Asase Ni (Land of Our Birth)," a Ghanian anthem in the Twi language. The best singers carried the tune while the others mouthed the words silently. It was a public relations coup of a high order, and *Time* magazine duly reported that the singing had moved the Ghanians deeply.

But *Time* did not report some other important facts: that the Volunteers' mastery of Twi was woeful; that few of them, if any, would use much Twi again; that Twi, the sole language taught in training, was only one of the three main indigenous languages of Ghana; and that most Volunteers would live in secondary school compounds that were isolated from Ghanian communities. In many ways, the first Ghana project would prove a model Peace Corps program, but there would always be a tension between what the Volunteers did in Ghana and what the American public thought they did.

Someone in Washington had started things off on the wrong foot in June by sending telegrams inviting these applicants to a Peace Corps teaching project in "Chana." At least one Volunteer's parents fretted that the Peace Corps intended to ship their daughter off to a godless Communist country in Asia. The mistake was straightened out after some phone calls to Washington, and the Volunteers soon showed up on the campus of the University of California in Berkeley for seven weeks of training for Ghana assignments.

Few Americans knew anything about Africa in those days, but the Volunteers were fortunate to have a training faculty headed by one of the most prominent of those few, David E. Apter. The thirty-six-year-old Professor Apter, who taught political science at Berkeley, had started his studies of Ghana when it was a British colony known as the Gold Coast, and his book *The Gold Coast in Transition* was a landmark in African studies.

Apter, meeting Sargent Shriver in his Chicago apartment, refused to take the job at first. He told Shriver that the idea of the Peace Corps— "a couple of thousand callow Americans running around Africa at this moment"—appalled him. In that case, Shriver countered, how would he like to design and run the first training program for Ghana and make it a model for all Peace Corps training? Apter, feeling pushed into a corner by the ever-enthusiastic Shriver, hesitated and muttered that he wasn't sure. "That's the trouble with you professors," Shriver said. "You won't shit or get off the pot." Apter finally gave in, but he set conditions—he would choose the entire faculty, Washington must not interfere with his curriculum, he wanted a pledge of no CIA involvement. Shriver agreed to everything.

"It was the best teaching I ever did in my life," Apter said almost a half-century later. The training focused on the history, politics, sociology, anthropology, and arts of Ghana and of Africa as a whole. "When we came to Ghana," a Volunteer said months later, "we knew more about Ghana than expatriates who have been here for years."

On top of the formal classes, the trainees tried to immerse themselves in Ghanaian culture. In the evenings, they danced the popular West African high-life. And since this was long before the age of "soccer moms" and suburban soccer play, "many of us," as Volunteer John Demos put it, "tried valiantly to learn how to play soccer" in the afternoons.

The program came close to an embarrassing disaster in early August. Reports from Accra indicated that President Kwame Nkrumah had changed his mind, evidently refusing to allow the Volunteers into Ghana. It would be a rude slap in the face to Shriver and the new Peace Corps and a terrible disappointment to the trainees.

Apter and another member of the training team, the renowned sociologist St. Clair Drake, decided to phone Nkrumah. African officialdom was very informal in those days. Apter phoned the president's secretary, Joyce Giddens, and she put him right through to Nkrumah.

Confirming that he had decided to refuse the Volunteers, Nkrumah stated he had agreed only because President Kennedy's brother-in-law was so insistent. Now, he didn't like the idea of so many Americans running around Ghana. They were unnecessary, he thought.

Apter felt that Nkrumah was hesitant but not definite. "Nkrumah was like that," he recalls. "He was pulled in various directions." He was moving leftward politically and therefore reluctant to become involved in a U.S. program.

"This is really an exceptional group," Apter told Nkrumah. "I give you my word, and you know me well enough that I wouldn't do this sort of thing if it wasn't OK." Drake, an African American who knew Nkrumah for many years, then took the phone. "Well, Kwame," he said, "you're going to have to do this." Nkrumah listened to their entreaties and wearily gave in.

The Volunteers did not know about the near disaster. When training ended, they presented gifts to the training staff—cigarette lighters with the awful pun, "Here today. Ghana tomorrow." The Volunteers assembled in Washington for a day of celebration before their departure for Ghana. Shriver, whom they had not met before, could not resist a kind of locker-room pep talk as he spoke to them in the State Department auditorium. "The President is counting on you," he told them. "Foreigners think we're fat, dumb, and happy over here. They don't think we've got the stuff to make personal sacrifices for our way of life. You must show them. And if you don't, you'll be yanked out of the ball game." His excitement was both challenging and infectious.

President Kennedy met the Ghana Volunteers in the Rose Garden along with twenty-four other Volunteers heading off to Puerto Rico for three-and-a-half weeks additional training for a road-building project in Tanganyika. It was a hot, sunlit, searing Washington day, and the Volunteers were outnumbered and crowded by the reporters, photographers, television crews, and White House aides who had shown up for so significant an event.

The president talked about the pioneer Volunteers as if they were goodwill ambassadors. "There are, of course, a good many hundreds of millions of people scattered throughout the world, and you will come into contact with only a few," he said, "but the great impression of what kind of country we have and what kind of people we are will depend on their judgment in these countries of you." Kennedy urged them to impress Africans with "your commitment to freedom, to the advancement of the interests of people everywhere, to your pride in your country and its best traditions and what it stands for."

But this troubled some of the Volunteers. Robert Klein, a Volunteer who had taught at a junior high school in Harlem for five years, told Tom Wicker of the *New York Times* that they had not been trained as political missionaries. Professor Apter, Klein said, had taught the Volunteers that each would go to Ghana as an "individual with his own ideas."

The Volunteers then lined up and walked through the Oval Office to shake hands with the president and say a few words. Most were too awestruck to say anything special. They muttered hello and their home state and whether their destination was Ghana or Tanganyika. He wished each person good luck. Newell Flather of Lowell, Massachusetts, mentioned that his brother was a roommate of the president's younger brother Ted at Harvard. Flather then said, "You've been under a lot of criticism, skepticism about the Peace Corps. We're going to serve you well." When Flather recalled the remark years later, it struck him as saccharine.

W. Q. Halm, the Ghana ambassador, threw a party for the Volunteers at his residence that evening. The merriment did not calm their apprehension about heading off to Africa and uncertainty the next day. After the party and some nightclubbing, four Volunteers took a taxi to the Shrine of the Immaculate Conception and prayed.

Once in Ghana, after conquering their apprehension, the Volunteers proved effective and necessary teachers. Nkrumah had decreed an expansion of secondary school education, and the Peace Corps enabled him to keep this pledge. Without the Peace Corps, Ghana would have had to close 22 of its 145 secondary schools. Almost half the Volunteers had come to the Peace Corps with teaching experience. For the others, facing a class for the first time was a daunting experience, but armed with their backgrounds and good sense, even they did well after a short while. The Ministry of Education was so pleased that it asked the Peace Corps to increase the number of Volunteers and replace them when their tours ended. By the close of 1962, Peace Corps Volunteers made up half of all the secondary school teachers in Ghana with at least a bachelor's degree.

The Volunteers were shocked by the degree of rote memorization. The students called their way of learning "chew and pour." They chewed their notes, memorizing every fact and piece of data, and then poured them out on the examination. Memorization was a way for desperate students to cope with strange subjects taught in the foreign language of the colonialists. Rote learning gave them a sense of power over the bewildering array of facts that seemed to have no relation to their African lives. So long as their success in school depended only on their scores on standardized tests, memorization worked. Since these examinations were based strictly on the syllabus, the students did not want their teachers to wander off the subject. "Please, this is not on the syllabus," they would say.

When the headmaster of Navrongo Secondary School, in the remote north near the border with Upper Volta, discovered that Volunteer Tom Peterson of Wilmette, Illinois, was a classics scholar, he assigned him to teach ancient Greek. That subject was offered by the British-designed syllabus, but, in Tom's view, it made no sense for the students in Navrongo. Yet it soon became the most popular course at school. All a student had to do was write down the Greek words and memorize them, a perfect course for chewing and pouring.

One major pedagogical problem for the Volunteers turned out to be their American accents. The students had a difficult time following English pronounced so differently from that of British and Ghanian teachers. This was compounded by the difficulty for Americans in understanding some of the usage in Ghanian English. When students interrupted Bob Klein at Sefwi-Wiawso Secondary School to say, "Please, sir, I don't hear you," Klein raised his voice. But no matter how loudly he spoke, the students kept making the same complaint. He discovered that "to hear" meant "to understand" in Ghanian English and realized that the students simply could not understand his New York accent.

Despite their demonstrated success as teachers, the Volunteers chafed at insinuations from some Peace Corps officials that they were flawed as Peace Corps Volunteers. In the view of the Volunteers, Shriver and the officialdom around him in Washington cared more about Madison Avenue hype than about reality. In the view of some officials, too many Volunteers had fallen into the mold of the colonial teacher in Ghana. In a report to Shriver written six months after the Volunteers arrived, Charles Peters, the director of evaluation, wrote that more had to be done "to correct the conviction of several Volunteers that doing a good job in the classroom is the extent of their role as Peace Corps Volunteers."

The issue centered on an obvious question that had a complex answer: What *is* a Peace Corps Volunteer? In their early discussions, Shriver, Wofford, Wiggins, Josephson, and others had tried to define a Volunteer by setting down three goals for the new Peace Corps. These were enshrined in the Peace Corps Act that Congress passed by overwhelming votes on September 21, three weeks after the pioneer Volunteers arrived in Accra:

1. To provide Volunteers, "under conditions of hardship if necessary," to help other countries "in meeting their needs for trained manpower, particularly in meeting the basic needs of those living in the poorest areas."
2. "To help promote a better understanding of the American people on the part of the peoples served."
3. To help promote "a better understanding of other peoples on the part of the American people."

Shriver and his aides did not want the Peace Corps to be just a supplier of cheap technical help to the Third World. The Volunteers, in the view of the founders of the Peace Corps, would break the image of the so-called Ugly American. They would be far different from the aloof, isolated, and insensitive Americans that Kennedy had criticized in his San Francisco campaign speech. Peace Corps Volunteers would be a new kind of overseas American. None of this was new to the Volunteers in Ghana, of course, for they had learned about the goals during training.

But the reality of the Ghana education system impeded the last two goals. Most secondary schools were boarding schools set in compounds apart from nearby towns and villages. The Ministry of Education assigned most of the Volunteers to comfortable staff housing on the school compounds. That made it very difficult to take part in Ghanian community life outside the schools.

Some quarters, originally designed for British teachers and their families at elite schools, were so comfortable that several Volunteers told a visitor from Washington that they did not have as nice a home in the United States. Not everyone experienced that kind of comfort, however, especially in new schools in remote areas. Klein, for example, was assigned to a six-room house with light fixtures and a toilet, but no electricity or running water.

The few Volunteers who lived outside the compounds had more opportunities to involve themselves in ordinary Ghanian life. Arnold Zeitlin and his wife, Marian Frank, took advantage of all the opportunities. They taught in O'Reilly School in James Town, the oldest neighborhood of Accra, but lived elsewhere in the city. They commuted to work by crowded buses, traveled everywhere in Ghana by mammy wagon and third-class train, haggled in the markets buying Ghanian food, enjoyed high-life dancing in local bars, supported Ghanian theater, had a growing number of Ghanian friends, visited the families of friends in upcountry villages, and on one occasion, trekked fifty miles through a Ghanian forest to reach the Ivory Coast.

An unanticipated and embarrassing scene sometimes awaited the Volunteers when they arrived at the schools. Laura Damon of Buffalo faced it on her first day at Opoku Ware Secondary School in Kumasi, the capital of the Ashanti region. "I was taken to my bungalow," she recalled, "and on the porch—it was five-thirty or so, just beginning to get dark—were sitting nine African young men, all hoping that I would hire him as cook-steward. The headmaster came over to welcome me. He had already hired somebody for me. I felt that was kind of an awkward beginning."

The headmasters expected teachers to hire servants so they could devote enough time to plan lessons, grade papers, tutor students, and supervise extracurricular activities. There was a logic to this. Without laundry machines, supermarkets, freezers, and packaged meals, teachers would otherwise be consumed by the everyday tasks of washing clothes, shopping in open-air markets, and cooking over a small stove. It was a practical solution, and the Volunteers did hire servants, but still, when they were awakened by houseboys at 6:00 a.m. with early-morning tea, the scene shattered the Peace Corps image.

The Volunteers identified themselves so much as expatriate teachers that some were upset to find they would not be allowed to take the regular eight- to ten-week vacation that teachers traditionally took when schools closed for the summer. George Carter, the Peace Corps director in Ghana, announced that they would be limited to taking four weeks and would not be allowed to vacation in Europe the way British teachers did. The Volunteers would be expected to work on summer school projects in their spare time. Carter evidently sympathized with the Volunteers and felt they should be treated like all other teachers, but he had to bow to what he called Washington's "let 'em live in the trees kind of policy."

Although the Volunteers were treated warmly by their Ghanian colleagues and acquaintances, the Peace Corps was often subjected to a barrage of vituperation by government-controlled radio and newspapers. The media, following the line of the Soviet Union, would accuse the Volunteers of working for the CIA as spies. It was obvious that Nkrumah was having new misgivings about accepting the Peace Corps.

In early December 1962, the Ministry of Education informed Carter that Nkrumah wanted to expel all Volunteers teaching subjects other than science, mathematics, English, and French. Although the Ministry had requested and placed Volunteers in subjects like history, the Peace Corps could hardly protest too loudly, since Nkrumah had admonished Shriver in the beginning that social science teaching was out of bounds.

Carter managed to persuade the Ministry not to expel anyone by promising that no future Volunteers would teach forbidden subjects. But he was sure that Nkrumah was looking for some excuse to oust Volunteers from Ghana, and he warned the Volunteers to tread carefully.

Yet, despite Nkrumah's ambivalence about the Peace Corps, he feted the first contingent of teachers with a farewell party on their last night in Ghana six months later. The party was held in Flagstaff House, the presidential office and residence, and Nkrumah mixed among his guests, chatting about their secondary schools.

Shriver visited Ghana during the second year and toured some of the sites. He seemed most taken by his overnight stop at the secondary school in Asankrangwa, a village with a population of fewer than 2,000. Volunteers Frank Guido of Philadelphia and Sam Selkow of New York took him and others from Washington through the village. Everyone seemed to know the Volunteers. They stopped at the Mexico Bar for high-life music and dancing, and they visited the chief's compound, which had several pictures of John F. Kennedy on its walls. In honor of the Volunteers, the chief gave Shriver a leopard skin to take back to President Kennedy. Guido gave Shriver a monkey.

Richard Goodwin, who was part of the entourage, told some Volunteers that they were having more impact in a post like Asankrangwa than in other schools, where Volunteers were tied to the school compound. "Well, doggone it, this made us mad," recalled George Coyne of Plainfield, New Jersey, who taught at Sunyani Secondary School in western Ghana. "Here we are, all right, so we aren't going out and we aren't wearing kentes and that sort of thing, eating foo-foo and all the rest of it . . . . The real impact is on the kids that you are teaching. These are the people who will be running the country later on."

According to John Demos, a Volunteer who would later win renown in the academic world as an historian at Yale University, Shriver "showed his dismay that we were not living a mud-hut life." That attitude made the Volunteers indignant. Shriver did not mean to give the impression that he valued image more than the job, but that was how it sounded, especially to those Volunteers who did not see how they could fit the image without shirking their work. "We had a job to do here," recalled Demos, who taught at Okuapemann Secondary School in Akroponga, "and that probably meant living in our houses on the school compound. There was a conflict between the needs of our job and the PR needs of the Peace Corps in Washington."

A reporter and a photographer from *Time* magazine showed up one day at the house of Tom Livingston in Dodowa, a village of 2,500. Tom, who had taught in Itasca, Illinois, was teaching in the Ghanata secondary school in Dodowa. He slept on a straw mattress on an iron bed under a mosquito net, shaved and bathed out of a bucket, and used a metal can embedded in a wooden box as a toilet. His house had the only electricity in town, but it worked for only three to four hours, and only at night. Tom wrote his family that he felt as if he were living in a "delightful summer camp."

Tom was closer to the image that Americans back home had of a Peace Corps Volunteer than most of his colleagues, which is precisely why the *Time* team showed up. "Can we get a picture of you drawing water from the well?" the photographer asked. Tom replied that he didn't know how to draw water from a well. His cook did that job.

"Come on," the *Time* man persisted, "let's get the picture."

Tom refused. "There may be other Volunteers who have to draw their own water," he said, "but I'm not one of them."

As several hundred Volunteers travelled to countries around the world during the first weeks, Shriver, despite his perpetual optimism, fretted that something could go wrong somehow, somewhere, and crush the wonderful mood in the United States of goodwill and admiration for the brave young Americans heading into the unknown. He knew that good moods and good publicity could be ephemeral and that the Peace Corps was politically fragile. One disaster could unleash the doubters, and the new agency might not be able to withstand a well-founded attack of derision.

And a crisis did come, a little more than six weeks after the first Volunteers arrived in Ghana. It took place in the nearby West African country of Nigeria. None of the nightmares at the Peace Corps headquarters in Washington had envisioned the kind of embarrassment that erupted. It was a complete and sudden surprise.

The first Nigerian contingent of thirty-nine Volunteers, all teachers, had arrived in Lagos at the end of September and moved to the University College of Ibadan fifty miles north for a few more weeks of training before heading to their schools. Ibadan was usually described as the largest indigenous metropolis in Africa. It had become a great city on its own, not because the British colonialists had decided to create a center of administration or commerce there.

Ibadan had modern neighborhoods with European-style structures—the university college, a grand hospital named after Queen Elizabeth II, and government buildings, including a new House of Assembly, to administer the Western region of Nigeria. But what impressed a newcomer most were the teeming dirt streets crowded with men and women draped in the blue-dyed cloth favored by the Yoruba tribe, the cacophony of cries from the open-air markets, the endless jumble of shacks in cement or mud brick with corrugated iron roofs, the paucity of sidewalks, and the smelly rivulets of open sewer that seemed to course the sides of every pathway a stranger took.

None of this escaped Margery Michelmore, a Volunteer from a Boston suburb with a great deal of potential. She was twenty-three and had graduated magna cum laude from Smith College. Peters, the director of evaluation, had met her while she was training for seven weeks at Harvard, and he wrote Shriver later, "Margery was as sensitive and intelligent a Volunteer as we ever had in the Peace Corps."

On Friday evening, October 13, 1961, Margery wrote a picture postcard to her boyfriend, Robert V. Storer, a young lawyer with the National Association for the Advancement of Colored People in Cambridge. The card had a scene of life in Ibadan on one side. She tried to cram her impressions of the city into a small space on the other side:

Dear Bobbo: Don't be furious at getting a postcard. I promise a letter next time. I wanted you to see the incredible and fascinating city we were in. With all the training we had, we really were not prepared for the squalor and absolutely primitive living conditions rampant both in the city and in the bush. We had no idea what "underdeveloped" meant. It really is a revelation and after we got over the initial horrified shock, a very rewarding experience. Everyone except us lives on the streets, cooks in the streets, sells in the streets, and even goes to the bathroom in the street. Please write.

Marge

P.S. We are excessively cut off from the rest of the world.

Margery could not recall later whether she had actually put the card with a group of others that she had deposited in a mail receptacle in her dormitory. She may have dropped the card on campus, or some postal clerk may have spotted it and passed it on to a student friend. In any case, the card never left Ibadan for the Boston area. Instead, a group of University College students mimeographed hundreds of copies of the postcard, distributed them throughout the university, and rushed to rallies to denounce the Peace Corps.

Copies were left at every place in the dining halls where Volunteers usually ate. The students were furious. Nigeria had been independent for only one year, and Margery's exaggerated description of primitive conditions in Ibadan stirred all the resentments about their inferior status when the British ruled them. The Students Union, in one rally, passed resolutions by acclamation that denounced the Volunteers as "America's international spies" and their teaching program as "a scheme designed to foster neo-colonialism." The Nigerians refused to eat at the same tables with the Volunteers and barred the Volunteers from the Students Union building. Some students chanted "Yankees, go home" at the Volunteers.

A crestfallen Margery wrote a letter to the students apologizing for her "senseless letter." The Volunteers mimeographed the apology and distributed it throughout the campus. But it did not temper the furor. A group of Volunteers rushed with the bad news to the home of Murray Frank, the nearest Peace Corps official in Ibadan. Frank, the associate director of the program in Nigeria, had left training in the hands of the university faculty while he checked on schools to make sure they had openings for the Volunteer teachers. Frank still had no telephone service in his home and drove to the U.S. Information Service library in Ibadan to phone Nigeria Peace Corps director Brent Ashabranner in Lagos. Ashabranner cabled Washington. Frank and Ashabranner agreed that it was best that Margery leave Ibadan as soon as possible. Joseph Greene, the U.S. deputy ambassador, was in Ibadan that day, and he drove Margery to Lagos.

The senior staff of the Peace Corps, fraught with panic and fear, frustrated by the distance and the lack of detail, gathered at headquarters in Washington on Sunday afternoon. They feared, as Wiggins recalled, that "the Peace Corps could be thrown out at any moment. It could be the domino theory—first we're kicked out of Nigeria, then out of Ghana, and so on. Anything was possible." Then a cable from Margery reached Shriver. She felt it would be best for both her and the Peace Corps if she resigned and returned to the United States immediately. That gave the staff direction, and arrangements began to bring her back.

By Monday morning, the postcard and the protests were worldwide news. Any hopes of Shriver and his aides that the fuss might make only minimal impact in the United States were dashed when they picked up their copies of the *Washington Post* that morning. An ominous headline on the front page glared at them. "Nigeria Students Urge Deportation of American Peace Corps Members," it said.

Shriver and his aides were obviously guided by four goals during the next few days. They wanted to whisk Margery out of Nigeria, to keep her away from U.S. press and television, to paint the protesting Nigerian students as communist-inspired and, finally, to demonstrate compassion by standing behind a Volunteer who had committed an indiscretion but did not deserve the wrath falling upon her.

Timothy Adams, who had left the *San Francisco Examiner* to join the Peace Corps staff, found himself heavily involved in damage control. The son of the renowned New York columnist Franklin P. Adams, Tim was a highly respected reporter and editor of great care and integrity. Shriver, in his public statements, tried to feign great calm about the notorious postcard, but Adams, a recent addition to the Peace Corps information office, said, "There was panic in Shriver's heart. There really was. That postcard had created a cause célèbre. It was temporarily the talk of the universe. So, above all, Shriver wanted to stop the talk. To do so, he felt he had to outsmart the press—divert them—get their minds off Margery and the Peace Corps and on to something else."

Shriver decided that Margery should fly from Lagos to London and then to Bermuda, accompanied by Dick Ware, an AID official in Nigeria who was joining the Peace Corps staff. Tom Mathews, a former *San Francisco Chronicle* reporter who was now Shriver's deputy director of information, waited in Bermuda to escort Margery to the Peace Corps training camp in Puerto Rico. There, Shriver hoped, Margery would spend a good number of days or even weeks talking to Volunteers about cultural sensitivity. That would keep her out of the limelight for a while.

But Shriver's elaborate and circuitous scheme collapsed when stormy weather shut down the Bermuda airport. BOAC decided to divert its flight to Idlewild (now John F. Kennedy) airport in New York. Adams managed to make his way to Idlewild before the BOAC plane landed. So did a horde of newspaper, magazine, and television reporters and cameramen from the New York area—so many, in fact, that Adams felt sure that they must have come for something else, perhaps the arrival of a supercelebrity like Grace Kelly. But when he asked why they were there, one of the press people replied, "It's the Peace Corps girl."

When Ware and Margery alighted, Adams maneuvered them to a Customs area separated from the reporters and photographers by glass. He phoned Shriver, who told him, "Tim, I don't want the press to talk to Margery."

Tim could see the impatient press people gesturing at him. "Sarge, there's no way to avoid that," he responded. Shriver did not reply.

Adams pleaded the case. "Sarge," he said, "Margery does not have two heads. She's a very intelligent girl. She's holding up. I have every confidence that she'll handle herself well." Shriver kept silent.

"Sarge, Margery will now meet the press. Gotta run." Tim hung up.

Adams rushed outside the Customs area, stood on a chair, and announced that Margery was fatigued but would reply to questions. She would spend five minutes with newspaper and magazine reporters and five minutes with television crews. Margery told the press that she thought the whole incident was "pretty much blown up." When asked if she agreed with Shriver's insinuations that communists had orchestrated the distribution of her postcard message and the protests, she replied that she had no idea who was behind it. She acknowledged her postcard was indiscreet and said with a wan smile that she should have written, "Having wonderful time. Wish you were here." Her boyfriend, Bobbo, had come to Idlewild and was near her as she spoke.

When she finished, Adams, who accompanied Margery on a flight from Idlewild to Puerto Rico, told other Peace Corps officials to tell Sarge that "she was so great that a lot of reporters ended up muttering, 'It must have been the goddamn Nigerians.'" Margery had been bolstered by a handwritten note from President Kennedy that was delivered to her in London. "We are strongly behind you," the president wrote, "and hope you will continue to serve in the Peace Corps."

Margery did not like the Puerto Rico assignment. Making her talk to trainees about cultural sensitivity felt like punishment to her. It was an Outward Bound camp, and the director insisted that she join the trainees in all their strenuous exercises. She demanded to return to the United States, and after a couple of days, the Peace Corps complied. She was hired to work in Washington, helping to put out the first issue of an official magazine for Volunteers. The six-page issue of the *Volunteer* included a four-paragraph factual account of the postcard incident. The story was headlined, "End of a Hubbub." In a few months, Margery resigned from the Peace Corps and married her boyfriend.

The postcard incident encouraged critics of the Peace Corps and political enemies of President Kennedy to gloat and heap scorn on the most celebrated and popular achievement of his administration. Some especially mean-spirited words came from former president Dwight D. Eisenhower. Addressing a Republican rally for the losing mayoral campaign of Louis J. Lefkowitz in New York City, Eisenhower derided the Peace Corps as a "juvenile experiment," and he cited "postcard evidence" that the Volunteers "did not even know what an undeveloped country was." "If you want to take a trip to the moon," he said in mocking tones, "send a Peace Corps there. It is an undeveloped country."

But the Peace Corps had many defenders as well. Poet Carl Sandburg, visiting the White House, dismissed Eisenhower's barbed comments as "easy and careless blast." In the *New Yorker,* novelist John Updike echoed the sentiment of many Americans when he wrote that "the fellow-student who picked up the dropped card and, instead of mailing it, handed it to the local mimeographer seems guilty of a failure of gallantry. One may or may not cook in the streets, but one does not read other people's mail and then demonstrate because it is insufficiently flattering."

The postcard incident also inspired a musical, *Hot Spot,* that reached

Broadway a couple of years later. The story centered, as the *New York Times* drama critic put it, on "a Peace Corps girl with a warm heart and a knack for getting herself and her country into trouble." Since the role was played by the delightful Judy Holliday, the Peace Corps could hardly complain about the attention. In any case, the musical folded after a few weeks, one of the most disappointing flops of 1963.

Once Margery left Nigeria in 1961, there was hardly any likelihood that the Nigerian government would throw out the Peace Corps. Abubakar Tafawa Balewa, the courtly, conservative prime minister, would not offend the United States just to please protesting students and noisy tabloids. In any case, the mood was changing. In Ibadan, Aubrey Brown, a Volunteer, announced that he would eat no food at all if the Nigerian students continued to shun the Peace Corps in the dining hall. Some Nigerians brought trays of food to his room, but he refused to take them. The students finally gave in and ended their boycott. The Volunteers and Nigerians dined at the same tables as they had before the postcard. In November, Prime Minister Balewa personally welcomed several members of another group of arriving Volunteers in Lagos.

About six months later, long after the Volunteers had left the campus for their teaching assignments, I spent ten weeks at the university as a Ford Foundation Fellow. The students and young faculty members that I met, whenever we talked about the incident, were a bit sheepish about their part in all the shouting and protesting, acknowledging now that they had overreacted.

Still, the postcard left its mark on Peace Corps history. At another Rose Garden ceremony in the summer of 1962, President Kennedy said farewell to almost 300 Volunteers heading off to Ethiopia with Harris Wofford, who had decided to leave his job as the White House special assistant on civil rights to direct the first Peace Corps program in that venerable African empire. At the end of the ceremony, Kennedy said to Wofford with a big grin, "Keep in touch, but not by postcard."

A few days after Christmas 1961, a third contingent of Volunteers arrived in Nigeria. Nigerian officials handed every Volunteer a welcome kit, containing maps, pamphlets about Nigerian life, and a few picture postcards with Nigerian scenes. A Volunteer accosted Ashabranner, the Peace Corps director in Nigeria, asking, "What are they trying to do, trap me?"

More than twenty years later, Warren Wiggins described the postcard incident in almost glowing rhetoric as a vaccination against far worse publicity. "The greatest thing that could have happened to the Peace Corps in the beginning," he told the writer Coates Redmon, "was a postcard from a Volunteer mentioning that people pee in the streets in Nigeria. It was like a vaccination . . . . Never again would a major newspaper, under the worst of conditions, streamer anything negative about the Peace Corps. Since then, the Peace Corps has had rape, manslaughter, bigamy, disappearances, Volunteers going insane, meddling in local politics, being eaten by crocodiles, but never again did it get a bad play in national news. The vaccination took; we were immune."

CHAPTER FOUR

The Battle of Britain

Shortly after the creation of the Peace Corps, Associate Director William Haddad, a former reporter for the *New York Post,* persuaded Sargent Shriver to set up an evaluation division. The idea was to send "our guys" to find out about the training at the universities and in the volunteer programs overseas. "If there's something wrong," Haddad told Shriver, "we'll be the first to know and correct it before the press gets onto it and starts screaming." As Shriver explained to an historian years later, he envisioned evaluation as "getting the *Time* magazine story before *Time* magazine."

They assigned Charles Peters to head the evaluation division. Peters was a thirty-five-year-old former West Virginia state legislator who had worked hard to help Kennedy win his state's Democratic primary. Influenced by his campaign boss, Bobby Kennedy, Peters had looked on Shriver as no more than a "nice lightweight." But the idea of the Peace Corps excited him, and he asked some contacts in the administration to help him work there. Shriver, who did not want his Peace Corps to become a dumping ground for politicians who were owed favors, was reluctant at first but finally accepted Peters. Shriver soon surprised Peters about "how good he was . . . what a great leader he was," and Shriver soon learned to respect Peters as far more than a politico.

Peters and his first evaluator, David Gelman, a former *New York Post* reporter, scurried around training sites in the United States and programs in the Third World to find out how the infant Peace Corps was doing. Their main sources were the Volunteers themselves. If Volunteers had problems, they were happy to gripe to an official from Washington who stopped by and asked how things were going. It helped even more if the evaluator struck them as unbureaucratic.

Robert Klein, one of the pioneer Ghana Volunteers, obviously found something simpatico about Peters even though he had advised Klein in training to get rid of his beard. "Charlie was soft-spoken," Klein wrote, "a Southern gentleman. He was short and stocky with a chubby-cheeked face, unevenly punctuated with an off-center grin that underlined crinkly, mischievous eyes. You half expected him to take you aside to tell an off-color story."

Ghana, the first Peace Corps country, struck Peters as well run, but he and Gelman found many woeful problems elsewhere. In Pakistan, only fifteen of the fifty-nine Volunteers assigned there had real jobs. "It was painful to see the idealism of the Volunteers squandered as they sat there with nothing to do," Peters wrote. In Somalia, Gelman discovered that the program was run by a director who did not like the Volunteers. He dismissed them as crybabies, man babies, mama's boys, and pains in the ass who went around Somalia yakketing, whining, sniveling, and behaving like six-year-olds. The program itself was a mess, with its teachers in only "minimum employment." The Volunteers were so ensnared by the pleasures of the old colonial expatriate life that all twelve Volunteers in the town of Hargeisa had joined or applied for membership in the British club that excluded Somalis.

The program in the Philippines underscored the fantasies of the "Towering Task" paper that had first encouraged Shriver to envision a very large Peace Corps. Warren Wiggins and William Josephson had proposed a model program of 17,000 teachers in the Philippines during five years. But there was no shortage of teachers in the Philippines, and the first group of 123 Volunteers came to the country as "teacher aides" in the elementary schools. The job was so ill defined that every Volunteer had to work out with the Filipinos whether to serve as helper, advisor, co-teacher, or supervisor of non-classroom activities.

The officials who set up and ran these programs bristled at all the carping from Peters. They felt he exaggerated problems, misunderstood what was accomplished, and listened too much to a few complainers. There might be a few problems here and there, but in their view, the Peace Corps was off to an exhilarating start. This view was espoused most of all by Wiggins, the associate director for program development and operations, a powerful figure in the early Peace Corps.

"It got to the point," Peters told the writer Coates Redmon, "where I knew . . . they wanted me out, and the sooner the better. I was feeling harassed and scared of their hostility to the point that I'd avoid them . . . . When I saw them coming down the hall, I'd duck into the men's room or slip into someone's office. I didn't want to think about them, and I didn't want them to think about me."

The problem of Peters was discussed at meetings of Shriver with his top managers, and Haddad warned Peters in the summer of 1962, "You are an inch away from being fired." A desperate Peters then came up with a desperate defense of his work. On the eve of Shriver's departure for a tour of sites in Africa, Peters prepared a ten-page memo. On one side of each page was a summary of what his evaluation division had said about a program; on the other side was a summary of the claims by the staff running the program. He asked Shriver to look closely in each African country and judge for himself whose description was right.

Shriver took the memo with him. While on the tour, he sent cables back to the senior staff in Washington discussing both his activities in Africa and pending business at home. One cable, sent from troubled Somalia, included the line, "Tell Peters his reports are right." That simple affirmation shut down any further talk about firing Peters and established the evaluation division as a powerful force within the Peace Corps.

By then, the role of evaluation changed significantly. Peters and his evaluators were vital to the Peace Corps, but not because, as Haddad and Shriver once hoped, they could help the agency clear up a problem before *Time* magazine found out about it. With its worldwide staff, *Time* had no trouble interviewing Volunteers and finding many foul-ups. In a long cover story in July 1963, *Time* described the frustration of "teacher aides" in the Philippines, the absence of jobs in Nepal, the nurses who showed up at a medical station in Bolivia only to find out that it no longer existed, and Volunteers in Colombia whose complaints about the inertia of local bureaucracy mocked the Peace Corps's public boasts about the success of the program there.

Yet the foul-ups did not turn *Time* against the Peace Corps. "The Peace Corps, then, is a loosely ruled, badly dressed, often complaining, yet highly motivated melting pot of individualists scattered through jungle, slum, and mountain peak in some of the most backward countries of the world," the article said. "At the same time, it is probably the greatest single success the Kennedy Administration has produced."

Peters and the evaluators were vital to the Peace Corps because they gave Shriver an outside view of what was going on. The staff people who developed, ran, and supervised the Peace Corps programs overseas were in no position to offer a cold and objective description of their work. The staff, for the most part, could not admit, accept, or even see its mistakes—in fact, that is the problem of any bureaucracy. A leader needs to go outside the chain of command for a clear view of reality, and so the evaluation division became Shriver's eyes and ears.

The system worked only because of Shriver. After all, the failures and the mistakes were at heart his failures and mistakes. He had approved the projects and hired the staff. But criticism did not upset Shriver. He had become a leader of great self-confidence who wanted and needed to know if something was going haywire in one of his far-flung and isolated stations. Moreover, he did not accept the evaluations as gospel. They provided him with a useful, outside look—no more. Sometimes he agreed with a report and acted on its recommendations, sometimes not.

Shriver would scribble his reactions in the margins of the report with a ballpoint pen. In the December 1962 evaluation of the Dominican Republic operation, for example, Peters reported that the Volunteers insisted that the hours in training devoted to "American Studies, World Affairs, and Communism" were a waste of time. Peters recommended that the Peace Corps abolish the course. This did not persuade Shriver. "I disagree," he wrote. "We've also found that many Peace Corps Volunteers don't know beans about American history, Communism, etc." On the next page, Peters suggested that, at most, "Communism as it exists in the host area could be discussed instead of abstract instruction on Marxism." "Fine," Shriver responded in the margin, "that's the way it should be *plus* the theoretical."

The importance of an evaluation report depended on Shriver's reception. A large number of Peace Corps people read these reports, often one hundred pages long, but only Shriver mattered. He was the audience. As the Peace Corps grew, Peters hired mainly journalists for his staff. Shriver would take the reports home to read in the evenings, and Peters kept them lively enough for Shriver to finish before falling asleep.

The evaluations were periodic, for an evaluator visited every Peace Corps country yearly, spending around a month assessing the work. That made it a unique operation in the U.S. government; many departments and agencies have inspectors-general, but they inspect only when there are accusations of wrongdoing or other whiffs of scandal.

Both Shriver biographer Scott Stossel and Peace Corps historian

Gerard T. Rice, looking back on the early years of the Peace Corps, described Peters as "the conscience of the Peace Corps," but as far as most of those evaluated were concerned, he was little more than a common scold. In fact, the evaluations were far more positive in tone than negative, but the staff chafed under any criticism by outsiders.

The system set up a perpetual antagonism between Peters and Wiggins, whose staff developed and ran all the overseas programs. "After the Shriver cable [to tell Peters his reports were right], Wiggins became publically respectful of Evaluation," said Peters recently. "He would even praise me at times at staff meetings. But the undercurrent always was that we were the enemy, and, of course, the evaluators thought that they were the enemy." As evaluator Phil Cook once said, "Charlie thinks we're the RAF and this is the Battle of Britain."

I was fortunate enough to become part of the evaluation staff for two and a half years during the mid-1960s. By then, Peters had assembled a formidable team. Most, like myself, were journalists. The newsmen had worked for the *Saturday Evening Post*, the *New York Herald Tribune*, the *Wall Street Journal*, CBS News, the *San Francisco Examiner*, the *San Francisco News*, and the Associated Press. There were also a lawyer, a Mobil Oil political analyst, and two stylish freelance writers who worked part time. The team was augmented by former Volunteers who had returned from the early programs in Pakistan, the Philippines, Togo, and Ethiopia.

In addition, Peters called on guest evaluators from outside the Peace Corps to look at the programs overseas. Most of the guests were well-known figures such as Richard Rovere of the *New Yorker*, novelists Fletcher Knebel and Mark Harris, and California politician Alan Cranston (a future U.S. senator).

Peters and the evaluators had an obvious influence on the Peace Corps in several important ways during the early years. They exposed the slipshod nature of many training programs and forced vital improvements. Evaluators, echoing the Volunteers, hammered away at the failure of training to hone the skills needed in the work overseas and at the failure to provide adequate instruction in the local languages. Under this barrage of criticism, the Peace Corps withdrew contracts from universities that ignored languages, refused to set aside time for practice teaching and other practical training, or hired staff with little experience in the countries hosting the Volunteers. The Peace Corps, in fact, gradually took over its own training, hired former Volunteers to staff the sessions, and moved the training overseas.

There were two main programs in the early days of the Peace Corps—teaching in Africa and community development in Latin America—and the evaluators played a major role in improving both. Although there was some question about the relevance of the elite colonial education systems to Africa, the evaluators generally supported the teaching programs. They provided useful work, and Volunteers found it easy to fit into those roles. The big problem was the danger of falling into the trap of living like a colonial, especially in school compounds. For example, I found it disconcerting on my first trip overseas to lunch with a couple of Peace Corps Volunteer teachers in Cameroon and watch one of them tinkle a little bell to signal an African servant to patter in and clear the dishes. Evaluators managed to persuade the Peace Corps to break up the clusters of Volunteers in schools and to improve teaching by encouraging the Volunteers to spend time in the countryside learning about the village life that produced their students.

The evaluators were divided about the value of community development. Peters was wary of the whole idea; he wrote in his memoirs, "The community development workers tried to organize the local people to carry out self-help projects. The possibilities were revolutionary. The volunteers could empower the powerless and array the heretofore helpless *campesino* against the oligarchies who were oppressing them. The catch was that actually accomplishing all this required a volunteer who was a combination of Jesus Christ and John Kennedy, with a little bit of Tip O'Neill thrown in."

Peters concluded that the community development Volunteers, with "a few heroic exceptions," accomplished little. "The concept was so vague that few of them had a clear sense of what to do when they got out of bed in the morning," he said.

But several of his most influential evaluators, such as David Hapgood and Meridan Bennett, were enamored with the idea of community development, though they scorned the way it was carried out by the Peace Corps. In their book *Agents of Change,* Hapgood and Bennett describe how the Peace Corps dropped Volunteers into the villages of Peru with the goal of stirring the disenfranchised and exploited Indian masses, but gave them little training and support. "At best," the evaluators concluded, "10 percent of the volunteers were creative enough and persistent enough to discover for themselves the way to go about the job." They also related the success story of a Volunteer who helped form a local committee that brought a water pipe to the village of Blanquita in Colombia for the first time. Yet, because of the daunting difficulties of community development, the water pipe stopped working a year and a half after the Volunteer left.

But evaluators did not demand an end to community development. Instead, they demanded an end to the practice of Peace Corps officials assigning community development Volunteers to the hinterland of a country as if they were throwing darts at a map. Evaluators insisted on thorough advance inspection of sites, intense training, the assignment of Volunteers alongside local community development agents, extensive Volunteer study of village life, and long spells of patience. These suggestions were generally accepted.

If there was a Battle of Britain between the evaluators and the rest of the Peace Corps, it was largely over what was known as the numbers game. In this, the evaluators won many skirmishes, but they could never win the whole battle. The Peace Corps would try to repair the damage caused by sending too many Volunteers to a particular country, but the drive to expand overall would not slow down in the early years. Despite the problems, Shriver wanted rapid expansion.

Peters understood Shriver's mood. "Part of Shriver knew that a good leader had to push to the maximum for growth," said Peters recently. "He was torn. He rightly understood the principle that if you don't grow, you go downhill." Peters and the evaluators were not against expansion in principle. They were against stupid expansion, and there was a lot of it going on.

I believe the evaluators became so exercised by the numbers game because they had fallen under the sway of the Volunteers. No one attached to headquarters in Washington spent more time talking with the Volunteers. No matter how hard-bitten, street smart, and skeptical they prided themselves, the ex-journalists usually felt inspired and excited by the young Volunteers who were devoting themselves for two years, in near-total isolation, to helping poor people of an unfamiliar culture. The evaluators felt anger at officials who, in their zeal to impress Shriver with expansionist numbers, hampered the enthusiasm of Volunteers by assigning them to sites that had little work for them.

The evaluators often brightened their reports with flattering portraits of wonderful Volunteers. In his 1963 report on Nepal, for example, Kevin Delany described how Dave Towle and Bob Murphy set out from Kathmandu with a herd of two rams, three ewes, three pigs, and a bull named Sarge. Their aim was to stock an animal husbandry demonstration station for Towle in Bhojpur in eastern Nepal. "They were warned by Nepalis and Americans," wrote Delany, "that they would never make it through the rugged terrain and across the swollen rivers during the monsoon season." But they insisted they could do it.

They began by taking a truck fifty miles over a rock-strewn dirt road to the Indian border. Then they boarded a train for a five-day ride through India to Biratnagar in Nepal. The Volunteers slept with the animals in a cattle car. A truck then took them another twenty miles. That was their last passable road. Joined by a third Volunteer, John White, at this point, they set out on foot over thirty-five miles of high mountain passes that took ten days to cross.

They had to ford streams six times, but their biggest problem was crossing the wide Arun River in a large dugout canoe paddled by six men. With Sarge, the bull, lashed to the side and the rest of the animals inside, they paddled the dugout upstream, then maneuvered it into the current and allowed it to drift downstream to the landing on the other side. "Frankly, the river crossing has to be seen to be believed," Delany wrote.

A tiger menaced them on the other side, but they scared it away with rocks and shouts. A final uphill climb brought them to Bhojpur. They had covered 350 miles in twenty-two days with one loss—a ewe dead from an ear infection. "The most important part of my job is over," said the twenty-two-year-old Towle. "It was getting the animals here." The demonstration project struck Delany as a success a few months later.

In my report on Cameroon in 1966, I included a portrait of Judy Erdmann, a vivacious young woman from South Dakota who was rated poorly in training, largely because of her weakness in French. Judy was assigned to the French-speaking area of Cameroon as a teacher of high school English. "On first glance, she might seem a sure bet to end up confused and lost in her town of Bafang," I wrote. "But beneath her innocence and woeful French is a tough little girl intent on succeeding as a Peace Corps Volunteer come what may."

Judy, the only Volunteer in town, made the most of her weak French. Luckily, her headmaster insisted that teachers of English in the lower grades like Judy use no French in the classroom. She was so popular with her students that pupils in a higher grade went on strike, demanding that she teach them as well. But Judy knew her limitations. Students in the higher grades must take a uniform examination that includes translations of English material into impeccable written French. They would be at a disadvantage with Judy in charge, and she declined taking on that class.

Her troubles with French did not hinder her everyday conversations. Judy rushed along in Bafang talking with everyone as if she were fluent. When the correct French word eluded her, she threw in the English word. Even the French expatriates in town, so particular about their language, always stopped to gossip with her. Judy said that her weakness in French even helped her relationship with African women. Their French was pretty bad as well, so they didn't feel inferior talking with Judy.

Judy was eager to know Africans—sometimes too eager. Soon after she arrived in Bafang, she waved and said "Hi" to a young soldier. He quickly sent her a gift of eggs and potatoes. She found out that that was the customary first step of a marriage proposal in Bafang. She stopped waving at him.

Unlike many other Volunteers in Cameroon, Judy never left her town on weekends. She loved Bafang. She also loved teaching in her overcrowded, old, rundown classroom and was growing more active in town. She taught an extra class in English at a nearby mission school and had plans to start a town library. "It's too early to tell the kind of impact Judy will have on Bafang," I wrote. "But I don't have any doubt there will be an impact."

As evaluators battled the expansionists, we felt like advocates for Volunteers like Judy Erdmann, trying to make sure that their experience would not be diminished by bureaucrats more interested in numbers than individuals. In 1965, I evaluated the program in Ethiopia with Richard Lipez (a former Volunteer in Ethiopia and now a successful mystery novelist). The program was faltering under the weight of numbers.

The Peace Corps had 550 Volunteers in Ethiopia, including 458 teachers who made up a third of the faculty of all the secondary schools in the country. The staff kept adding teachers as if the need could never be satisfied. A batch of more than a hundred had arrived a few months before the evaluation, and a quarter of them were still underemployed. Despite this, the staff was requesting even more teachers for the future. Some schools had so many Volunteers—fourteen or more—that the Ethiopian headmasters felt that the Peace Corps was usurping their authority.

Over half the Volunteers lived in five towns. In the capital, Addis

Ababa, there were 159 Volunteers, the largest Peace Corps concentration in the world. There were more Volunteers in Addis Ababa, in fact, than in twelve of the other Peace Corps countries in Africa. The Volunteers spent almost all their leisure time with each other. They had almost no social contact with Ethiopians. To make matters worse, there was a breakdown in relations between the staff and the Volunteers. The staff had little time to visit the Volunteers because so much of their energy was devoted to drawing up expansion plans for the future.

After a month in Ethiopia, Lipez and I sat down with the Peace Corps director in his office in Addis Ababa to discuss some of the problems. We concentrated on underemployment, low Volunteer morale, poor staff-Volunteer relations, and clustering of Volunteers. But he did not seem to listen. We had scarcely finished our comments when he eagerly pulled out a fancy chart with his projections for a double-sized Peace Corps in 1968. We were exasperated.

India was an example of how a first-rate program could be weighted down by White House pressures to expand. In 1966, India had more than 700 Volunteers, the largest Peace Corps program in the world. In March, Indian prime minister Indira Gandhi visited Washington, and President Lyndon B. Johnson decided to make a dramatic gesture of help at a time of impending famine in India. He promised to ship 6 to 7 million tons of food grains to India and, in a message to Congress, proposed sending U.S. agricultural experts to India as "part of an agricultural training corps or through an expanded Peace Corps."

Warren Wiggins, by then deputy director, seized on Johnson's words. He quickly cabled Jack Hood Vaughn, Shriver's successor as director, who was at a conference in New Delhi. "I believe situation in India as dramatized by Prime Minister's visit and President's message," Wiggins wrote, "offers unique opportunity to respond in full to need for agricultural experts and corpsmen through dramatic expansion in size and emphasis PC/I [Peace Corps/India] program." He proposed sending a massive group of a thousand more agricultural Volunteers before the end of 1966.

The evaluation division felt that India could be expanded, but only if it solved its problems of inadequate program planning and site selection, a severe shortage of staff, and poor relations between Indian officials and the Volunteers. "We are afraid they [the problems] will be ignored in a dramatic White House drive to help India," an evaluation report said.

Brent Ashabranner, the careful and competent country director in India, was even more pessimistic. He protested that the Wiggins expansion would court disaster. But Ashabranner, about to leave India to take up a new post as director of all Peace Corps training, was regarded as a lame duck and ignored. Wiggins won the day.

In 1967, a team of evaluators led by Hapgood studied the result. They reported that "the Peace Corps' attempt to save India . . . seems to have failed." In all, seven hundred new Volunteers had been sent to India in six months. Wiggins had envisioned that a portion of them would be experienced specialists who would lead the others, but these experts could not be recruited. Almost all the Volunteers were generalists with a BA degree and no agricultural background. They were trained hurriedly and poorly. There was not enough staff in India to check out whether there were real jobs for them at every site. A bitter joke went around that the staff had placed the Volunteers with a Ouija board. Indian officials were fed up with Volunteers they could not use. "They don't want any more Volunteers shoved up their ass with a Ouija board," said a member of the staff.

A minority of the Volunteers managed to find some kind of work for themselves. But, as Ashabranner wrote in his memoirs, "The majority either resigned and came back to the United States or spent their two years in India with the frustration of knowing that they had not really been a help to the Indians."

The evaluators found that idle Volunteers would divert themselves with drug use, heavy drinking in public, escapist travel to areas like the beaches of Goa, and an obsession with purchasing extra things for themselves, like monkeys and big refrigerators. They also suffered more bouts of illness than other Volunteers.

One Volunteer sent a bitter letter to the Peace Corps magazine the *Volunteer* after she and her husband failed to find work for a year. "How many other Volunteers are stuck without jobs, were sent into 'unstructured' programs and told to be 'creative,' and found only emptiness?" she wrote.

In 1967, Vaughn tried to use evaluation as a weapon to destroy the excesses of a program even before it really got started. The Peace Corps was sending more than five hundred Volunteers to Micronesia, a loose grouping of ninety inhabited islands and another 2,000-odd uninhabited islands in the Pacific that was shoddily run by the U.S. Department of Interior as a U.N. trusteeship. A recruiting leaflet, titled "The Peace

Corps Goes to Paradise," called for Volunteers to take on the troubles in this Paradise—poverty, poor schools, inadequate health care.

The program, planned under Shriver, was the creation of Ross Pritchard, the director of East Asia–Pacific regional operations of the Peace Corps. Pritchard, a future university president, embraced numbers as much as Wiggins. Ashabranner wrote that Pritchard "firmly believed that the Peace Corps could not make an impact in a country without a large Volunteer presence which would form a 'critical mass' for promoting new ideas." In a memo to Shriver promoting his plans for Micronesia, Pritchard said the Peace Corps would have a chance "to play a major formative role in a revolution that would be almost completely in our hands."

Vaughn was wary of the swollen new program that he had inherited. He took the unprecedented step of asking the evaluation division to send an evaluator to Micronesia right after the first Volunteers arrived. He hoped that the evaluator would call attention to any problems before they got out of hand. In a turn of bureaucratic gamesmanship, however, he asked us not to reveal that he had ordered the evaluation.

By then, I was deputy director of the office of evaluation and was assigned by Peters, my boss, to write a letter alerting the team in Micronesia that an evaluation was imminent. I prepared a rather shameless composition for delivery to the new country director as he arrived in Micronesia. I explained blandly that, as he knew, every Peace Corps program was evaluated once a year and that Micronesia's turn will come up in a couple of weeks. I tried to make that sound routine, kind of ho-hum.

The letter had to be cleared by several officials in Washington, including Pritchard. I knew he would become enraged and would storm into Vaughn's office, rant against me for daring to evaluate a program so soon, and demand that the letter be squelched. I wondered what Pritchard would say and do when Vaughn told him that the letter made sense to him.

But Vaughn could not face up to Pritchard's anger. For the sake of bureaucratic peace, he tore up the letter and cancelled the evaluation that he himself had secretly ordered. When the program was evaluated a year later, it proved as disastrous as the hurried, massive program to turn back the famine in India. Many years later, when both of us had long left the Peace Corps, Vaughn and I were sipping drinks in a bar in Mexico City. He acknowledged, a little wistfully, that he should never have cancelled that early evaluation of Micronesia.

The biggest complaint about evaluation by Peace Corps staff overseas was that the reports were too sprightly. "This may be good journalism," said one country director about the report on his program, "but it's poor evaluation." They resented being judged by journalists and other professional writers rather than by their peers.

Tom Quimby, who was named director of African operations after serving as the Peace Corps representative or rep (as the country directors were known) in Liberia and Kenya, praised the evaluation division because "it's good to have a burr under the saddle." "But," he went on, "one of the things that bothered me was the emphasis on getting good writers to go out in the field and write highly readable reports, rather than getting good development people to go out and analyze the development problems. I thought that too much attention was being paid to getting down on paper the fine phrase that would titillate Sarge."

In 1967, the staff in India invoked an awful pun to defend their program against the latest evaluation. Alluding to the notion that evaluation reports supposedly read like pages from Henry Luce's *Time* magazine, the staff accused the evaluation division of publishing "its newsmagazine exposés of Luced prose where cuteness of expression and pre-stated conclusions take precedence over accuracy of content and objective investigation."

Peters resigned from the Peace Corps in 1968 to found a magazine called the *Washington Monthly*. His plan was to evaluate the machinations of the agencies and departments of the U.S. government just the way he had evaluated the operations of the Peace Corps. Vaughn appointed Lawrence J. O'Brien to take his place.

O'Brien, who had run unsuccessfully in 1962 as a Democratic candidate for the state senate from New York City, was a brilliant staff officer overseas, serving as deputy director in Cameroon and a director in Gabon. But he came to the evaluation division with all the attitudes of an overseas staffer. His first symbolic act was to cancel an evaluation trip by the *New Yorker* writer Calvin Trillin. He did not want reports by professional journalists. He wanted them written by people "with some interest in the technical part of development." And he wanted the evaluators, rather than acting like complete outsiders, to take part in the planning of future programming through their reports.

His ideas, very far from the Peters concept of hard-hitting, smoothly written evaluations by outsiders, were never fully tested. The Nixon administration took over in 1969, and the new director of the Peace Corps,

Joseph Blatchford, did not show much interest in evaluation reports. O'Brien resigned in August of that year. The Peace Corps maintained some kind of unit called "evaluation" for the rest of its history, but evaluation never again had the power, influence, and importance of the early years. It takes a powerful, self-confident director to put up with the continual blandishments of someone like Charlie Peters. It is much easier to listen to underlings tell you what you want to hear.

CHAPTER FIVE

Friday, November 22, 1963

In Huarocondo, 11,000 feet high in the Andes of Peru, Nancy Norton and her roommate liked to sleep in on Saturday mornings. The two schoolteachers had to wake at 6:00 a.m. on schooldays. On this Saturday, an incessant knocking on the door woke them at seven. It was a Peruvian friend, Vilma.

"Tu presidente está muerto," Vilma shouted.

"Whose president?" asked a bewildered, barely awake Nancy.

"Señor Kennedy."

After Vilma left, the two Volunteers reassured themselves that it was only a rumor, but nonetheless, they dressed and headed for the train station to buy a newspaper.

On the way, several teary-eyed teachers from the school stopped them to express sympathy. The sobbing mayor met them at the station, and the Indian women selling food there were unusually quiet. When the Cuzco train arrived, everyone rushed towards the newsboy to buy a paper. The headlines were large and very black. DEATH OF JOHN KENNEDY—THE WORLD MOURNS, they said, in Spanish. He had died the day before, eighteen hours ago. A student came over to the two Volunteers. "Señoritas," he said, "please, don't cry." But he, too, was crying.

The two Volunteers returned to their home and donned black. The townspeople came by all day to express sympathy. Several students, very subdued, sat by the Volunteers. The church bells tolled. A special mass was planned for Sunday.

"The paper said the whole world is mourning," Nancy wrote to her parents that night. "I don't know about the whole world, only about

Huarocondo. Huarocondo is mourning. Everyone knows the President of the United States. They would be stricken if we weren't here. But they know we are here because of John Kennedy. They know we are sad because he is dead. They loved us, so they are sad, too. Were I not here, I would never have believed that the world really cared."

When the first batch of Volunteers arrived in Togo in the fall of 1962, they were welcomed personally in Lomé by Sylvanus Olympio, the courtly, well-educated president, a hero of African independence. Four months later, Olympio died in a military coup led by disgruntled soldiers. It was the first of many coups in independent African countries that would disillusion outsiders about the future of the continent. Olympio was assassinated on January 13, 1963, as he ran towards the U.S. embassy in hope of refuge.

In Atakpamé in southern Togo, Peggy Anderson, a Volunteer teacher and a future best-selling author, recalls the mood as "desperately sad." "Our Togolese friends could hardly function," she says. "I remember people moving stunned and slow around the school grounds, where . . . they'd come just to be with colleagues. We consoled them as best we could with our poor French and our grossly inadequate emotional language. Deep down, I—and no doubt others among us in the Peace Corps—gave silent thanks that nothing like this could ever happen in America."

On November 22, ten months later, Peggy was a teacher in Kpalimé, another town in southern Togo. She was visiting a young French professor across the street from her house when she noticed a Peace Corps jeep stop at her front door. Sylvia Feinman, a Volunteer, had driven there from her village six miles away. She was accompanied by Mr. Anthony, who ran the only shop in Sylvia's village, selling basics like tomato paste, tinned sardines, palm oil, and kerosene.

It was near midnight, and Peggy wondered what could have brought them to her house so late.

Wearing a muumuu that she had made from royal blue, printed cloth bought in the local market, Peggy rushed across the sandy, unpaved road. As she neared them, Sylvia said, "The president's been killed." Peggy turned to Mr. Anthony, struggling to find the right words to console him for his second loss so soon after the first. "No," Sylvia said, "our President Kennedy."

"The next day," Peggy recalls, "it was the Togolese who consoled me.

And with every premise of my life suddenly jolted off its moorings, I realized as if lightning had struck that we really are all together in this small boat—that whether rich or poor, black or white, African or American or whatever else, we are bound as humans by the capriciousness of the universe and our helplessness in the face of it. That was the profoundest lesson I learned in the Peace Corps and probably in life."

In Iran, Volunteer Donna Shalala, future university president and secretary of Health and Human Services, spent all night listening to the funeral services. The next day a beggar approached her in the street. "No, I don't have any money," she said. He replied, "I don't want money. I just want to tell you how sorry I am that your young president died."

Kennedy was assassinated while Dick Lipez was at the movies in the old Haile Selassie I theater on Friday night in Addis Ababa, Ethiopia. Knowing nothing of it, he went to bed, awoke Saturday morning, and headed off to do his weekly shopping at the Italian grocery in the Cherkos Kebele neighborhood near the Shimelles Habte school where he taught. At the grocery, an Ethiopian whom he did not know walked up to him and asked, rather brusquely, "Sir, are you an American?" Wary, Dick said he was.

Lipez, now a well-known writer of detective novels under the pen name Richard Stevenson, recalled recently, "This place was near the insane asylum, and some of the inmates sometimes wandered around the neighborhood. I figured this guy was a probably 'a mad,' as the students would have called him. He looked at me and announced, 'Your president is dead!' More annoyed than anything, I asked him what he meant by that. He said Kennedy had been shot and killed."

Dick turned to the Italian manager of the shop. She looked fearful, stricken, near tears, and she nodded once. Dick paid for his groceries and headed home, passing the headquarters of the U.S. Military Assistance Advisory Group on the way. The building's U.S. flag was at half mast. Inside, a stunned soldier showed him a U.S. Information Service dispatch about the killing. Dick read that the assassin was named Lee Harvey Oswald. Who? What? He thought it was surreal.

At home, he sought more news on the radio but was continually interrupted by visitors, mainly students and fellow teachers. The Ethiopians spoke quietly of their sorrow over his loss. "All of these people felt Kennedy's death as a loss, too," said Lipez. "Kennedy was famous and well liked. He was young and looked like he belonged in a movie—which until the Peace Corps arrived was how most Ethiopians got their information about America—and he was an internationalist and he sent people in rockets in space and he welcomed the Ethiopian emperor and took him seriously."

The U.S. embassy held a memorial service a few days later. "I think I went," said Lipez, "but I have no clear memory of it. I just remember the madman and the Italian grocery lady and the sorrow that was felt all over Cherkos Kebele."

A few hundred Volunteers had already completed their overseas tours when Kennedy was assassinated. Among them was Maureen Carroll, who years later would serve the Peace Corps as director of the Botswana program and as director of the Africa region.

Maureen had worked as a teacher's aide in the Philippines. She recalled that small children in her barrio, when they wanted the Volunteers to pay attention to them, would chant outside the windows of the Americans, "Ken-ne-dee. Ken-ne-dee."

A few weeks before the assassination, Maureen had received a letter from a Filipino schoolteacher. "No American during the fifty years they governed us could really fathom the true Filipino," the letter said. "It was President Kennedy who sent you [the Peace Corps] to establish the true friendly relationships that were only assumed previously."

Maureen wrote about her feelings in the Peace Corps's *Volunteer* magazine. "I feel that the Peace Corps is a living and breathing answer to Kennedy's famous, 'Ask not what your country can do for you—ask what you can do for your country,'" she said. "One source of consolation for me over the loss is that I was in the chorus that answered him."

Jack Hood Vaughn, then director of the Latin American region for the Peace Corps, was lunching on Friday with several Volunteers and staff in a restaurant in San José, Costa Rica. For more than a year, a nearby volcano had been spewing ash over the city. Every step anyone took sent up bursts of ash that stuck to their clothing.

A fire siren began to sound during their meal. They listened for it to stop, but it kept wailing. The incessant noise persuaded Vaughn that there had been some calamity. He left the restaurant and headed for the U.S. embassy four blocks away.

"By the time I got to the door," he told Coates Redmon, "people were running around just screaming and waving their arms. The ash was flying everywhere. You could have choked to death on it. I tried to get through the door of the embassy but they were just closing it. Bam. That was it.

"All of a sudden I was surrounded by about fifty people—charladies, paperboys, vendors—who were all falling to their knees in front of the U.S. embassy on the sidewalk, praying and crossing themselves and moaning. It was mad. It was ghoulish. It was out of Dante. I just stood there, frozen, at the door of the embassy. But now I knew. Kennedy was dead."

Sargent Shriver was lunching at the Lafayette Hotel on Friday with Eunice and their four-year-old son, Timmy. The old hotel, which no longer exists, was near both the White House and Peace Corps headquarters. Eunice was then six months pregnant.

The lunch was interrupted by a phone call from Shriver's secretary Mary Ann Orlando. Shriver left the table to take the call. When he returned, he told Eunice, "Something's happened to Jack." He said her brother had been shot. A second call followed quickly, telling Shriver that the president's condition was critical.

The Shrivers rushed across Lafayette Park to the Peace Corps building. Eunice phoned her brother Bobby, the attorney general, who told her, "It doesn't look good." A Peace Corps official then brought them the dreaded wire service flash: the president was dead in Dallas. The Shrivers and two Peace Corps staffers knelt by Shriver's desk and chanted "Hail Mary, full of grace."

Shriver assembled a dozen tearful senior staffers in his office and assured them that the Peace Corps would continue running as normally as possible. He ordered similar reassurance cabled to all posts overseas. Shriver said later that he did not want Volunteers "to worry that the Peace Corps had died with the President." There were now almost 6,000 Volunteers overseas.

The Peace Corps, of course, did not die with John F. Kennedy. But the assassination would affect the Peace Corps in significant ways. First of all, the emotional anguish that raged for weeks, even months, would make Americans embrace all things that bore the stamp of their beloved and martyred president. Nothing bore that stamp more than the Peace Corps. For a young American, joining the Peace Corps would become a way of trying to infuse some meaning into an awful, senseless death. It would be a way of making a sacrifice, of performing a powerful service, at the calling of the fallen hero. The "ask not" mantra would have more meaning and more verve than even before.

As a result, the Peace Corps could expand with relative ease. Thousands of young people were more ready than ever to volunteer, and the naysayers in Congress were less ready than ever to carp against a program so favored by the revered late president.

The assassination, however, would also push Sargent Shriver away from the Peace Corps. This would leave the agency and the Volunteers without their charismatic leader, without the symbol of their celebrity chief so linked by family to John F. Kennedy. Shriver would leave the Peace Corps slowly, reluctantly, step by step, and the departure would come as he found himself caught in both family and White House politics.

As soon as Kennedy died, Shriver took charge of all the complex and massive arrangements for the extraordinary funeral in Washington. It was natural that he do so. Bobby Kennedy stayed close to the president's widow, Jackie Kennedy, in the White House, relaying her many wishes for historical flourishes to Shriver. Senator Ted Kennedy, the other surviving son, and Eunice flew to Hyannis Port to comfort their parents. As the senior Kennedy son-in-law, Shriver was left to run the most important and sensitive family business of that moment.

He did so with extraordinary skill and care. One of the most delicate and difficult aspects of his role was the negotiation of the demands of the family with the demands of Lyndon Johnson, the new president. The family, especially Bobby, looked on Johnson as a usurper moving too swiftly to push aside the heroic president. To demonstrate the continuity of office, Johnson wanted to move into the Oval Office right away, but Shriver persuaded him to wait a few days because the grieving family still looked on it as Kennedy's hallowed office. Johnson wanted to address Congress on Tuesday, the day after the funeral, but Bobby wanted him to wait until Wednesday. Johnson asked Shriver to try to persuade Bobby to change his mind, but Bobby turned down his brother-in-law with a brusque, "Why does he tell you to ask me?" Johnson waited until Wednesday.

Johnson knew that most in the Kennedy family, especially Bobby, would never reconcile themselves to Johnson taking the place of the martyred son and brother. Bobby, in fact, before his own assassination in 1968, would break with Johnson, oppose the war in Vietnam, and run for the Democratic nomination for president. Shriver, on the other hand, had worked with Johnson in the early days of the Peace Corps and treated him with the respect and honor that Shriver believed he deserved as president of the United States.

But it was more than gratitude that led Johnson to look on Shriver as a significant member of his new administration. Shriver was useful to him. Johnson could feud with Bobby and yet demonstrate his loyalty to Jack Kennedy and his admiration for the Kennedy family by favoring Shriver. Two months after the assassination, Johnson decided that he wanted Shriver to organize and lead the War on Poverty that would be a centerpiece of Johnson's Great Society. It struck Johnson as an inspired choice. The success of the Peace Corps had favored Shriver with the aura of a national celebrity. The success also demonstrated that Shriver knew how to mold a new organization out of the sparsest beginnings. And, of course, Shriver was Kennedy family.

Johnson practically bullied Shriver into the job, while dangling hints of promises, even the vice presidency, before him, and warning him that he had enemies (presumably Bobby most of all), who wanted to block his way to higher office. Shriver was reluctant, but not reluctant enough to stand up to the vaunted Johnson treatment.

Johnson announced his War on Poverty in his first State of the Union address on January 8, 1964. A few weeks later, while Shriver was visiting Peace Corps sites in Asia and handing letters to world leaders from the new U.S. president, Johnson summoned Bill Josephson, now the agency's general counsel, to the White House. Budget Director Kermit Gordon and Civil Service Commission Chairman John Macy, who served Johnson as a talent scout, also attended the meeting. The president told Josephson that he intended to name Shriver head of the poverty program. Josephson was handed two black briefing books on the new program. He was ordered to absorb their contents, find Shriver, and describe the plans to him.

Josephson flew to Hawaii, where Shriver planned a stopover on the way home. Shriver descended from the plane carrying a pink-and-white pagoda, more than two feet high, encased in a glass box. His honorary doctorate from Chulalongkorn University in Bangkok was inscribed on the pagoda. Josephson showed his boss the briefing books and announced that Johnson had tapped him for the poverty job. "He was not exactly happy," Josephson recalled years later.

On the flight home, Josephson summarized the main themes of the books and tried to persuade Shriver to absorb some of the contents. But it was not easy. "When Sarge did not want to hear something, he was very good at trying to avoid hearing it," said Josephson. "My recollection is that the last thing he wanted to hear from me was that he was to head the War on Poverty or what the details of that program were." When they reached Andrews Air Force Base outside Washington, a presidential car was waiting to rush Shriver to the White House.

Johnson took him for a walk in the Rose Garden and told him, "Now you know we're getting this War on Poverty started, Sarge. I'd like you to think about that, because I'd like you to run the program for us." It sounded like the president was giving Shriver time to make up his mind, but that was not Johnson's intent.

Johnson phoned Shriver at home the next day, Saturday, February 1. "Sarge, I'm gonna announce your appointment at that press conference," he said.

"What press conference?"

"This afternoon."

Shriver pleaded for a delay. Throughout this phone call and others with Johnson that day, the usually self-confident and articulate Shriver would sound diffident and hesitant. "God," he said. "I think it would be advisable, if you don't mind, if I could have this week and sit down with a couple of people and see what we could get in the way of some sort of plan."

That made no sense to Johnson. "I want to announce this and get it behind me . . . . You've got to do it. You just can't let me down. So the quicker we get this behind us the better . . . . Don't make me wait till next week, because I want to satisfy the press with something. I told them we were going to have a press meeting."

Shriver, now pleading he needed more time to prepare the Peace Corps, asked Johnson, "Could you just say that you've asked me to study this?"

"Hell no! They've studied and studied. They want to know who in the hell is going to do this, and it's leaked all over the newspapers for two weeks that you're going to do this, and they'll be shooting me with questions."

"The problem with it is that it'll knock the crap out of the Peace Corps," said Shriver, who then asked if he could remain as Peace Corps director.

"I am going to make it clear," replied Johnson, "that you're Mr. Poverty, at home and abroad, if you want to be. And I don't care who you have running the Peace Corps. You can run it? Wonderful. If you can't, get Oshgosh from Chicago and I'll name him . . . . You can write your ticket on anything you want to do there."

Then Shriver asked a couple of housekeeping questions. He wondered if the poverty program ought to be run by the Department of Health, Education, and Welfare (HEW). Michael R. Beschloss, who has edited and annotated the taped telephone conversations of Johnson, believed that Shriver may have been "gently suggesting" that he should be secretary of HEW. Johnson, perhaps encouraging Shriver, said any placement of the poverty program within HEW would have to wait until after the 1964 presidential election.

Shriver also asked if he could have Bill Moyers back as deputy director of the Peace Corps. The highly regarded young Moyers had left the Peace Corps to work in the White House with his old boss, Johnson, right after the assassination. But Johnson squelched any idea of Moyers returning to the Peace Corps. "I need him more than anybody in the world right here," he said.

After the call, Shriver, according to his biographer Scott Stossel, told Eunice, "I don't really want to run this thing." In that case, Eunice told him, make that clear to Johnson. Shriver phoned the president, reaching him a half-hour before the news conference.

But his reluctance wasn't strong enough to allow him to insist that he did not want the job and demand that Johnson choose someone else. Instead, Shriver repeated that it was a bad time for him to abandon the Peace Corps. Johnson reminded him he did not have to give up the Peace Corps. Shriver then repeated he needed more time to prepare. That argument made no more impression on Johnson than it had before. Johnson was dismissive.

"Why don't you let me leave it where we were?" said Johnson. "Now I'm here with all this staff trying to get ready for the three o'clock meeting, and I haven't had my lunch . . . . I need it for very personal reasons."

After Johnson announced the appointment at the televised news conference, Shriver phoned the White House again. This time Moyers took the call first. Shriver mused to his former deputy about the jobs he'd rather have—secretary of HEW, governor of Illinois, or "this Vice President thing." "What I would look to do sometime is talk to him and find out where I stand," he said.

Then Johnson took the phone. First of all, the president explained why he had to make the announcement so swiftly. "Now I don't want to make you feel bad," he said, "because you're too successful and I'm too proud of you to ever pour cold water on you. But up to one minute before I appeared, I was meeting violent protest to naming you. Now I couldn't let that grow and continue."

Johnson described the ringleader and his associates as "about as powerful people as we have in this government." Both Beschloss and Stossel interpreted this as a hint that the opposition had been led by Bobby Kennedy.

Then the president offered Shriver wisps of future rewards. He praised Shriver, insisting "I think that as an administrator and as a candidate [presumably for vice president] that you have great potentialities." If Secretary of Defense Robert McNamara ever left the administration, Johnson said, "you could have the damned job—tomorrow. And we got few of them we can rely on that way, Sarge." In another phone call that day, Johnson kidded Shriver that Moyers is "in there swinging every hour" to persuade Johnson to pick Shriver as his vice presidential candidate later that year.

Johnson never named Shriver secretary of defense, secretary of HEW, or his vice presidential candidate (though Shriver would run for vice president in 1972, when Democratic presidential candidate George McGovern selected him to replace Senator Thomas Eagleton after the latter admitted he had received electric shock therapy for mental illness). Shriver tried with spirited energy to carry both jobs—Peace Corps and the War on Poverty—at the same time for two years. He tried to devote Mondays, Wednesdays, Fridays, and Sundays to the War on Poverty and Tuesdays, Thursdays, and Saturdays to the Peace Corps. He carted two briefcases of poverty business and two briefcases of Peace Corps business in his car at all times. He still read all Peace Corps evaluation reports and commented freely in the margins. His senior staff meetings at the Peace Corps were still as lively and far-ranging as ever, but they were far less frequent.

But the demands of the two posts, especially the War on Poverty, became too troublesome for a part-time director, as mayors complained bitterly about young organizers stirring up trouble and as unfriendly members of Congress kept looking for signs of scandal and waste in the programs. On March 1, 1966, Shriver invoked the five-year term limit rule on himself and resigned from the Peace Corps to devote himself fully to the War on Poverty. It was the fifth anniversary of the day President John F. Kennedy signed the executive order creating the Peace Corps. In three months, at the end of the fiscal year, the Peace Corps would boast that it now had more than 15,000 Volunteers and trainees serving forty-six countries.

CHAPTER SIX

U.S. Troops Invade
the Dominican Republic

The Peace Corps has always brimmed with pride over the deportment of the Volunteers during the U.S. invasion of the Dominican Republic during a civil war in 1965. The Volunteers in the capital of Santo Domingo refused to leave despite heavy fire and bloody mayhem. They rushed to hospitals that were bereft of power and supplies and, amid awful, searing scenes, cared for the wounded, some cut down by U.S. marines and paratroopers. Despite muzzles from Washington, they sided with their impoverished Dominican friends and cried out against U.S. intervention. It was a glowing moment in Peace Corps history.

In *Dominican Diary,* his book-length account of the invasion, *New York Times* correspondent Tad Szulc singled out seven Volunteer nurses as "the real heroines of the civil war." And he dedicated his book as a whole to "the Peace Corps volunteers in Santo Domingo."

More recently, the Sargent Shriver Peace Institute commissioned Josef Evans, a young playwright with the Bedlam Theatre in Minneapolis, to write a play about the Peace Corps in the Dominican Republic. His play, *The Only Americans Welcome,* which was performed twice in 2008, at George Mason University in Virginia and the University of Maryland in Baltimore, depicted the Dominicans revering the Peace Corps despite their anger against the Yankee invaders. In lines that give the play its title, Lt. Col. Francisco Caamaño, the leader of the Dominican constitutionalists, as the rebels called themselves, announces, "Peace Corps Volunteers will be allowed through all Constitutionalist checkpoints. From this point forward they are the only Americans welcome in our section of the city."

Yet a harsh and uncomfortable reality has long lain beneath all the glory of the Peace Corps in the Dominican Republic. The U.S. intervention demonstrated the fragility of Peace Corps independence. Throughout the crisis, President Lyndon Johnson made it clear that he regarded the Peace Corps as an instrument of his policies. He tolerated the Peace Corps, in fact, largely because it served to show the soft side of a harsh, bellicose United States. The vaunted independence of the Peace Corps was at best ambivalent, at worst a sham.

Frank Mankiewicz, the director of Peace Corps operations in Latin America, filled a significant role during the crisis. A Los Angeles lawyer who was the son of *Citizen Kane* screenwriter Herman J. Mankiewicz and the nephew of *All About Eve* director Joseph L. Mankiewicz, he had become a luminary of the early Peace Corps and one of the most fervent advocates of the employment of Volunteers as community development workers—the main job of the Peace Corps in the Dominican Republic. Mankiewicz believed that community development Volunteers could become "a revolutionary force" that would give the masses of poor peoples in Latin America "an awareness of where the tools are to enable them to assert their political power." His belief in community development remained unshaken, even strengthened, but the Dominican invasion disillusioned him about the independence of the Peace Corps and made him unhappy in his work.

Mankiewicz had long taken a pledge of Secretary of State Dean Rusk at face value. Soon after the creation of the Peace Corps, Rusk cabled all ambassadors in countries with incoming Volunteers, "The Peace Corps is not an instrument of foreign policy because to make it so would rob it of its contribution to foreign policy." But the Dominican crisis clouded that. Mankiewicz was continually pressured to shut off the comments of Volunteers to U.S. reporters. "I got a sense that when push came to shove," he recalled recently, "that while it might not be an instrument of U.S. policy, it sure would not be an instrument against U.S. policy." Mankiewiz left the Peace Corps a year later to become the press secretary of Senator Robert F. Kennedy.

Perhaps Mankiewicz expected too much. Even in its beginnings, the Peace Corps did not demonstrate total independence. It is true that President Kennedy, at the insistence of Sargent Shriver, ordered the CIA to keep its hands off the Peace Corps and make no attempt to infiltrate the staff or Volunteers. And Shriver bravely resisted all pressure from his brother-in-law to send Volunteers to newly independent Algeria as a way of getting a U.S. foothold there after its long war with France.

But there were also moments when Shriver felt forced to bow to political pressure. In December 1962, Shriver announced that the Peace Corps would shift its emphasis and start assigning more Volunteers to Latin America than to any other region. Although Shriver would not acknowledge it, the Peace Corps was obviously meshing its policies with the White House campaign to shore up Latin American democracies against Fidel Castro's influence.

In August 1961, several members of Congress demanded that Shriver dismiss a Peace Corps trainee who had been thrown out of a Rotary Club meeting in Miami during the showing of the movie *Operation Abolition*. The House Committee on Un-American Activities had made the movie in an attempt to prove that riots against the committee in San Francisco a year earlier were inspired by communists. Showings of the movie were often met by youthful protests throughout the country, and Charles Ka-men, a twenty-one-year-old graduate of Brandeis University, was ejected, according to club officials, for laughing and applauding at the wrong times. This happened before Kamen was invited to enter training at Penn State University for the Peace Corps in the Philippines.

Shriver refused to heed the congressional calls to dismiss Kamen immediately. "The integrity of the selection process was at stake," the Peace Corps declared proudly in its *First Annual Report*. "The Peace Corps took the firm position that if it reacted to pressures or pressure groups in the determination of who should or should not be a Volunteer, the fundamental selection concept of the Peace Corps—that of selection based on merit—would be destroyed with disastrous consequences."

Despite these high-minded sentiments, Shriver overruled his selection officials when they found Kamen qualified to serve with the Peace Corps in the Philippines. Shriver felt he could not afford to offend members of Congress while the bill authorizing the Peace Corps was still pending. He secretly ordered that selection officials change their decision and reject Kamen or, in Peace Corps jargon, "select him out." There was dismay among the senior staff in Washington when they realized what had happened.

For the Peace Corps in 1965, the Dominican crisis followed two story lines. One played out in the Dominican Republic, especially the capital, Santo Domingo. The other played out in Washington. There were 108 Volunteers in the country, 34 of them in Santo Domingo. The Santo Domingo contingent comprised 25 urban community development workers and 9 nurses operating clinics. All worked in the barrios, the poorest neighborhoods of the city.

No one from the Peace Corps took part in the deliberations about Dominican policy in Washington. But two former Peace Corps officials played important roles. One was Bill Moyers, who had been deputy director of the Peace Corps before the assassination of President Kennedy. His old boss, Lyndon Johnson, had pulled him into the White House, and now he was a trusted special assistant to President Johnson, taking part in most White House deliberations.

The second was Jack Hood Vaughn, who had preceded Mankiewicz as director of Peace Corps operations in Latin America. Vaughn was now assistant secretary of state for Latin American affairs, an office he had held for only a few weeks when the crisis erupted. Johnson would later name Vaughn to succeed Shriver as director of the Peace Corps, and the Dominican crisis would have a good deal to do with putting Vaughn there.

The Dominican troubles were rooted in the brutal dictatorship of Gen. Rafael Leonidas Trujillo, who ruled from 1930 until his assassination in 1961. Juan Bosch, an exiled writer who had opposed Trujillo for many years, was elected president, taking office in February 1963. But seven months later, the old guard of the military, the backbone of the Trujillo dictatorship, overthrew Bosch in a bloodless coup and eventually set up a military-backed government with a civilian president, Donald Reid Cabral, in charge.

Since President Kennedy had regarded the Bosch administration as a showcase for new democracy in Latin America, he broke off relations and withdrew all U.S. aid programs (except the Peace Corps). But this break lasted only a few weeks. Soon after Kennedy's death, President Johnson resumed diplomatic relations on the strength of a promise by the new Dominican government to hold national elections in 1965. Although Reid Cabral's government was unpopular, American diplomats and military officers maintained friendly relations with him. In fact, they did not grasp the extent of his unpopularity.

On April 24, 1965, junior officers of the Dominican army staged a countercoup, overthrowing Reid Cabral while demanding a revival of constitutional government and the return of Juan Bosch as president. Colonel Caamaño emerged as the leader of the rebels or constitutionalists. Crowds took to the streets chanting the name of Juan Bosch for hours. The American embassy had no inkling of the countercoup ahead of time and no links with Colonel Caamaño and the other rebel leaders. In fact, Ambassador W. Tapley Bennett Jr. was visiting his mother in Georgia when Colonel Caamaño and his associates rose up.

Large right-wing elements of the army and air force, who did not want Bosch back, resisted the countercoup, and Santo Domingo was soon engulfed in civil war. The leader of these senior officers was Brig. Gen. Elias Wessin y Wessin, who had led the overthrow of Bosch in the first place. Most of the population of Santo Domingo, many armed by the rebels, appeared to support the counter coup, and it is likely that Colonel Caamaño's forces would have defeated General Wessin's forces and Bosch returned to the presidency if the United States had not interfered.

In fact, the U.S. intervention astounded many Peace Corps Volunteers, for they had assumed that if the United States did send troops, it would be to assist the rebels who were demanding the return of the democratically elected president. But the ignorance of the U.S. embassy and the White House about Caamaño and his fellow plotters led to fears that they were communists, or influenced by communists, or susceptible to manipulation by communists.

In their ignorance, the Americans reinforced each other's suspicions. It was the height of the Cold War. Fidel Castro had come to power in Cuba only six years earlier. The Cuban missile crisis—with the United States and the Soviet Union edging to the brink of war until Moscow finally removed its missiles from Cuba—had taken place only two years earlier. President Johnson was determined not to allow another Castro Cuba to emerge in the Caribbean. Bosch was regarded as an ineffective intellectual who would surely fall under the control of the supposedly communist rebels if he returned to the Dominican Republic. Johnson did not want him back.

Johnson ordered more than five hundred Marines into the Dominican Republic, supposedly to evacuate Americans and other foreigners. But once that job was done, the Marines stayed and, in fact, were augmented by Army paratroopers. By the end of the first week of May, there were almost 23,000 U.S. troops in the Dominican Republic.

It was a shocking moment for Latin America. The United States had supposedly given up those early-twentieth-century days when it mounted military expeditions to Haiti, Nicaragua, the Dominican Republic, and Mexico to restore order, collect debts, and punish bandits. President Franklin Roosevelt had pulled out the last American occupation troops soon after he took office in 1933 and initiated a Good Neighbor policy. Even the Bay of Pigs fiasco of 1961 had been a CIA-assisted and financed invasion of Cuba by Cuban exiles, not a blatant U.S. military intervention.

Johnson justified the Dominican invasion as a defensive blow against communism. He told the American public that the revolution by the colonels had taken "a tragic turn," with communists assuming "increasing control." While insisting that the United States supported no leader or faction in the Dominican Republic, the president said, "Our goal . . . is to help prevent another communist state in this hemisphere."

But the United States was hardly neutral. There is no doubt that the U.S. troops squelched any chance for victory by the Bosch supporters. The United States pressured the right-wing military to create a junta with a general less reactionary than Wessin y Wessin in charge, and the Americans then surreptitiously aided the right-wing troops in hopes that they could put down the rebellion by the Constitutionalists and their civilian supporters. But this junta failed both in squelching the rebellion and attracting popular support.

Almost every action of the Americans, ostensibly there to save lives, served to hurt the rebels and strengthen the right-wing junta. The Americans seized the Duarte Bridge that the rebels were attacking as a gateway to their enemy. The bridge crossed the Ozama River that separated the city of Santo Domingo from the area that housed the military camps of the anti-Bosch troops. After pushing the rebels back, the Americans set down an "international security zone" across downtown Santo Domingo that kept the Bosch rebels within the populous southern barrios of the city. Even when a cease-fire was signed, the Americans helped the anti-Bosch troops with supplies, military advice, and access to positions on the other side. This eventually led to occupation of the northern sections of Santo Domingo by the right-wing troops.

The Johnson version of events in the Dominican Republic bore little relation to what the Volunteers saw and heard around them. Kirby Jones, a twenty-four-year-old Volunteer from Bedford, New York, kept a detailed diary during those violent days, and it makes clear that many Volunteers lived in a milieu that welcomed and supported the pro-Bosch coup.

Jones had achieved a good deal in his fifteen months in Santo Domingo. He had been told while training for urban community development that if you "inject a foreign element into a community, stuff happens," and stuff had happened on his watch. Jones and his fellow Volunteer, Joe Morrison from Buffalo, began by organizing eight- and nine-year-old kids into baseball teams. The games soon attracted older brothers who formed teenage and youth teams, and the teams turned into social clubs. Parents and other adults came to some of the meetings, and in a few months, Jones and Morrison could boast that their baseball teams had evolved into a community association.

In their first political action, the members of the association, with the help of the Volunteers, trudged to the offices of the mayor and petitioned him to give their streets names and put numbers on their homes. Without these, the barrio had not been able to receive normal mail. The mayor agreed. One of the new streets was named Calle Cuerpo de Paz. Pleased with this triumph, the association planned new campaigns for paved streets and running water in the barrio.

Jones had taken on an extra job on Saturdays. He and a Volunteer nurse telecast a public health program every week on Radio Santo Domingo. But when he showed up on Saturday, April 24, 1965, his Dominican boss shooed him away. "There's no program today," the boss said. "The equipment isn't functioning." This station official obviously knew what was coming. The rebel officers seized Radio Santo Domingo later that day, igniting the revolution and civil war.

When the fighting erupted, the Peace Corps decided that the Volunteers in Santo Domingo would be safest remaining in their barrios where people knew them well. But the barrios became a kind of battleground. "The streets began filling up with guys with guns," Jones recalled years later. "A lot of the guys with guns had been playing on our baseball teams the week before." The rebellious fighters and their supporters in the barrios did not harm the Volunteers. But planes of the anti-Bosch Air Force bombed and strafed the barrios. "Am back in my house," Jones wrote in his diary, "lying in bed, listening to all machine guns and rifles going off all around." "Flares are going up to light the sky," he wrote the next day. "Vigilantes are roaming around. I'm alone and a bit scared."

Communication with Peace Corps headquarters was very difficult. Jones had no phone. Only one phone existed in the whole barrio, in the home of a police officer. Peace Corps staffers drove through the barrios from time to time with messages and news. The Volunteers were impressed by the bravery of Associate Director Roberta Warren, a twenty-four-year-old former Volunteer in Peru. Warren, who was known by her family nickname of B. J., would show up in her jeep during some of the most embattled hours. Word reached Jones on the fifth day that the Volunteers should head to the closest hospital. Jones and Kay Deming, another Volunteer in the barrio, pasted red crosses on their Peace Corps medical kits, as if they were hospital workers, and hitched a ride to a hospital.

At the hospital, Jones carried the wounded from an ambulance to the doctors and carried bodies from the wards to the morgue. He held a patient down while doctors performed a tracheotomy. He folded bandages and carried in the meager supplies that were delivered occasionally. "Saw eight-year-old girls," he wrote, "shot through the back, breast, legs, lying on beds, crying for their mothers, suffering—for what?"

"In the hospital," he went on, "there are no lights, no water, no food, no linen, no medicines, just a few exhausted doctors, many lazy nurses, five PC [Peace Corps] nurses that do everything, [Volunteers] Steve and I, Elaine, Fran, Karen—an incredible mess." The scenes grew more horrifying. "A little girl was brought in with her face blown up and hand half cut through." After a few days, Jones "knew I'd had it. I could not take this any more." Bob Satin, who ran the Peace Corps program in the Dominican Republic, agreed that he should leave the hospital.

Jones joined several other Volunteers at the Hotel Embajador in the security zone that had been carved out by the U.S. troops. The Volunteers drove trucks carting food from CARE into the isolated barrios. A CBS crew accompanied Jones on one trip to tape a segment for Walter Cronkite's evening news show. The rebel soldiers in a barrio imposed order on the hungry, anxious crowd and distributed the food. Jones did not try to hide his familiarity with the rebel soldiers from the CBS camera. That kind of scene, however, would trouble some Americans who had been told by their president that the rebels were Castro Commies and thus enemies of the United States.

The Embajador was the headquarters for many American journalists covering the war, and Volunteers, including Jones, talked freely with them. The journalists also sought out the views of the young Americans elsewhere in Santo Domingo and the Dominican Republic. The result was an ample amount of publicity for the Peace Corps in the Dominican Republic.

Some of it was welcomed in Washington. Satin, the thirty-four-year-old Peace Corps director, was hailed as a hero in news dispatches. Wearing his white panama hat and a yellow anorak, Satin was able to drive in and out of the rebel areas without harm. On one trip, he spotted two wounded Marines and persuaded the rebels to release them to his care. On another occasion, the rebels notified U.S. military authorities that they would let several captured Marines go if Satin drove into the zone to pick them up. In all, Satin brought back six U.S. servicemen and the bodies of two others to the American lines. He also served as a kind of neutral go-between, setting up a meeting between rebel leader Caamaño and U.S. negotiators. Satin received a letter of commendation from the Secretary of the Navy for his heroics during the crisis.

Some Volunteers were troubled by Satin's role. In his diary, Jones complains that Satin has been acting as a "big cheese" instead of concerning himself with the Volunteers. Jones doubts whether acting as the intermediary between Caamaño and the U.S. embassy is a proper Peace Corps role. He contrasts Satin with other members of the staff who "have risked their personal safety to protect the PCVs." Some staff members also felt troubled by Satin's activities. "He had the idea that his responsibility was to his country," Warren said recently. "I thought that his responsibility was to the 120 Volunteers."

The critics may be too harsh on Satin. He felt that he could perform useful and peaceful service as one of the few U.S. officials trusted by the rebels. In the early stages of the war, so many American diplomats were away from the embassy that as the senior official on the scene, he surely knew more about the rebels than any other American in the embassy.

Ambassadors regard the Peace Corps director as part of the "Country Team," like the AID director, U.S. Information Agency director, CIA station chief, commercial attache, military attache, and representatives of other agencies. The team meets periodically with the embassy's top diplomats, usually once a week. In the event of a crisis, the ambassador expects all members of the Country Team to take part in dealing with it. The ambassador usually assumes that he or she has some authority over the Peace Corps director, especially in a crisis. During the Dominican invasion, Satin assumed he was performing his duty as part of the Country Team.

The issue raised by Satin's critics is one that will come up often in Peace Corps history. Can the Peace Corps really go its own way overseas? How much can the Peace Corps divorce itself from the embassy? Peace Corps independence is not unlimited. But the nature and extent of the limits are often ambiguous.

Although Washington officialdom hailed reports about Satin, they did not appreciate news reports with Peace Corps quotes that echoed the Dominican antipathy toward the U.S. invasion. Nurse Alice Meehan told the *Washington Post* that the invasion "has set back the image of the United States that we were trying to build by fifty years." Joan Temple, a twenty-four-year-old nurse from Trimont, Minnesota, told the *Chicago Daily News,* "I don't think the people are opposed to the American people, but many of them are against the American government. Some of them will bring you a baby or someone else who's been shot. They'll say it was shot by Marines and they'll ask, 'Why are you doing this?'" She said this happened even when the wounds were probably caused by anti-Bosch Dominican soldiers.

While many Dominicans did not let their anti-Yankee feelings get in the way of their admiration for the Volunteers, some lumped all Americans together. "Our pupils are scared to work with us," a Volunteer teacher in a small provincial town in the Dominican interior told the *Washington Post.* "It isn't considered proper now to associate with Americans."

Some Americans were upset by the news reports of the Peace Corps's continued work in areas controlled by Dominicans fighting the U.S. invasion. The *Richmond News-Leader* complained about Volunteers "giving aid and comfort to an enemy at the same time the enemy's troops are still shooting at American soldiers in the streets of Santo Domingo." Warren, the associate director of the Peace Corps in the Dominican Republic, defended the humanitarian work of the Volunteers. "We are giving whatever help we can to anybody who needs it—without asking their politics," she told the *New York Times,* "and most of us have been accused of being Communists by the GIs." A correspondent of the *New York Herald Tribune* wrote, "This is a war in which the U.S. War Corps is at odds with the U.S. Peace Corps."

The ubiquitous quotes from the Volunteers irritated the Johnson administration. There evidently had been very little pressure to remove the Volunteers after the fighting erupted. Satin had persuaded Washington that the Volunteers were safe so long as they remained among the Dominicans who knew them. Moreover, he offered to evacuate any Volunteer who wanted to leave. Only a handful accepted. From the point of view of the administration, the Volunteers were a useful symbol. The Peace Corps was very popular in the Dominican Republic, and its continued presence might help persuade Dominicans and, in fact, other Latin Americans that, despite the military intervention, the United States harbored only the best intentions toward the country.

The issue was raised at a meeting of the Dominican Republic task force in the White House on May 6. Participants included Secretary of Defense Robert McNamara, National Security Advisor McGeorge Bundy, Deputy CIA Director Richard Helms, Undersecretary of State Thomas Mann, Bill Moyers, Jack Vaughn, and several other policymakers. The group, according to the minutes, "discussed the problem of the Peace Corps people in the Dominican Republic who are giving interviews that are damaging our interests." Moyers assured everyone that Sargent Shriver was dealing with the problem, but that did not end the discussion.

"While the group saw certain advantages in bringing the Peace Corps back to the U.S.," the minutes went on, "they also saw a number of disadvantages—e.g., Peace Corps people would hold their interviews in the U.S., which would also hurt; it would be a blow for the Peace Corps people all over the world if we quashed their right to speak freely."

In the end, the task force decided to "leave them there" but added "we should give the Peace Corps people some background on the Dominican situation." Bundy suggested that John Bartlow Martin, the magazine writer and former ambassador to Santo Domingo, and Harry Shlaudeman, the Dominican desk officer at the State Department, talk to the Volunteers.

But Moyers and Shriver decided it was best to send one of the Peace Corps's own, and Frank Mankiewicz was selected for the job. "You'd better go down there and shut those guys up," Moyers told him, "or the President's going to pull them out."

Moyers invited Mankiewicz to lunch at the White House, and, when they finished, they were summoned to the living quarters, where President Johnson was lunching with some guests. Undersecretary of

State Tom Mann joined the group. A fellow Texan and probably the president's most influential advisor on the Dominican crisis, Mann told Johnson, "The whole problem, Mr. President, is left-wing newspapers such as the *Washington Post*, the *New York Times,* and the *New York Herald-Tribune,* which always take the Communist side."

"I couldn't believe it," Mankiewicz recalled years later, "but I *did* believe it."

Mankiewicz's view of the intervention was colored by the reports he had read from Satin and his own understanding of the problems of Latin America. Later, his view would be reinforced by his conversations with the Volunteers in the Dominican Republic.

"I was very disturbed about the Dominican intervention," he recalled. "It seemed to me wrong in every way, particularly since I'd been reading all the cables . . . . It was clear to me from the beginning that we were putting those troops in not to preserve order, but to . . . put the right-wing military back in power . . . . I thought we were on the wrong side . . . politically and spiritually."

After he arrived in the Dominican Republic, he was astonished at the lack of contact between U.S. officials in the embassy and the pro-Bosch rebels in the Dominican army. He was just as struck by how little embassy officials, unlike the Volunteers, understood the masses of poor Dominicans who supported the rebels. He attended some of the U.S. military briefings for the press and was shocked by their dishonesty.

"It turned me off on Vietnam," Mankiewicz said. "I mean I had no particular thoughts about Vietnam until around May or June of '65. I didn't like it too much, I was a little suspicious, but I really didn't like a lot of the people who were so strongly in opposition, and I felt there must be something to the government's argument. And then I went to the Dominican Republic and I saw Army spokesmen saying what was happening when, in fact, precisely the opposite was happening. I saw the mentality and the spirit of the State Department and AID and the military guys . . . . And it suddenly occurred to me that maybe they weren't telling the truth in Vietnam, either."

Mankiewicz was obviously a reluctant censor. But he met with about twenty Santo Domingo Volunteers in the abandoned Catholic girls' school that had become Peace Corps headquarters during the war. The school straddled both the U.S.-controlled security zone and the rebel-controlled southern barrios of the city. Mankiewicz warned Volunteers that President Johnson would probably withdraw the Peace Corps from the Dominican Republic if there was another rash of anti-intervention quotes from the Volunteers. He urged them to stop talking to reporters.

The numbers of published Volunteer quotes diminished after that, though this may have been due more to lack of press interest than to Volunteer discretion. In any case, the discretion was never strong enough to satisfy critics of the Peace Corps in Washington. In late May, a month after the invasion, Volunteers sent a letter to the White House that surely would have closed down the Peace Corps in the Dominican Republic if it had been published. The letter, addressed to the president of the United States, was signed by thirty-two Volunteers.

The letter accused U.S. military forces of backing the rightist military juntas against the rebel or constitutionalist forces that "have overwhelming popular sympathy." The Volunteers said that the U.S.-imposed cease-fire had "stopped the 'rebels' on the threshold of victory, and allowed junta forces, in violation of that cease-fire, to eliminate mercilessly 'rebel' control of the northern part of the city."

On top of this, the Volunteers made it clear they did not agree with Johnson's main rationalization for his invasion. Their letter accused the United States of perpetuating "the junta's generalization that the full 'rebel' movement was communist."

The Volunteers supported what they called the Johnson administration's "diplomatic efforts to form a government acceptable to the true Constitutionalist Movement." By this time, the United States was trying to create a caretaker government that would be accepted by both sides in the war. But the letter set down a catalogue of examples where U.S. military actions, by favoring the right-wing forces, veered in a different direction from the diplomatic maneuvering. "We urge your immediate attention in making our military actions consistent with our diplomatic efforts," the Volunteers said.

In a covering note to Shriver and other Peace Corps officials, the Volunteers said they would release the letter to the press if they felt it was ignored by the president. Two days after the letter was sent, Mankiewicz was dispatched to talk the Volunteers out of going public.

The letter was drafted by Kirby Jones and two other Volunteers while they were in Puerto Rico for what is known as their "termination conference." The Peace Corps holds these conferences whenever a group of Volunteers nears the end of a two-year tour. The Volunteers, meeting with officials from Washington, sum up their accomplishments and problems, and make recommendations for future programs. In this case, the conference was held in Puerto Rico because of the war.

Mankiewicz was persuasive. "To say the least," Jones wrote in his diary, "he made a masterful presentation of his position .... Frank started off by complimenting us on the letter, saying that it was very well received and that the message had indeed reached the President, and that if this is what we had wanted to accomplish, we had succeeded." Mankiewicz did not say that Johnson had actually read the letter, and there is no evidence now that he had. It is possible that Moyers or other aides kept it from him.

Mankiewicz then presented his argument for withholding the letter from the press. "He pointed out the fact," Jones wrote, "that in other countries there were also military juntas and strong executives who might interpret the letter as the PC [Peace Corps] actively participating in revolutions and that the PCVs [Peace Corps Volunteers] in their respective countries were working to overthrow them. This, in turn, might very well result in the retiring of PC from quite a few countries." Jones thought that Mankiewicz's argument was sound.

Not every Volunteer agreed. "I had nothing but contempt for Frank Mankiewicz," Lynda Edwards, a Volunteer in Santo Domingo, told writer Karen Schwarz. "I had heard him say more than once that if there was ever a revolution, he expected to see the Volunteers on the barricades. I later understood that he was keeping us from getting kicked out, but at the time I thought he was a hypocrite and a windbag. It must have been very difficult for him to ask us not to give the letter to the press." In the end Mankiewicz prevailed, and the Volunteers agreed not to release the letter.

Five months later, McGeorge Bundy sent a memorandum to Lyndon Johnson that reflected a blatant attempt at politicization of the Peace Corps. The document provides clear evidence that the White House and the State Department intended to oversee Peace Corps programming in the Dominican Republic to make it serve U.S. foreign policy and public relations.

"I know you have been cautious on this," Bundy wrote, "but I believe myself it is now time to act. The Peace Corps is popular in Santo Domingo, and if it behaves with proper discipline, it can be a very useful balance to more hardheaded activities which clearly will be necessary as we go ahead."

Bundy proposed almost a doubling of the Peace Corps program to 210 Volunteers—80 in community development, 50 in public health, 50 in rural elementary schools, and 30 in town administration. He recognized the administration's irritation with the tart comments of the Volunteers to newspaper reporters after the intervention. But he said he had discussed the problem with Mankiewicz, who is "smart and good on the political problems involved."

"I have his assurance," Bundy went on, "that he will make a special effort himself to ensure that Volunteers understand the sensitive nature of their work. After all, it is quite simple: if they start criticizing U.S. policy down there, they will simply shut down the Peace Corps in the Dominican Republic and give the whole operation a bad black eye."

Bundy asked, "Can we go ahead?" Johnson replied yes, but "subject to Bill Moyers's supervision."

This was an outrageous involvement of the White House in the placement of Volunteers in a country. The White House did not completely usurp the responsibility of Peace Corps programmers and attempt to assess the Peace Corps needs of the Dominican Republic itself. Bundy's figures were based on a report sent to him by Mankiewicz two weeks earlier. But the episode reflected an unprecedented decision by the president to approve a suitable number of Volunteers, not because they were needed for economic development but because they were needed to balance the "more hardheaded activities" of the U.S. troops.

The Peace Corps, however, was a willing victim, and its leaders, especially Shriver and his deputy, Warren Wiggins, went overboard in their zeal to serve the president by trying to bloat the numbers of Volunteers in the Dominican Republic. At one point, they had even contemplated sending more than a thousand Volunteers there.

This plan stemmed from some fanciful remarks by Teodoro Moscoso, the former coordinator of the U.S. Alliance for Progress, the vast Kennedy program of assistance to Latin America, and Jaime Benítez, the chancellor of the University of Puerto Rico. They had remarked that there ought to be as many Volunteers as soldiers in the Dominican Republic; in short, that the U.S. Peace Corps should be as large as the U.S. War Corps. Since Johnson had dispatched more than 20,000 troops, their musings about a balance between soldiers and Volunteers were obviously exaggerated to make a point. But they did believe that a "massive Peace Corps involvement" could help stabilize the Dominican Republic.

The Moscoso-Benítez idea was immediately embraced by Peace Corps officials obsessed with numbers. They began to talk of proving the Peace Corps "can make a difference" by rushing in quantities of Volunteers that made the largest Peace Corps programs elsewhere seem piddling. Mankiewicz said that between 500 and 1,500 could be dispatched within a year, and "Operation 1500" was launched.

But the plan was absurd. The little Caribbean country could not absorb that many Volunteers. Former Dominican Volunteers working in Washington opposed the expansion. The staff in Santo Domingo felt foolish trying to persuade Dominican officials to request such large numbers of Volunteers. "It was a ridiculous exercise," says Warren, "and I was embarrassed." According to a study written a decade later by Peace Corps officials Kevin Lowther and C. Payne Lucas, the Dominican director of community development "could barely contain his laughter" when he was pressured to sign an official request for several hundred community development Volunteers. "I thought it was the funniest thing I had ever heard," he said later.

Operation 1500 collapsed of its own inanity. When evaluator Jack Rosenblum arrived in the Dominican Republic a year after the invasion, there were only seventy Volunteers in the country—a third as many as Bundy proposed, and even fewer than the number at the time of the invasion. Volunteers were still popular. In one rural area where Volunteer Casey Case worked, youths had organized an anti-U.S. march with a banner demanding, "Yankees Go Home but Casey Stay." Rosenblum wrote that almost all the Volunteers, even those who arrived afterwards, spoke of the U.S. intervention "with great bitterness."

But with the fighting over, Rosenblum noticed some troubling signs about the relations between the Volunteers and the U.S. soldiers. "The spectacle," he wrote, "of thirsty PCV boys ambling across the street for a 15¢ American beer at the army base or of lonely PCV girls dating GIs tends to create confusion in the Dominican mind about the autonomy and separate identity of the Peace Corps." That problem would have been exacerbated, of course, if 1,500 Volunteers had arrived in the Dominican Republic.

The troops would not be a Peace Corps problem very long. The last U.S. troops departed in September 1966. The United States had succeeded in putting together a caretaker civilian government, acceptable to both sides, which paved the way for new elections. In those elections, held in May 1966, Joaquin Bellaguer, who had once served the Trujillo regime, defeated Bosch. The Johnson administration decided it was safe to pull out all the troops four months later.

It was easy for Lyndon Johnson to regard the Peace Corps as an instrument of his foreign policy. After all, Peace Corps operations were paid for by congressionally appropriated U.S. funds, and the officials who ran the Peace Corps served at his pleasure. He understood that the Peace Corps deserved some independence, but not enough to get in the way of what he regarded as patriotism.

The Dominican intervention was not the only time he tried to bend the Peace Corps to his political will. In late 1965, he suspended foreign aid to both India and Pakistan as punishment for their war over the territory of Kashmir. When he issued his edict, a group of Volunteers was on its way to India. Johnson, declaring the Volunteers a part of U.S. foreign aid, refused to let them continue. The Volunteers shuttled from Israel to Guam to the Philippines as Shriver implored the president not to use them as punishment. Finally, after six weeks, Johnson relented and allowed the Volunteers to fly to India.

The Dominican intervention also taught Johnson that the Peace Corps, though an instrument of foreign policy, could backfire. Johnson was in an angry mood at his office on the LBJ ranch in Texas one night in November 1965 when Bill Moyers reached him on the phone. Johnson had read a news report about a Peace Corps recruiter encouraging anti–Vietnam War protestors at the University of Michigan to join the Peace Corps. "He is going to reward these folks who want to destroy our democracy," Johnson told Moyers. He instructed his assistant to get a report from Shriver on the incident.

"This is what we ran into in the Dominican Republic," Johnson went on. "They [the Volunteers] were the first ones to jump us."

CHAPTER SEVEN

Johnny Hood

President Lyndon Johnson needed a Peace Corps–type ambassador to repair some of the damage in Panama. The U.S. Canal Zone lay across Panama like a swath of imperialism, the last Big Splinter from Teddy Roosevelt's Big Stick. According to the treaty imposed upon Panama at the turn of the century, the United States would control the canal and five miles on either side "in perpetuity." This presence of the U.S. Canal Zone in an era of diminishing empires caused a good deal of tension, and the United States agreed in 1962, as a goodwill gesture, that the Panamanian flag would always fly alongside the U.S. flag within the Canal Zone. But that agreement kept tempers down for only a couple of years.

In January 1964, American students, defying U.S. officials, raised the U.S. flag in front of Balboa High School inside the Canal Zone and stood guard to prevent anyone from putting up a Panamanian flag. Crowds of Panamanian students rushed into the zone to confront the young Americans and attempt to raise their own flag. This provoked rioting that was finally put down by U.S. troops stationed in the Canal Zone. At the end, twenty Panamanians and three Americans died in three days of violent riots.

Panama broke off diplomatic relations. They were not resumed until April, when the United States agreed to open talks that might lead to a renegotiation of the Panama Canal treaty. Special White House Assistant Bill Moyers, who had been deputy director of the Peace Corps until Johnson succeeded Kennedy, suggested that the president nominate Jack Hood Vaughn as the new ambassador. Vaughn was then director of Latin American programs for the Peace Corps.

"You met in Senegal," Moyers wrote to Johnson. "He is bi-lingual, has worked long years in Latin America, yet is young and lean and tough. Take my apologies, too, for always recommending Peace Corps people— but they are good people." Moyers added an official Peace Corps biography that reminded the president that Vaughn had been the featherweight champion of Michigan as an amateur and fought professionally in Mexico as "Johnny Hood."

Johnson had first encountered Vaughn in Dakar while on a vice-presidential trip to Africa in April 1961. Vaughn, then the AID director for Senegal, led Johnson on a half-day tour of fishing villages up-country. Johnson did not like Vaughn's thin brush of a moustache but otherwise found the ex-boxer a congenial guide and interpreter. Johnson enjoyed politicking among the Senegalese, handing out old Johnson Senate campaign pens and promising to send one village a new Johnson outboard motor. When the motor arrived a month later, villagers paraded it in Dakar and up and down the coast.

Vaughn, who had worked for the U.S. foreign aid program in Panama for several years, brashly told the vice president that it was a mistake to let the Pentagon set policy for the Canal Zone; diplomats should be running the zone, not generals. Johnson made it clear that he felt bored as vice president and confided, according to Vaughn, that he regarded Bobby Kennedy, then attorney general, as a "piss-ant little runt." Vaughn enjoyed his adventure so much that, as he wrote later, "I was beginning to question my lifelong Republican inclination and knee-jerk voting."

Johnson had not met Vaughn since then, but he obviously had good memories of the day, for he quickly accepted the suggestion of Moyers and nominated Vaughn as ambassador. During his years as a foreign aid officer in Panama, Vaughn had arranged grants for a thousand Panamanians to pursue postgraduate studies in the United States. When he arrived in Panama City as ambassador at 4:00 a.m. on April 17, 1964, ten young Panamanian professionals stood at the airport despite the hour and unfurled a twenty-five-foot canvas sign that read, "Jack, the scholarship holders remember your work and greet you."

Vaughn quickly developed a reputation as a sensitive ambassador who immersed himself in the country, dealing with the complexities of Panamanian poverty as well as the tensions of the Canal Zone. He did so well that he was promoted ten months later to the position of assistant secretary of state for Latin American affairs.

Vaughn took up his new job in Washington a few weeks before the Dominican invasion. He was not a major player in the crisis. His predecessor as assistant secretary, Thomas Mann, now an undersecretary of state, took charge as Johnson's main State Department advisor. Vaughn had a supporting role, handling assigned tasks and defending the administration's policies before Congress.

One of his assignments turned disastrous. Johnson had invaded the Dominican Republic without consulting the Organization of American States. That broke at least the spirit of the treaty creating the OAS. So Johnson phoned Vaughn a few days later and ordered him to write "a complete scenario" of how Washington had urged individual members of the OAS before the invasion to do something about the civil war in Santo Domingo. Johnson said he wanted the report to include "everybody we talked to and everybody we urged to do anything."

Putting together such a report proved exceedingly difficult for Vaughn, mainly because its premise was false. Johnson had not consulted any other government before dispatching troops. Vaughn set up a cot in his office and worked on the report without coming home for three nights. He listed every contact, in Washington and overseas, between a State Department official and a Latin ambassador or minister, no matter how perfunctory, no matter what was discussed. His drafts sounded tentative and bland. He finished eight versions, each one fatter and worse than the one before.

The president met with members of his Dominican task force three days after his phone call to Vaughn. When he entered the room, Vaughn found Secretary of State Dean Rusk, Secretary of Defense Robert McNamara, Deputy CIA Director Richard Helms, and a dozen other officials along the lengthy table. Johnson sat at one end of the table, a copy of Vaughn's report in his hands. Vaughn took a seat near the other end. He thought the president looked "very sad and ugly."

Johnson said that "the news media don't know that we notified OAS and urged them to act." Vaughn's report, the president lamented, would never change that impression; it was a failure. He excoriated Vaughn in vivid Johnsonian imagery. "He really reamed me," Vaughn recalls. "He cast aspersions on my genealogy, patriotism, and manhood." The president then tossed the report across the table, bouncing it into Vaughn's lap.

Vaughn stood up, pale and shaking. "You will have my resignation, Mr. President," he said, "as soon as I can get to a typewriter."

An exasperated Johnson stared at Vaughn and told him, "Sit down, you little shit." Vaughn sat down, and the president went on to other business.

Moyers slipped a note to Vaughn. "Welcome to the club," it said. A second note came from another presidential assistant, Jack Valenti. "You are now a celebrity," said Valenti (who would go on to become the president of the Motion Picture Association of America). "I want to be your agent."

President Johnson was notorious for his brutal chastisement of staff. They were expected to shake off the expletives and continue to serve, and this episode did not seem to harm Vaughn's career. Vaughn continued to serve loyally. Although critics of the Dominican invasion usually castigated Undersecretary Mann as the main villain who had persuaded Johnson to launch the adventure, there is no evidence that Vaughn ever disagreed with Mann on the subject. Like Mann, Vaughn, with hardly any evidence, reported to Johnson soon after the rebels rose up, "Involvement of communist elements in this has become clearer and clearer."

As assistant secretary for Latin American affairs, Vaughn, a soft-spoken man with occasional flashes of temper, had to defend the invasion in public. These defenses annoyed the main critics in Congress, including Senator Robert F. Kennedy.

Vaughn shared the anti–Bobby Kennedy sentiment that emanated from Johnson and pervaded the White House. He did not know Senator Kennedy well but harbored at least one unpleasant memory. When he worked for Shriver at the Peace Corps, he had attended several interagency meetings chaired by Kennedy as attorney general. After the first session, he walked alongside Kennedy and asked him, "Mr. Kennedy, why do you keep referring to your brother-in-law and my boss, Sargent Shriver, as the Boy Scout?" Kennedy, according to Vaughn, replied, "None of your fucking business. You Peace Corps types are all the same. Haven't grown up yet."

In November 1965, Senator Kennedy and his wife, Ethel, embarked on a heavily publicized three-week tour of five countries in South America. Before setting out, Kennedy attended a briefing at the State Department. Vaughn, in charge, assembled a large team of specialists, including State's desk officers for the five countries and representatives from AID, the U.S. Information Agency, the Peace Corps, and other agencies. Mankiewicz, who would soon become Kennedy's press secretary, represented the Peace Corps.

"The briefing was a calamity," Mankiewicz recalled years later. "Jack Vaughn was extremely hostile, completely out of character.... Just set a very angry tone right at the beginning." Vaughn agrees it was "an ugly meeting." But he blames Kennedy, insisting that the senator was trying to bait him with questions that seethed with unfair attacks on Johnson administration policy. Vaughn felt that he had to defend the policy.

In one exchange, Kennedy asked what he should say when Latin Americans questioned him about the Dominican invasion. Vaughn replied, "Well, you could always tell them what your brother said at the time of the Cuban missile crisis."

"Which comment of President Kennedy's was that, Mr. Vaughn?" said Senator Kennedy.

Mankiewicz did not hear Vaughn make any reply. But Vaughn recalls he said that President Kennedy told the world he would react to the missiles in a way dictated by our national interest.

"I hope you are not quoting President Kennedy to support your intervention in the Dominican Republic," Kennedy admonished him.

Kennedy also was angered by Vaughn referring to the assassinated president as "your brother." The senator evidently regarded that as disrespectful and offensive. He wanted Vaughn to call his brother "President Kennedy." Yet Vaughn, according to Mankiewicz, ignored Senator Kennedy's obvious displeasure and kept referring to "your brother."

The exchanges grew worse, and, according to Mankiewicz, reached their nadir when Kennedy, bristling with sarcasm, said to Vaughn, "Well, then as I understand it, what the Alliance for Progress has come down to is that you can lock up your political opposition and outlaw political parties and dissolve the Congress, and you'll continue to get all the aid you want from us; but if you mess around with an American oil company, we'll cut you off without a penny. Is that right?"

Vaughn stared at him and replied, "Well, that's about the size of it, Senator."

The two men were so angry at this point that it is doubtful they could hear each other clearly. Vaughn, in fact, says he wanted to punch Kennedy in the mouth. "It was a very messy thing," said Mankiewicz, "and I thought at the time that Vaughn probably was put up to it ... probably by Thomas Mann." But no one needed to put Vaughn up to this. He had looked on Bobby Kennedy as a bully for a long time—a feeling that only increased under the influence of Lyndon Johnson; he felt that Bobby was trying to bully him during this confrontation, and Johnny Hood was not going to stand for it.

After the briefing, Vaughn walked unsteadily to his office. He was shocked at his own behavior, surprised at himself. He had almost punched a U.S. senator in the face. His career might be at its end. "I really blew it," he decided. Then his phone rang. It was a call from the White House. Someone at the briefing had reported all the details of the ugly meeting. The operator told Vaughn that the president was on the line. "Good going, son," said Johnson.

Vaughn did not campaign to succeed Shriver as director of the Peace Corps. He did not ask anyone in the White House for the job, and he never expected an offer. The most logical choice was Bill Moyers. There is no doubt that Moyers, who was recently appointed White House press secretary, would have liked to return to the Peace Corps as director. But, as Shriver put it later, "Johnson knew exactly how valuable Moyers was to him, and he had no more intention of letting Moyers out of the White House to do anything, including running the Peace Corps, than he did of jumping into the Potomac River."

A good number of candidates were discussed at the White House, including G. Mennen Williams, the former governor of Michigan who was now assistant secretary of state for African affairs; John Bartlow Martin, the magazine writer who had served as ambassador to the Dominican Republic; and Congressman John Brademas of Indiana, the future president of New York University. All were better known nationally than Vaughn.

In the end, however, Johnson surprised Vaughn by selecting him. In fact, the president gave Vaughn only three hours' notice before making the announcement at a news conference. Vaughn believes the deciding factor was Bobby Kennedy's contempt for him.

As evidence, Vaughn, in his memoirs, cites a recorded phone call between Johnson and Undersecretary Mann in January 1966 in which they discuss the possibility of Vaughn taking over the Peace Corps. "From his own point of view," Mann said, "it's time for a change." The reason, Mann went on, was that "Bobby and some of the other boys are trying to get him." They were trying to force him out of his position as assistant secretary for Latin American affairs. Mann, under Johnson's questioning, identified the "other boys" as Senators J. William Fulbright of Arkansas, the chairman of the Senate Foreign Relations Committee, and Wayne Morse of Oregon. Mann said both Democrats were under Bobby's influence. The conclusion that Vaughn draws from the transcript of the call is "that I owe Bobby a very big debt."

There is no doubt that Vaughn's distaste for Bobby Kennedy may have been a strong influence in Johnson's choice. But even more important was Vaughn's friendship with Bill Moyers. Moyers had worked with Vaughn at the Peace Corps and always had a high regard for his good sense and commitment.

Many Peace Corps officials had been gossiping for months about the possible candidates for director. Some thought that Johnson would ask Shriver to appoint his successor. But Charles Peters, the director of evaluation, told Peace Corps publicist Coates Redmon at the time, "Shriver is a lame duck . . . . So forget all those people that Shriver is supposed to be appointing. Only the White House can appoint. And that means Moyers. Because who else at the White House has the interest or the power to appoint a new Peace Corps director?" Johnson usually deferred all Peace Corps matters to Moyers and surely relied on his advice more than anything else in the decision to name Vaughn.

Vaughn, in any case, did not boast in Peace Corps circles about his tattered relations with Bobby Kennedy. By 1968, most of the Peace Corps community—staff, current and returned Volunteers, and former staff—had become followers of Senator Kennedy in his opposition to the war in Vietnam and his quest for the Democratic presidential nomination. Kennedy, like his brother, was a Peace Corps hero, and, when assassinated like his brother, he became a Peace Corps martyr as well. There is no evidence that Vaughn, who was still a registered Republican, ever tried to persuade his colleagues or the Volunteers that their faith in Bobby Kennedy was misplaced.

As director of the Peace Corps, Vaughn lacked the dynamism, charisma, influence, and national standing of Shriver. But so did every other director who followed Shriver in the past half-century. Shriver was the last director with pizzazz. Vaughn, who served only three years, endowed the Peace Corps with steadiness and maturity. He knew the Peace Corps well. He understood the worth and needs of the young generalist Volunteers and initiated significant changes in training and job assignments. He traveled often, spending a third of his time meeting staff, Volunteers, and trainees throughout the world. He seemed always low-key, always attentive, seeking the views of all. In many ways, he became a model of competence and foresight.

In his perceptive memoir, Brent Ashabranner, who served Vaughn as deputy director, wrote, "It has always seemed to me that Shriver was most preoccupied with the image of the Peace Corps—as I think in those formative years he should have been—and that Jack Vaughn became most concerned with the substance of the Peace Corps: how to be sure that there was a real piece of work for Volunteers who were sent overseas, how to see that they were best prepared for that work, how to give them the best support possible."

One night, Ashabranner and Vaughn sat in the director's office discussing the probable decline in the size of the Peace Corps. Numbers would decline as the staff learned to scrutinize Volunteer job assignments more closely, training became tougher and more intense, and the growing resentment over the Vietnam War dampened enthusiasm for joining any U.S. government program. Ashabranner and Vaughn wondered what the press and Congress would make of a decline. Vaughn, lighting his pipe, said, "They'll say we're losing our charisma and that the fire is gone. But what I'd like to do is make the Peace Corps as good as Sarge said it was."

CHAPTER EIGHT

The Specter of Vietnam

On January 6, 1966, two Peace Corps officials embarked on a secret, reckless trip to Vietnam. The goal of their mission was to find out whether Vietnam might be a suitable country for a Peace Corps program. That goal was foolish and fanciful. President Lyndon Johnson had already dispatched thousands of combat troops to South Vietnam and ordered the continual bombing of North Vietnam. Antiwar rallies were already dominating campus life on universities throughout the United States. Peace Corps Volunteers were joining protests. Any attempt to place Volunteers in Vietnam would have crippled the Peace Corps. Even news of the exploratory trip would have damaged the Peace Corps badly.

The two officials were Warren Wiggins, deputy director of the Peace Corps, and Ross J. Pritchard, director of Far East regional operations. Within the Peace Corps, Wiggins and Pritchard were known as the most fervent players of the numbers game—they relentlessly promoted massive new programs without worrying about meticulous planning. But it was not their idea to go to Vietnam.

Wiggins, who died in 2007, never discussed the Vietnam adventure publicly. But Pritchard, retired in Tennessee, says they flew to Vietnam because Johnson ordered them to go. Pritchard says he and Wiggins knew that a program in Vietnam "would ruin the Peace Corps, absolutely wreck it. Because of the mood on campuses, it would cut us off at the knees." But Bill Moyers, the former Peace Corps deputy director who was now White House press secretary, told them that Johnson insisted they go. According to Pritchard, "We went with great, great reluctance."

They should have resisted. But Johnson's insistence came at a time when the Peace Corps bureaucracy was weak, practically rudderless. Sargent Shriver was in his last weeks as director, spending most of his time on the War on Poverty. Wiggins, who had almost no influence at the White House, was acting director much of the time. Jack Vaughn would be nominated to succeed Shriver a few weeks later but would not take over the agency until March 1.

Despite their reluctance, Wiggins and Pritchard sent a rather enthusiastic cable to the U.S. embassy in Saigon announcing their arrival. The cable, written by Pritchard, boasted, "Peace Corps elsewhere and its ability to provide significant numbers of Volunteers suggests there may be a useful role in Vietnam."

"While it is important for the Peace Corps to maintain an independent, nonpolitical stance in order to avoid jeopardizing its worldwide acceptance," the cable went on, "the ability of the Peace Corps to work with and attract host country participation may have potential in Vietnam now and more especially in the future."

The two officials provided a cover story and assured their hosts that the Peace Corps was prepared to lie about the mission. "We desire to avoid publicity for this visit," they said. "If questioned here [Washington], the Peace Corps will take the position that both men are in vicinity Southeast Asia on business and interested in exploring possible role for Peace Corps Volunteers and/or other international Volunteers with refugee work in Vietnam." There was no need to invoke the cover story. The press never spotted the adventure. In fact, hardly anyone in the Peace Corps itself knew that Wiggins and Pritchard had left for Vietnam.

In Saigon, Ambassador Henry Cabot Lodge Jr. welcomed them and promised that the U.S. embassy would show them whatever they wanted to see. Wiggins and Pritchard looked at six sites, including the battleground city of Hue. In each case, their plane would spiral downward while landing to avoid gunfire.

Wiggins and Pritchard decided to explore neighboring Laos as well. Their reception from Ambassador William H. Sullivan in Vientiane was far different. Sullivan was supervising what would become known as the "secret war" in Laos. CIA agents were leading guerilla units against rebels and North Vietnamese troops. U.S. military pilots, wearing civilian clothes, were flying missions in support of the Laotian government. Sullivan did not want independent-minded Peace Corps Volunteers stepping into the cauldron.

"Sullivan was absolutely adamant that this was the stupidest idea he had ever heard of," Pritchard recalls. "He chewed our asses out."

After their ten-day trip, Wiggins and Pritchard wrote a report. They could not resist sounding expansive about the future. "Under different circumstances, you could put a thousand Volunteers into Vietnam," they wrote, according to Pritchard. But in view of the dangers of the war and the backlash that a Vietnam program would unleash elsewhere in the Peace Corps, they strongly recommended against launching a program there.

The conclusions of the report did not matter in any case. Vaughn, the new director, made it clear: No Volunteers would go to Vietnam, no matter what the report recommended, no matter what Johnson demanded.

At Vaughn's swearing-in ceremony at the White House, President Johnson made his case for the Peace Corps in Vietnam someday. While soldiers struggled to halt aggression by North Vietnam and Viet Cong insurgents and provide security in South Vietnam, he said, "other workers of peace . . . must lay the foundation for economic and social progress." He counted on the Peace Corps to do just that in the future. "The day, I hope, will soon come," the president said, "when the Peace Corps will be there, too. It must somehow find the day and the time that it can go and make its contribution when peace is assured."

In at least four meetings during the next three years, Johnson pressured Vaughn to send Volunteers to Vietnam. Johnson promised they would work only in the "pacified" areas. The president said he would be satisfied even with a program of only ten to fifteen Volunteers. But Vaughn turned him down each time.

Yet even as it kept out of Vietnam, the Peace Corps could not escape the war. Gerald Berreman, an anthropologist at the University of California at Berkeley, warned students in 1965, "The government wants the Peace Corps to be a playpen for activist students to keep them out of the kitchen while the adults are cooking up the war in Vietnam." He urged them to stay out of the Peace Corps and protest the war instead.

Some idealistic Volunteers hoped that the leaders of the Peace Corps would stand up to such criticism by forthrightly defying President Johnson and denouncing the war themselves. Marlyn Dalsimer, a former Volunteer in the Ivory Coast, wrote a letter to Jack Vaughn. The letter, Dalsimer recalled later, told Vaughn that "I had observed his never having made a public statement about the war in Vietnam. I told him that as head of an organization with 'peace' in its name, I expected him to. We always hoped the Peace Corps would be different." The Peace Corps *was* different, but not so different that its director could oppose the president openly and keep his job.

In 1965, an article opposing the war appeared in a Volunteer newspaper in Malawi. The article was written by Paul Theroux, a Volunteer teacher who would become one of the most distinguished American novelists of the next half-century. The article infuriated U.S. Ambassador Sam P. Gilstrap. He ordered the expulsion of the Peace Corps director, Michael McCone, for allowing the newspaper to publish a diatribe against U.S. policy. (Theroux, chastened but not otherwise punished, was later thrown out by the Malawi government for delivering letters for friends who were opponents of the dictator Hastings Kuzuma Banda.)

As the war intensified and the awful casualties mounted, Vaughn was forced to field protests from every side of the Peace Corps—even from his own staff. Kirby Jones, the Volunteer who helped write the letter of protest to Lyndon Johnson about the Dominican invasion, worked for the Peace Corps in 1967 as the Ecuadorean desk officer. Allard Lowenstein, the militant anti–Vietnam War protester and future congressman, persuaded Jones to join him in drafting a protest letter to President Johnson. Jones then started collecting signatures from returned Peace Corps Volunteers.

Vaughn asked him to stop, but Jones refused. "Then he [Vaughn] went through this long song and dance," Jones recalled, "about how long it had taken him to establish credibility in the White House, since Johnson had always thought of the Peace Corps as a Kennedy creation, full of Kennedyites, and that this was going to adversely affect the relationship between the Peace Corps and the White House."

"You're going to have to fire me, because I'm not going to stop," Jones said

"I'm not going to fire you," said Vaughn.

The most publicized protest case involved a Volunteer who taught music at the University of Concepcíon, in Chile. Bruce Murray and more than ninety fellow Volunteers signed a letter in 1967 protesting the bombing of North Vietnam and calling for negotiations to end the war. The Volunteers planned to pay for the publication of the letter as an advertisement in the *New York Times*. But after local Peace Corps officials discovered what was going on, Ambassador Ralph Dungan warned the

Volunteers they could be thrown out of the Peace Corps if the letter were published. A similar warning came from Vaughn.

Faced with these threats, the Volunteers abandoned their project. But Murray was angered by Vaughn's restrictions on the rights of the Volunteers to speak out on American issues. In a letter to Vaughn, Murray accepted the stricture that Volunteers "should not meddle in the politics of the host country." But he argued that this restriction should not prevent Volunteers from speaking out on "international policies of the United States which may be of interest to the host country." He sent a copy of this letter to the *New York Times*, but the newspaper did not publish it.

The news agency United Press International (UPI) found out about the controversy and released an article describing the suppression of Volunteer antiwar protests by the Peace Corps. The article was published in the newspaper *El Sur* of Concepción. Murray felt that the UPI article did not state the position of the Volunteers fully, and he sent *El Sur* a Spanish translation of his letter to Vaughn. The Chilean newspaper published it.

The Peace Corps retribution was swift. Country director Paul Bell ordered Murray home, ostensibly for "consultations." When Murray arrived in Washington, he found that no consultations were scheduled. He had already been dismissed from the Peace Corps.

"I was very distraught," Murray recalled later. "I really loved Chile and wanted to stay another year . . . . People at the university were upset, too, because my dismissal was a contradiction of everything the Peace Corps had been saying—that we were independent agents and not called upon to toe the government line. I had voiced a protest and was gone—in the middle of a semester."

The American Civil Liberties Union took up the case, and Murray filed suit against the Peace Corps for wrongful dismissal. Federal Judge Raymond Pettine in Providence heard the case and ruled against the Peace Corps. While the judge understood that the Peace Corps had "an interest in remaining apolitical with respect to host country politics," he called the dismissal "a shocking, unconstitutional act on the part of the Peace Corps." The government, in the judge's view, could prove no national interest in preventing Murray from speaking out "about matters of vital interest to him as a human being, a United States citizen, and a Peace Corps Volunteer."

In the wake of the Murray controversy, Vaughn retreated. He set down regulations, revised them, and, in any case, no longer disciplined anyone. As the war ground on, killing many young Americans and many more Vietnamese, the pressure on Volunteers to cry out intensified. Vaughn decided to trust in the good sense of the Volunteers.

A formula of sorts evolved. The Peace Corps administration agreed that the Volunteers, unlike members of the armed forces, had the right to speak out and protest U.S. policy if they saw fit. In turn, the Peace Corps wanted the Volunteers to accept two limitations on their freedom of speech: They must not interfere in the internal politics of the host country, and their actions must not harm the Peace Corps.

But the formula was fragile, dependent on interpretation. When Murray was dismissed, a spokesman for the Peace Corps had said, "The Vietnam War is a major issue in Chile, and it has been the policy of the Peace Corps not to get involved in any local political issue." This, of course, was a good deal of a stretch—it would be difficult to find any controversial U.S. foreign policy that was not a political issue in most other countries.

The second problem of interpretation centered on what would harm the Peace Corps. Peace Corps officials tended to find any publicity about a protest "embarrassing" and therefore harmful to the agency. They feared that members of Congress might find the protests offensive and slice the budget. They told Volunteers that an angry White House might lose confidence in the Peace Corps.

Many Volunteers, in any case, tried hard not to embarrass the Peace Corps with their demonstrations. In 1968, for example, when President Johnson visited El Salvador, Volunteers Mark Schneider and his wife, Susan, organized an anti–Vietnam War protest. All Volunteers had been invited to a reception at the residence of the U.S. ambassador in San Salvador. Within the compound, the protesting Volunteers lined a small driveway leading to the house. When the president's car drove by, they held up signs condemning the war. Then they put the signs away and joined the reception. The protest, out of sight of journalists, was not reported in either the Salvadorian or U.S. press. (Mark Schneider would be appointed director of the Peace Corps thirty years later.)

Peace Corps demonstrations intensified as the war continued under President Richard Nixon. From the beginning, the Nixon administration decided that it had to meet the Peace Corps protests with new toughness. Secretary of State William Rogers cabled every embassy and consulate in May 1969, "President Nixon and I have determined that the twin goals of service and mutual understanding can best be served if the Peace Corps continues to remain strictly apolitical . . . . Volunteers will be expected to refrain from all political activities in the countries in which they are stationed."

A few months later, Joseph Blatchford, the new Peace Corps director, sent a letter to all country directors clarifying what the Rogers directive meant. While the Peace Corps continued to guarantee "the basic freedoms" of every Volunteer, Blatchford wrote, "we simply cannot have it both ways; we cannot both claim to be apolitical and insert American foreign policy issues into the host country scene." In short, despite the ruling in the Murray case, the Peace Corps would regard a Volunteer's public protest against the U.S. role in Vietnam as interference in the internal politics of the country in which the Volunteer served. If the Volunteers protested privately to the U.S. ambassador, however, there would be no disciplinary action, and their protest would be relayed to the White House or State Department.

By April 1970, Blatchford reported to Congress that he had dismissed twelve Volunteers and one staff member for publicly demonstrating against the war in four countries. Yet this did not dampen the fervor of many other protesting Volunteers. At least once a month, Peace Corps officials would read a dispatch in U.S. newspapers reporting a Volunteer antiwar demonstration overseas.

Several were especially embarrassing. In Afghanistan, a group of Volunteers wore black armbands and read an antiwar statement in front of the U.S. embassy just before the arrival in Kabul of Vice President Spiro Agnew. In Tunisia, a few Volunteers turned their backs on Secretary Rogers while he was addressing members of the U.S. mission.

These incidents drew adverse comments from critics of the Peace Corps. Richard Wilson, a columnist with the *Washington Star,* wrote, "The President, the Vice President, and the Secretary of State have now had enough experience with the high spirits of the politically turbulent Peace Corps to wonder if this experiment in spreading youthful idealism over the world has not gotten badly off the tracks." "These people were not hired to demonstrate either for or against our government," said Representative William Scherle, a Republican from Iowa. "They should either shape up and do the job expected of them, or ship out."

The most embarrassing Peace Corps incident came in early May 1970 in Washington, not overseas. This followed a week of political turbulence. Student protests had erupted on campuses throughout the country after Nixon ordered the invasion of Cambodia to shut down Viet Cong supply bases. Nixon, in turn, derided the protesters as "bums blowing up campuses."

Then, in a terrible moment, National Guardsmen fired on protesting students at the Kent State campus in Ohio, killing four and wounding eleven. A photograph of an anguished student, kneeling by a fallen comrade and calling for help, made the front pages of newspapers throughout the country. Tens of thousands of protesters poured into Washington during the next few days. An insomniac President Nixon, shaken by the Kent State killings, even made his way to the Lincoln Memorial before dawn one night to talk with protesters.

On May 8, two dozen former Volunteers entered the Peace Corps building, rushed to the fourth floor, the quarters for the Asian operations of the agency, ordered everyone to leave, and hung a huge Viet Cong flag from the windows of the building that faced Lafayette Square near the White House.

The protesters, members of a militant organization called the Committee of Returned Volunteers (CRV), remained in the building and issued a bitter anti–Peace Corps statement. "Once abroad, we discovered we were part of the U.S. worldwide pacification program," it said. "We found that U.S. projects in these countries are designed to achieve political control and economic exploitation to build an empire for the United States. As Volunteers, we were part of that strategy; we were the Marines in velvet gloves." The demonstration infuriated Nixon and his staff.

After Washington reporters and television crews rushed to the scene, H. R. Haldeman, the White House chief of staff, and John Ehrlichman, the domestic affairs adviser, continually demanded that the Peace Corps throw the interlopers out. But Blatchford made the decision to do nothing so long as the demonstration was peaceful. "If I had thrown them out," Blatchford recalls, "the White House would have thought I was the greatest thing since Spiro Agnew." But Blatchford's mind was chock-full of images of Kent State and rioting at the 1968 Democratic convention and massive demonstrations at the University of California in Berkeley. "I didn't want the Peace Corps to become a casualty of the Vietnam War," he says.

Ehrlichman urged Blatchford several times to issue an order for the forcible evacuation of the demonstrators. But Blatchford replied he would do so only if expressly ordered to by President Nixon. Ehrlichman never came back with such an order.

Haldeman kept phoning Thomas F. Roeser, the Peace Corps public relations chief, inside the building. "The president wants them the hell out of there," Haldeman ordered on the first call. "He wants you to get a few staffers together, go to the fourth floor, get off the elevator there, grab the intruders, and remove them bodily the hell out of there. That's an order." Roeser, who thought erroneously that the occupiers were armed, warned Haldeman that the White House order might provoke the killing of Peace Corps staffers. "Get back to you," said Haldeman.

Haldeman wrote notes to himself that show how the feelings in the White House changed during the day. "Bust the Peace Corps. Get it rough," he wrote at first. Then, as the model of Kent State began to trouble the White House, he added, "No soldiers do anything—let the kids break windows." But the mood shifted again. "Get Peace Corps out," he wrote.

Finally, the White House gave up and was rewarded for its patience. In the middle of the second night, the demonstrators slipped out of the building. Ehrlichman phoned Blatchford the next morning. "Why did they leave?" he asked. Blatchford replied sarcastically, "I don't know. I'm pissed because they didn't call me."

Although the Peace Corps never did serve in Vietnam, not even after the war ended, it did find itself intertwined with the Vietnam War in one program overseas—the operation in nearby Thailand. Throughout the war, the Peace Corps kept 200 to 420 Volunteers in Thailand. The U.S. military, meanwhile, used Thailand as a staging base for air raids into North Vietnam and as a rest and recreation center for worn out soldiers. Almost 50,000 airmen and airwomen operated the base while 6,000 troops came to Bangkok and other tourist sites every month for R and R. On top of this, an unknown number of CIA operatives used Thai territory as headquarters for various missions throughout Southeast Asia. As Michael Schmicker, who arrived in Thailand in 1969 as a Volunteer teacher, put it, "The 'War Corps' dwarfed the Peace Corps in Thailand."

Sometimes a Volunteer foolishly poked into U.S. military and even intelligence business. In his second year, Schmicker began moonlighting by writing articles for the *Bangkok World*. One assignment took him to neighboring Laos, where he boarded a small Air America plane that dropped ninety-pound sacks of rice to CIA-backed guerrillas who were fleeing from the communist group Pathet Lao. As everyone, including Schmicker, knew, Air America was a supposedly civilian airline owned and operated by the CIA throughout Southeast Asia.

When the article appeared in the *Bangkok World*, it sported a phony byline; Schmicker had adopted a *nom de plume*. But that did not fool Kevin Delany, the Peace Corps director in Thailand. Since its founding, the Peace Corps had taken extraordinary measures to make sure that it had no entanglements with the CIA, and Schmicker had jeopardized all this. Delany called Schmicker into headquarters for a lecture and punishment.

"I had done an incredibly stupid thing," Schmicker wrote in his memoirs. "Imagine the communist propaganda headlines if something had happened, the plane went down, and I got picked up by the Pathet Lao instead of the good guys. How about 'CIA Plane Carrying Thai Peace Corps Volunteer Downed Outside Luang Prabang.' I felt sick to my stomach. My selfishness and stupidity could have had disastrous consequences."

Delany informed Schmicker that he would be thrown out of the Peace Corps. The Volunteer begged for a second chance. "I didn't think it through," he explained. "I just knew it would make a hell of a story, so I went for it." That rationale struck a chord with Delany, a professional newsman who had worked with the *New York World-Telegram & Sun* and CBS News before joining the Peace Corps staff. He relented but warned Schmicker, "OK, but if I ever catch you doing something that stupid again, you're gone."

The temptation to fraternize with fellow Americans was greatest near the U.S. air base in the northeast. James I. Jouppi, a Volunteer civil engineer who came to Thailand in 1971 to help build dams for fish ponds, was assigned to Nakorn Panome province, not far from the base. "A few months after I arrived, I began making GI friends," he wrote in his memoirs. "I'd sometimes visit them in the evening, and when John [another Volunteer] arrived to see me, he'd want me to pay them a visit so that he could tag along and talk to them. The GIs I knew had a standard evening routine. They'd gather around a marijuana bawng and talk about what was on their minds which, as often as not, involved the trials of being part of the American machine when they didn't believe in the War."

The proximity to Vietnam encouraged Volunteers in Thailand to continually examine the rationale for the war; mostly, they found it wanting. Several Volunteers wanted to stage a protest march on the U.S. embassy, but faced with a threat by the Thai government to shut down the Peace Corps, settled for a two-hour meeting with the U.S. ambassador instead. When Vice President Spiro Agnew arrived in Bangkok for an official visit, six Volunteers greeted him with protests against the war.

The greatest impact of the Vietnam War on the Peace Corps was surely on the size of the agency. In 1966, the year Shriver gave up the helm, the Peace Corps counted 15,556 Volunteers and trainees in the field. The total began to decline after then, dropping by 1,000 to 1,500 a year, until it dipped below 10,000 in 1970. By the time the North Vietnamese army captured Saigon in 1975, the total number of Volunteers and trainees had dropped to 7,015. For the rest of its first fifty years, it would never reach the numbers of the Shriver era again. In fact, it would never climb over 10,000 again. The Peace Corps's numbers would remain in the 5,000 to 8,000 range.

There are a number of reasons for the long decline, including the insistence by Vaughn and his deputy director, Brent Ashabranner, that no Volunteer go on post until the Peace Corps was sure that a real job existed and the Volunteer was thoroughly trained for it. The suspension of the draft also cut down the number of male applicants.

But the two most important reasons were the enmity of President Nixon and the war in Vietnam. Nixon did all he could to cut the budget of the Peace Corps and subsume it underneath another agency. As we will see, the blows against the Peace Corps by the Nixon White House were brutal and incessant, but the Peace Corps might have recovered if it were not for the specter of the Vietnam War.

The furor over the war and its seeming senselessness rendered the Kennedy call for service both quaint and specious to many young Americans. If you asked yourself, Kennedy-style, not what your country can do for you but what you can do for your country, the answer left a bad taste. You knew what your government wanted. It wanted you to serve by killing Vietnamese and risking a terrible death yourself. Joining the Peace Corps, in the view of many young Americans, would only help divert attention from the American guilt in Vietnam.

In a thunderclap, the war shut down the optimism and hopes that had emanated from the brief Kennedy years. Applying to the Peace Corps was no longer chic, fashionable, or, for some, even honorable. There was something disdainful, in fact, about working for any agency of the federal government. Applications to the Peace Corps dropped from 42,000 in 1966 to just under 14,000 in 1977. Of course, not every young American felt this way. As the furor over Vietnam dissipated, the anti–Peace Corps and anti-government rhetoric dissipated as well. But this did not bring back the old Peace Corps buzz and the old Kennedy magic.

But in some ways, the slimmed Peace Corps was a stronger Peace Corps. Training was more intense and meaningful. Officials, no longer focused on the numbers game, examined job openings with more intelligence and care. The small Peace Corps did not make the kind of major impact that Shriver and his colleagues once envisioned. But it still performed significant work and continued to produce a cadre of Americans with unusual sensitivity, insight, and experience in the desperate problems of the poor nations of the world.

CHAPTER NINE

The Wrath of Richard Nixon

President Richard M. Nixon had every reason to despise the Peace Corps. Even before it started, he had denounced it as a haven for draft dodgers. John F. Kennedy's espousal of the idea in the final days of the campaign probably contributed, at least in a small way, to his defeat of Nixon in the close 1960 election. The outburst of youthful enthusiasm for the agency and the fawning attention by the press had made the Peace Corps a showcase for the enchanted Kennedy era. For many onlookers, the Volunteers were still the children of Kennedy. That made it difficult for Nixon and his White House to embrace them.

After a year in office, Nixon assigned speechwriter Pat Buchanan and former Des Moines Register reporter Clark Mollenhoff to investigate, as Buchanan put it, "the Peace Corps's egregious blunders with an eye, as we understand, to doing away with the thing."

Buchanan, a future candidate for the Republican nomination for president, was young, right-wing, tough, and master of a style so aggressive and harsh that even Nixon sometimes felt it necessary to tone him down. In the case of the Peace Corps, however, Buchanan counseled slow steps and patience.

"As for abolition," he wrote in a February 20, 1970, memorandum to Nixon, "I would not counsel such drastic action. It would put us crosswise with a number of our friends who have swallowed the propaganda that this is the greatest thing since sliced bread. Also, the Kennedyites would create a real storm." Instead, he proposed leaking tales of Peace Corps blunders to members of Congress "again and again to create a climate of opinion that would receive the executive [*sic*] a little better."

Buchanan's advice took hold and the White House soon embarked on a campaign that would not abolish the Peace Corps in a swoop but would try instead to render it impotent through a thousand cuts. Mollenhoff sent Nixon a report on what the White House regarded as the Peace Corps's most egregious blunder: It had become a hothouse of protest against the war in Vietnam. Mollenhoff reported that Volunteers had become involved in "political demonstrations in more than a dozen countries in the last two years."

Mollenhoff proposed more thorough FBI background investigations "to avoid selection of Peace Corps Volunteers who are likely to become involved in defiance of the rules." He also suggested that the Peace Corps needed an influx of new staff "who will be able to spot potential problem areas and deal with these problems with restraint and balance."

The idea of a Peace Corps with different Volunteers and staff appealed to Buchanan. He endorsed Mollenhoff's report with a memo to Nixon that proposed "changing its [the Peace Corps's] nature to a more altruistic outfit than it seems to be today with the young leftists dominant."

A few weeks later, in mid-March, Nixon was angered by a lengthy article in the *Wall Street Journal* that described the work of the CRV and its argument that the Peace Corps serves "as an insidious way of furthering questionable 'imperialistic' aims of the U.S. government." The article quoted Paul Cowan, a disillusioned ex-Volunteer from a hapless community development project in the slums of Guayaquil, Ecuador. Cowan concluded that Peace Corps projects like his own were just tokenism—they did nothing to solve the problems of a poor country but instead prepared young Americans to serve later in the foreign policy establishment of the United States.. "It's a kind of graduate school for imperialism," Cowan said.

The article appeared a couple of months before the CRV would infuriate the White House by seizing a floor of the Peace Corps building to dramatize its opposition to the war in Vietnam. But the article was enough to reinforce Nixon's distaste for the Peace Corps. The president issued a directive to phase it out. For good measure, he coupled VISTA (Volunteers in Service to America), the domestic volunteer program of the War on Poverty, with the Peace Corps, aiming for the two organizations to suffer a similar fate. The directive, which came in the form of a memo to Henry Kissinger, the national security adviser, and John Ehrlichman, the domestic affairs assistant, stated that the president "feels a quiet phasing out of the Peace Corps and VISTA is in order. He notes that the place to begin is to get the appropriations cut. He requests that you have Mr. [Bryce] Harlow begin to work quietly on this." Harlow was the White House liaison with Congress.

Harlow received his instructions in a memo attached to a copy of Nixon's directive. In the memo, presidential aide Lamar Alexander, the future governor of Tennessee and senator, advised Harlow, "Because more young people are interested today in solving problems in America rather than abroad, and because the Peace Corps is not working out as well in foreign countries as it once did, there may be some room here to get a cutback in appropriations."

This set off a bizarre maneuver in which the Republican White House quietly tried to persuade the Democratic Congress to appropriate less money for the Peace Corps than the White House had requested in its own budget. The maneuver encountered snags from time to time.

The Nixon White House, of course, could count on Otto Passman, a powerful member of the House Appropriations Committee, who luxuriated in the role of an implacable, irascible, and obsessive foe of foreign aid. This Louisiana Democrat never had joined all the oohing and ahhing over the Peace Corps. "I say without fear of contradiction or any factual statistics to the contrary," he told Congress, "that the so-called misnamed Peace Corps is the most useless and, in all probability, most detrimental to our foreign policy of any agency in our federal government."

Yet the Peace Corps still had enough congressional admirers to prevent crippling slashes of its budget. A disappointed White House staffer reported to Ehrlichman in mid-May that "we didn't do as well as expected" when the appropriations committee voted more money for the Peace Corps than the White House wanted. But that did not discourage Nixon. H.R. Haldeman reported in his diary in July that the president still "wanted to cut Peace Corps and Vista budget down far enough to decimate them."

The conspirators in the White House kept one key administration official in the dark about their plot to squelch the Peace Corps. Joseph H. Blatchford, the director of the Peace Corps, knew that the White House wanted to cut out wasteful spending by the agency. He also knew that Nixon believed the Peace Corps staff was chock-full of liberal Democrats. In a meeting with Nixon, Blatchford reported he was hoping to reach the goal of a 30 percent reduction in staff by the end of the administration's first year in office. "The president responded," according to an official account of the meeting, "by requesting Mr. Blatchford to keep on cutting, to get more young men like Mr. Blatchford and 'to get rid of the other sort.'" But Blatchford was never told that Nixon wanted to get rid of the Peace Corps itself.

Blatchford seems to have been beguiled by Nixon. Whenever he met the president, the president appeared pleased by the Peace Corps and positive about his work. "He never said a thing negative about me and the Peace Corps," says Blatchford. "I always thought I had the support of the president." The president invited Blatchford and his wife to dinners at the White House with the president of Colombia and with the president of Venezuela. "When I met him in the Oval Office," Blatchford recalls, "he gave me a lot of time." Blatchford realized that Nixon had been annoyed by the anti–Vietnam War protests by Volunteers overseas and by the former Volunteers in Washington, but Blatchford assumed he was satisfied with the Peace Corps's disciplinary action and new recruitment policies. Blatchford knew that some people around Nixon scorned the Peace Corps. "But," he says, "I didn't think there was any intentional plan to get rid of the Peace Corps."

It was a stealth campaign. Nixon wanted to rid himself of the Peace Corps but not be seen doing so. In 1972, Blatchford found himself embroiled in a public fight with Passman, the chairman of the foreign aid appropriations subcommittee. Passman had cut so much out of the Peace Corps budget that Blatchford insisted he would have to recall more than 4,000 Volunteers from their posts overseas. Nixon could have remained aloof and let the Peace Corps fall apart. But that would have made it obvious where he stood. So instead he transferred emergency funds to the Peace Corps, making himself look like the savior of the Peace Corps, not its nemesis. That made it harder for Blatchford to regard him as anything but a friend.

The appointment of Blatchford had not been welcomed by the Peace Corps staff. Jack Vaughn, a registered Republican, had hoped that the new Republican administration would let him remain as director. Secretary of State William Rogers, in fact, had told Vaughn to inform the Peace Corps staff that he was "staying on." This set off happy celebrations at headquarters. But Rogers had meant Vaughn was staying only until a new director was named. In March 1969, the White House announced the nomination of Blatchford, a complete outsider. The appointment was looked on by the Peace Corps as a great betrayal.

In other circumstances, Blatchford might have been regarded as a welcome choice. He could boast a lot of Peace Corps–like credentials. He was a thirty-four-year-old Los Angeles lawyer who had founded a private volunteer program in Venezuela known as Acción. He had first visited Latin America as part of a touring band of jazz musicians from the University of California at Los Angeles (UCLA). Since he was also a member of UCLA's championship tennis team, Blatchford competed with Latin tennis players wherever the band traveled. He enjoyed motorcycle riding, and after his confirmation, he often showed up for work on a Yamaha motorcycle, parking it in the lobby of the Peace Corps building.

The White House had no doubts about his party loyalty. He had run for Congress as a Republican in a heavily Democratic district in southern California in 1968 and come close to an upset. But Nixon wanted Ehrlichman's office to "come up with some proof as to his strength of character and his general 'toughness'" before final approval. Ehrlichman evidently did so, but Nixon would continue to harbor some doubts about his toughness.

Blatchford was not the White House's first choice. Ehrlichman had first offered the job to a classmate at Stanford Law School, Lewis H. Butler, a Republican lawyer in San Francisco. Butler would probably have been welcomed enthusiastically by the Peace Corps, for he was one of its own. He had served as the first director of the Peace Corps in Malaysia and later worked for Charles Peters at the evaluation division. But Butler turned down Ehrlichman's job offer. Butler had been assigned temporarily to the Department of HEW and liked the work there. "Besides," as he now recalls, "who wants to run the Peace Corps in the middle of the Vietnam War with Richard Nixon as president?" It was a prescient attitude. Butler instead accepted an offer to serve as assistant secretary of HEW.

Once he became director, Blatchford felt the need to put his personal stamp on the agency and issued a series of "New Directions" during his first year supposedly designed to help the Peace Corps, born in the 1960s, catch up with the 1970s. The most important was his call for more skilled and mature Volunteers. After his first trip abroad as director, to Kenya, Libya, and Iran, he told his staff, "Everywhere the cry was for men and women with higher-priority skills—who can also work with people—to fill higher-priority development needs."

Blatchford may have put too much stock in what he was told by officials in these countries. It was easier for Third World officials to request highly skilled technicians than to acknowledge a need for young Americans just out of college. The officials may simply have been asking for as much as they could. But there is no doubt, in any case, that they gave Blatchford an earful.

Recruiting skilled technicians was not as novel an idea as Blatchford made it sound. The Peace Corps had long been interested in attracting older Volunteers with special skills—agricultural specialists, doctors, nurses, experienced science teachers, and so on. But they were difficult to recruit. They would have to give up two years of lucrative pay for the pittance the Peace Corps set aside for them as Volunteers. The Peace Corps would have to make special arrangements for those with families.

Some country directors did not favor older Volunteers, who often had a more difficult time learning a foreign language than younger Volunteers. Even more important, some older Volunteers tended to fester with frustration if their expertise were not fully utilized. These disadvantages, in the view of other country directors, were more than balanced by the popularity of older Volunteers among younger Volunteers, who depended upon them for advice and support.

But Blatchford's recruiting campaign was much stronger than those in the past. He enlisted the aid of labor unions and the Smithsonian Institution to spread the word among skilled laborers and scientists that they were welcome. He encouraged families. At one news conference, he showed off a dozen Volunteers and spouses and their twenty-five children, en route to Ghana.

The publicity generated by Blatchford's recruiting campaigns had one major drawback. It tended to denigrate the role of the BA generalist who still made up the bulk of the numbers of the Peace Corps. Even Henry Kissinger was troubled by this. After Blatchford presented his plans to the White House, Kissinger warned in a memo to Nixon that the recruitment of older, skilled Volunteers "blurs image of a highly motivated and youth-oriented undertaking." In some instances, Kissinger went on, the Peace Corps would be creating "a virtual counterpart to the local AID operation."

Blatchford also used the image of an older Peace Corps to ward off complaints that the Peace Corps had become a hotbed of young anti–Vietnam War radicals. After Col. Alexander Haig, Kissinger's military assistant, asked for reaction to the Volunteer protest during Vice President Spiro Agnew's visit to Afghanistan, Blatchford wrote to Haig, "We have sharpened our focus in selection procedures so as to encourage greater cross-section of skilled Americans with emphasis on maturity."

In a similar way, Blatchford sent a memo to the seventeen Republican members of the House Foreign Affairs Committee, listing the steps that he was taking to deal with the rash of Peace Corps protests. He devoted a good deal of space to the "initiation of a policy of recruiting different types of Volunteers—people with more maturity, greater experience, and training such as skilled technicians from the ranks of labor, farmers, professional people in the fields of engineering, architecture, etc."

Blatchford's recruitment drives did change the makeup of the Peace Corps somewhat. The average age of the Volunteers rose, and the Peace Corps could boast about a new array of skills. Moreover, though the recent liberal arts graduate remained the mainstay of the Peace Corps, Blatchford's emphasis on skills reinforced the intense training that had started in the last years under Vaughn. New Volunteers might not be the experienced professionals that foreign officials wanted but most would be sufficiently trained for the middle-level jobs they filled.

Blatchford's call for older, more skilled Volunteers would be echoed afterwards every ten years or so by Peace Corps directors acting as if they were announcing a brand new idea. In 2008, for example, the *Christian Science Monitor* ran a story from Addis Ababa quoting Ethiopian officials who demanded Volunteers with "expertise, not youthful zeal." Director Ronald Tschetter had already moved in that direction, the story went on, recruiting through the American Association of Retired Persons (AARP) and organizations of retired teachers. "The same kind of passion that . . . young people have, these people have . . . but they have thirty years of experience to bring along with it," Tschetter said.

(Yet the Peace Corps, as always, would remain youthful. Although almost 7 percent of the 7,761 Volunteers and trainees in 2009 were more than fifty years old, including one aged eighty-five, the median age was twenty-five.)

There is a strong possibility that Nixon and his aides began to look on Blatchford as almost a "liberal," taking on attitudes from an agency steeped in idealism, naivete, and fervor. Soon after Blatchford took office, Nixon was upset by a *Foreign Affairs* article that accused the Volunteers in Micronesia of meddling in local politics. The president asked Blatchford "to investigate this situation carefully and recommend corrective action."

Instead, Blatchford sent back a well-reasoned defense of the work of the Micronesia Volunteers. Micronesia was a unique Peace Corps venue, for it was not a foreign country at all. A group of 2,100 islands (only 90 inhabited) scattered across an enormous area of the Pacific Ocean, Micronesia was a U.N. trusteeship administered by the United States. Before World War I, it had been a German colony. After Germany's defeat, it became a mandate of the League of Nations administered by Japan. After Japan's defeat in World War II, the United States took it over. So the Volunteers were dealing with a people subject to U.S. colonial masters. These colonial masters were officials of the Department of Interior that administered the trusteeship for the United States.

Although the population of Micronesia was only 100,000, there were more than 500 Peace Corps Volunteers there. Some were lawyers who helped both Micronesia legislators and private citizens prepare petitions, reports, and letters to the U.N. Trusteeship Council. This upset Interior Department officials, who bore the brunt of the complaints. It also upset the State Department because the Volunteers, by helping Micronesians communicate with the United Nations, were interfering with U.S. foreign policy.

In his memorandum, Blatchford cited the case of one Volunteer who had helped the people of Bikini Island petition the United Nations for the right to return to their island. They had been evacuated years earlier to make way for American nuclear testing there. "By a strict interpretation of Peace Corps policy of non-involvement in politics," Blatchford wrote, "this resolution should never have been written. But as a Peace Corps Volunteer with a commitment to the people he serves, it was a move which will ultimately be of great benefit to the Bikinis."

Blatchford's defense was not well received. Ehrlichman told him that the report had been reviewed by both Nixon and Kissinger, and that "Dr. Kissinger remarked that the most troublesome element in Micronesia apparently is a group of young attorneys in the Peace Corps who have made themselves obnoxious to the Micronesia government and to the (Interior) Department people."

In September 1969, Blatchford sent an unsolicited paper to Ehrlichman and Kissinger, setting down his views "on the need for a new dynamics in U.S. policy on Latin America." Basing the paper on his own experience, Blatchford concluded that "the attitude of the United States must be one which respects Latin culture, which treats Latin Americans as friends, and which encourages them to manage their own development."

These high-minded sentiments on Latin America surely made no impact on a White House proud of its realpolitik. Far from fretting over the need to make more friends in Latin America, Nixon and Kissinger would soon become obsessed with the election of left-wing President Salvador Allende in Chile and the need to get rid of him.

In late 1970, Blatchford received word from George Schultz, the director of the Office of Management and the Budget, that the Peace Corps budget for the new year would be slashed by 30 percent. "I was really stunned," says Blatchford. "But I didn't think Nixon was behind this. I blamed it on Schultz."

A puzzled Blatchford then lunched with Assistant Attorney General Robert Mardian, who would become involved later in the White House cover-up of the Watergate burglary. "There are people who think you're another Leon Panetta," Mardian told him, "that you're kind of a liberal." Panetta, a Republican, had been accused by right-wingers in the administration of applying too much zeal to his post as director of civil rights in the Department of Health, Education, and Welfare. Panetta quit and switched to the Democratic party. Blatchford protested to Mardian that he was a conservative Republican. "I knew in my heart," Blatchford recalls, "that Nixon didn't think of me that way [as a liberal]."

But by mid-1971, there was evidence in the diaries of Haldeman that Nixon looked on Blatchford as lacking right-wing toughness. The president, Haldeman wrote on May 24, is "worried about the Peace Corps and thinks we're making some mistakes there." To deal with this, according to Haldeman, Nixon proposed "that we should really look into this; put a tough guy on it who hates the left-wing press and do something about it." None of this lack of confidence was communicated to Blatchford.

Schultz's office had been considering ideas to streamline the executive branch and make it more efficient. The suggestions included the possible merger of the Peace Corps and VISTA. Blatchford says he decided to write a memorandum to Schultz embracing this idea. "I thought it would protect both Peace Corps and VISTA," he says. He believed they would be less vulnerable to budget slashers if they were out of sight. The White House soon announced the merger.

Many Peace Corps advocates feared that the merger would bury the Peace Corps. Sargent Shriver asked Congress to block the reorganization, but Congress refused. On July 1, 1971, Nixon created a new agency, ACTION, that combined the Peace Corps with VISTA, the Foster

Grandfather Program, the Retired Senior Volunteer Program, the Senior Corps of Retired Executives, and the Active Corps of Executives. Blatchford was named the first director of ACTION.

He did not last very long. On the day after Nixon was elected to a second term in 1972, the White House asked the head of every government agency to submit a letter of resignation. Not all of them were accepted, but Blatchford's was.

The days at ACTION were humbling days for the Peace Corps. While Volunteers overseas were still identified as part of the Peace Corps, the organization in Washington was officially "the International Operations Division of ACTION." Peace Corps directors, now known as associate directors of ACTION, could not use the Peace Corps logo on their stationery. Several Peace Corps officials were reprimanded, staffer Deborah Harding recalls, for announcing "Peace Corps" when they picked up their phones. A procession of associate directors in charge of the International Operations Division came and left, little known to the public. Shriver complained, with some regret and some scorn, "Peace Corps isn't even listed in the phone book anymore."

But it was never tested whether Nixon intended the burial of Peace Corps within ACTION as a first step toward oblivion. Nixon had far more to worry about in his second term. He and the White House became obsessed with the Watergate burglary, the cover-up, the threat of impeachment, and finally, his resignation. With all that to contend with, the machinations of the International Operations Division of ACTION hardly mattered.

The Peace Corps managed to survive the administrations of Nixon and his successor, President Gerald Ford. Blatchford deserves some credit for this. He was a strong believer in the Peace Corps and felt a need to protect it. Despite all his talk about New Directions, his most noteworthy achievement was to reinforce the best ideas from the past.

The Peace Corps enrollment of Volunteers and trainees continued to slide from a little more than 12,000 in 1969 to a little under 6,000 in 1976. From now on, the Peace Corps remained a small but significant operation—never again reaching as many as 10,000 Volunteers and trainees in the field, but never falling as low as 5,000, either. It would never again face a danger as great as the twin threats of Nixon and the Vietnam War. And the Peace Corps enjoyed a growing constituency of former Volunteers who would staff, train, lobby for, and protect it.

CHAPTER TEN

The Fall of the Lion of Judah

For better or worse, no country has ever felt the impact of the Peace Corps as much as Ethiopia did in the 1960s and 1970s. A generation of educated Ethiopians grew up in which every member had been taught in high school by at least one Peace Corps Volunteer, and probably many more. These educated Ethiopians spoke English better than any generation that came before or afterward and pondered modern and democratic ideas that were both exciting and subversive in the hoary empire of Haile Selassie I. A case can be made that the Volunteers contributed to the revolution that brought down the emperor. But the Peace Corps has never boasted about this.

Ethiopia was then one of the most impoverished and least educated nations on earth, and it was still ruled by one of the icons of the tumultuous years that prefaced World War II. Haile Selassie had stood in the hall of the League of Nations in Geneva in June 1936 and called on the world to save his country from the poison gas and marauding troops of Italian dictator Benito Mussolini. The plea pricked the consciences of many but not enough to galvanize their governments into action, and the Italians soon occupied Ethiopia, one of the last independent lands of Africa. Haile Selassie remained in exile until British troops drove out the Italians in 1941 during World War II.

Except for the few years of Italian occupation, Ethiopia had escaped colonialism. That had helped instill a stubborn self-confidence in many of its people but left the country with few paved roads, schools, clinics, or modern ideas. Haile Selassie ruled a people hampered by ways that seemed to belong in medieval feudal Europe. In 1968, 70 percent of Ethiopian farmers were tenants who paid for the use of the land by turning over large portions of their crop to landlords, sometimes as much as half. They saw little point in adapting new techniques that would enrich their landlords.

Ethiopia had a parliament, a cabinet, and other democratic trappings, but the autocratic emperor ruled by fiat. He reigned over a court of schemers and whisperers and sometimes made decisions based only on the insinuations of favored courtiers. By tradition, he supposedly could trace his lineage to the seduction of the Queen of Sheba by King Solomon, and official proclamations of the state described him as "Conquering Lion of the Tribe of Judah, Haile Selassie I, Elect of God, Emperor of Ethiopia."

The United States served as a bulwark of the regime. U.S. aid to Ethiopia, including both military and economic, was the largest for any country in Africa. The Ethiopian army of 39,000 and its air force of 2,300, with more than 100 planes, would be crippled without U.S. support. U.S. policymakers looked on the large assistance program as the rent they had to pay for the Kagnew communications base in the northern province of Eritrea. U.S. officials were always vague about the purpose of Kagnew, but it was obvious that this U.S. base, in an era before space brimmed with satellites, was eavesdropping on the Soviet Union, trying to decipher secret messages. More than 3,000 Americans worked at the base.

Another 3,000 Americans worked elsewhere in Ethiopia. Some were U.S. special forces advising the Ethiopian army in its perennial campaign to stifle guerilla warfare in Eritrea. Eritrea, a former Italian colony that Ethiopia annexed after World War II, chafed under the rule of Haile Selassie and his Amharic people. Most Americans, however, were civilians, largely employed by AID. AID projects included dam and power station construction, training for Ethiopian Air Lines, and the creation of an agricultural college, a public health college, and a business school.

Support of modern education, in fact, was a major U.S. contribution, and, as a result, the United States became both the major support for the traditional authoritarian rule of the emperor and the major agent of change leading young Ethiopians away from traditional ways. Fellowships for study in the United States were awarded to five hundred Ethiopians a year. Haile Selassie I University in Addis Ababa, supported by both AID and the Ford Foundation, was heavily staffed by Americans.

The dean of its law school and much of his faculty were American. And the Peace Corps, with one of its largest programs in the world, became the backbone of secondary education throughout Ethiopia.

The first contingent of almost three hundred Volunteers arrived in Ethiopia in September 1962. The importance of the program was underscored by the appointment of its director, the thirty-six-year-old civil-rights activist Harris Wofford. Wofford was already well known as the campaign worker who had come up with the idea that presidential candidate John F. Kennedy phone Coretta King when her husband, Martin Luther King Jr., was jailed in Georgia. Wofford was also one of the pioneers who had helped Shriver set up the Peace Corps, and he had joined the White House staff as special assistant to President Kennedy on civil rights. The Peace Corps looked on his dispatch to Ethiopia as a grand coup.

The Volunteers regarded Wofford as an inspiring visionary. In his view, "Every Peace Corps Volunteer—like Mark Twain's Connecticut Yankee in King Arthur's Court—became a 20th-century revolutionary example in Ethiopia for they were pluralist, secular and full of can-do American enthusiasm."

In an early achievement, Wofford persuaded the Ethiopian government to create a Peace Corps of its own. Under the scheme, every Ethiopian university student was obliged to take a year off and teach in an Ethiopian secondary school alongside the American Peace Corps teachers. Many students, from elite families, did not know the countryside outside Addis Ababa. "They were shocked by the bureaucracy and poverty and misery and became radicalized," says Wofford.

The emperor, who wanted to modernize his country without altering his traditional authoritarian rule, welcomed the Volunteers with a reception at his Jubilee Palace. Later, whenever his Rolls Royce passed a Volunteer in the streets of Addis Ababa, he would nod at the American. The Volunteers were easy to spot because they only bowed to the emperor—unlike his subjects, they did not fall to their hands and knees when he passed by. By prearrangement at Christmastime, a group of fifty Volunteers assembled below the windows of the palace and sang carols. He invited them in, served champagne and Ethiopian tej, a honey wine, and, seated on his throne, received each one for a few moments of Christmas greeting.

The Peace Corps kept growing in Ethiopia and began to display all the flaws of an oversized program. By 1965, a year after Wofford returned to Washington, the number of Volunteers had almost doubled to 550. More than 450 were teaching in the secondary schools, more than 30 at the university. The Volunteers made up more than a third of all secondary school teachers in Ethiopia, and more than half of all secondary school teachers with a university degree. "While it is not always good to be dependent on so many Americans," said Tegegne Yeteshawork, the editor of the government newspaper, the *Ethiopia Herald,* "Ethiopia cannot help itself. The Peace Corps is indispensable to us. By 1970, we may need 4,000 Volunteers."

Yet the size was already making it difficult for the Volunteers to break away from each other and experience Ethiopian life fully. The clusters were enormous. Addis Ababa alone had 159 Volunteers, more than any other city in the world. In fact, the contingent in Addis Ababa alone numbered more than the full Peace Corps program in twelve other countries in Africa. Throughout Ethiopia, many Volunteers enjoyed a varied social life, playing poker, riding horses, seeing movies, playing tennis, watching television, drinking beer, and vacationing—almost always with other Volunteers.

Despite the problem of the large clusters, many Volunteers maintained an intensive relationship with their schools and their pupils. Ethiopia did not have the isolated school compounds and dormitories of the boarding schools in the former British colonies. Pupils came to town, often from far-off villages, and fended for themselves while attending secondary school in town. Many Volunteers allowed pupils to live in their houses in exchange for household chores. Others were hired by the Volunteers as Amharic teachers. The Volunteers handed out books to the young Ethiopians and, in many cases, paid for them to continue their schooling.

Unlike Ghanian schools, the Ethiopian secondary schools did not have comfortable bungalows for their teachers. The Volunteers lived in functional, nondescript houses in town, and many pupils, whether they lived with the Volunteers or not, hung around.

The Ethiopian children had to learn in English, a foreign language. Although English was one of their subjects of study, they felt ill at ease with the language. In their desperation, they memorized great chunks of subject matter to parrot back on examinations. Volunteers tried hard to break down this rote learning. They admonished their young Ethiopians to think for themselves, to find solutions though their own ingenuity, to analyze subject matter instead of memorizing it.

The Volunteers, sometimes through demonstration, also taught their pupils to question authority. That, of course, was one side of the admonition to think for themselves. The pupils would also see the Volunteers challenge Ethiopian headmasters to expand the curriculum, or speed up the mimeographing of examinations, or stop beating pupils. This example would not be lost on the Ethiopian university students teaching in the secondary schools as well.

All those ideas that came naturally from American teaching—think for yourself, question what you are told—were subversive ideas in a country where one man, elected by God, possessed the authority to make all decisions. Americans imparted these ideas without even realizing it. Some Volunteers went further, expanding the curriculum to include Western ideas that they knew (or should have known) challenged the emperor, his court of whisperers, and his feudal world.

"At Shimeles Habte School in Addis," Richard Lipez, a member of the first contingent of Volunteers, recalled recently, "I taught a unit in ninth-grade English on the techniques and uses of propaganda. I never mentioned the emperor, of course, or maybe Ethiopia at all, but these kids were soon up to their eyebrows in Orwell. And they could put two and two together.

"I also led an after-school seminar, for those top students who wanted to participate, on Great Books and Documents. I can't remember all the literature we read and discussed; availability was one of the factors in choosing what to take on. But I do remember Alan Paton's *Too Late the Phalarope* and—God, what was I thinking?—the American Declaration of Independence . . . .

"The students I had," Lipez went on, "were hungry for ideas and for the kind of societal change that would give them more opportunities to get ahead. Maybe the most radical idea we promoted, consciously or unconsciously, was that merit was what mattered, not tribe or family or class. I wonder if Haile Selassie knew what he was doing when he invited us in."

In 1969, students began to strike and demonstrate against their government. At first, their demands focused on the woeful weakness of the Ethiopian school system. Almost 80 percent of the pupils who entered sixth grade dropped out of school before the twelfth grade. Those who made it through high school found an economy too frail to provide enough jobs for them. Only a handful were admitted to the university in Addis Ababa.

Their demands grew more universal as the strikes continued. "Land for the tiller"—a demand for land reform—became a familiar student battle cry. They also demanded parliamentary democracy, freedom of speech, and an end to corruption and nepotism. The students continually drew up lists of demands. But as one militant university student acknowledged, "If the government gives in to our fifteen demands, we will have thirty more. Our real aim is the overthrow of his majesty's government."

The students also wanted Ethiopia to rid itself of the foreign forces that propped up the emperor. These were mainly American and, in the school system, mainly Peace Corps. As one Volunteer teacher put it, "We are liked as Peace Corps, admired as teachers, but we are Americans."

The strikes would usually begin at the university, spread to the high schools in Addis Ababa, and then reach the schools in the countryside. Communication was eased by the program—first proposed by the Peace Corps—that put university students into the secondary schools for a year of teaching.

The government of Haile Selassie dealt with the strikes mainly by suppressing them. The emperor and his cronies convinced themselves that foreign communists had subverted the minds of the students. Two Soviet journalists and three Czech diplomats were expelled from Ethiopia in March 1969. Suppression worked, but only as a temporary palliative. The student demonstrations would subside, but then, after a few weeks, they would burst forth again.

In late December, Tilahan Gizaw, the president of the university student union, was shot and killed while walking near campus. Students carried the body to campus and staged a demonstration against the government. Five trucks arrived, crammed with soldiers of the emperor's imperial guard. Officers of the guard demanded that the students relinquish the body. When the students refused, the guardsmen fixed bayonets and marched forward, determined to clear the campus grounds of students. At least twenty students, but probably more, died in the melee.

Joseph Murphy, a thirty-six-year-old former professor of political science at Brandeis University, was then director of the Peace Corps in Ethiopia. For months, he had tried to persuade senior U.S. officials to understand the significance of the student strikes.

Ethiopia allowed very few channels for open dissent. Political parties did not exist. Labor unions were weak, practically ornamental. Newspaper editors and reporters either wrote their articles as directed or tried to anticipate what would please the emperor and his court. But students at the university had the privilege of a student organization, a student newspaper, and a tradition among their American teachers that encouraged dissent. Their complaints often echoed the complaints of the silent in Ethiopia.

But Murphy failed to persuade U.S. officials of the significance of the student demonstrations and the need for the emperor to modernize his corrupt and inert feudal government quickly. Like the emperor's bureaucrats, U.S. officials tended to look on the student demonstrations as isolated bursts of youthful exuberance. They believed that the emperor, a stalwart anti-communist ally during the Cold War, would eventually control the restless students.

A month after the killing of the students at the university, Murphy resigned as Peace Corps director in Ethiopia. In a letter that soon circulated among the Volunteers, he wrote he could no longer work in a dictatorship "which cannot establish a social order with better answers to its problems than shooting and beating young people." "The recent incidents at the university and other places throughout the empire," he went on, "have pretty well convinced me that we do no service in teaching Ethiopian youngsters how to ask questions about their physical and social world when they live in a society in which the answers to those questions are bayonets and clubs." Murphy would return to academic life, most notably as chancellor of the colleges of the City University of New York.

Perhaps the resignation should have been treated by U.S. officials as a signal that the time had come for the U.S. government to exert pressure on the emperor to give up his absolute power in favor of a democratic constitutional monarchy. But that was too much to expect at a time when the minds of U.S. policymakers were clouded by the priorities of the Cold War and the need to keep the Kagnew military base. Shoring up the emperor seemed like the best insurance for maintaining the base. Most U.S. officials treated Murphy's resignation as a minor personnel change brought on by rowdy, undisciplined students.

The waves of student strikes intensified, and Peace Corps Volunteers often found themselves the object of student anger and resentment. The

Volunteers may have helped carry western enlightenment to young Ethiopians, but, far more important to many students, the Volunteers were the most visible manifestation of U.S. support for the despised emperor.

In the town of Harar, in eastern Ethiopia, once the fabled home of the nineteenth-century French poet Arthur Rimbaud, the secondary school was in continual turmoil. "Teachers were often shouted out of class," Volunteer Eleanor Shumway wrote in a report. "Peace Corps Volunteer teachers got particular abuse about our cultural imperialism, involvement in Vietnam, and the students' certainty that we were CIA agents intent on making Ethiopia a second Vietnam." On two occasions, the pupils threw rocks at the Volunteers.

"We feel our continued presence here," Shumway said, "is a hindrance to the political development of Ethiopia. This is an internal problem and the Ethiopians are constantly demonstrating to us they want to solve their own problems without our interference." Ten of the thirteen Volunteers in Harar resigned.

In the historic northern town of Adowa, where Ethiopian soldiers had halted the march of Italian colonialism in 1896, forty eleventh-grade pupils set upon Volunteer teachers Craig Johnson and Dick Obermanns one afternoon. The young Ethiopians were angry that one of them had been disciplined in class, but the encounter soon turned into one of anti-American fury.

The students pummeled the Americans with sticks, stones, and their fists, leaving them bruised and bleeding. "While we remain in Ethiopia," Johnson wrote in a report, "we will only remain conspicuous targets for the very real frustrations young Ethiopians feel about their political and economic systems. No matter how good a job we feel we are doing as individuals, our experience has made it clear that we are first and foremost symbols of an oppressive American presence which nationalist-minded young Ethiopians deeply resent." Four of the five Volunteer teachers in Adowa resigned after this incident.

In all, by early 1970, 70 of the 235 Volunteer teachers in Ethiopia had resigned. Teaching had become halting and exasperating throughout the country. For long stretches, university classes had no more than 25 percent attendance, the high schools of Addis Ababa were shut down, and teaching in most schools outside the capital had become a farce. The Peace Corps announced that it would reduce the numbers of Volunteer teachers to 100 in 1971. The numbers dwindled even more after that.

Haile Selassie and his security forces were unable to contain the relentless movement of the students. The government even tried trucking university students into the countryside and herding them into concentration camps. But, when released, the students returned to demonstrations and strikes. Other Ethiopians started marching with students throughout the country. The government's woes were exacerbated by a famine that the emperor refused to acknowledge. Photos of him feeding meat to his dogs while Ethiopians starved added fury to a growing national resentment. The government's stability quivered as the army continued to fail to squelch the insurgency of Eritrean nationalists in the north.

The revolution reached a climax in 1974. A mutiny by junior officers and noncommissioned officers led to a military takeover of the government. The soldiers put Haile Selassie under house arrest in his palace and ruled through a military committee known in Amharic as the Derg. The eighty-two-year-old emperor, close to senility, dismissed his government and issued whatever decrees the soldiers demanded.

At first, it did not seem as if the soldiers had seized control of the revolution from the students. The two groups were very close. Most of the noncommissioned officers were recent secondary school graduates who had joined the army because they could not find any other job. Many of the junior officers were graduates of the non-elitist Holetta Military School, which admitted poor youngsters after a year or two of secondary school. The students served as the intellectual guides of the soldiers.

The students, in fact, were more radical than the revolutionary soldiers, at least in the beginning. The students wanted a complete end to the reign of the emperor and all the regime's trappings. Yet the Derg continued to issue its decrees "in the name of the Conquering Lion of the Tribe of Judah."

Western education and the English language opened channels to far more subjects than English literature, Enlightenment philosophy, and U.S. history. Students could delve into Marxism and Leninism as well. This was especially attractive during a Cold War when young Ethiopians looked on the United States as an enemy. Although many students still advocated parliamentary democracy for Ethiopia, others organized two communist-style political parties.

Major Mengistu Haile Mariam soon emerged as the strongman of the revolution, taking the post of vice chairman and then chairman of the

Derg. He was thirty-six years old in 1974—too old to have studied with any Peace Corps Volunteer teacher before entering the Holetta Military School. Although the cause of the emperor's death is still a mystery, one theory holds that Mengistu ordered his personal physician to smother Haile Selassie to death in 1975 with an ether-doused pillow. By 1977, Mengistu was the ruthless ruler of Ethiopia, and the Peace Corps withdrew the last of its Volunteers.

Mengistu's reign, which lasted fourteen years, was one of the bloodiest in Africa. Not only did he kill hundreds who had once worked for the emperor, but he also wiped out one of the student communist parties because it advocated civilian rather than military rule. Yet he declared himself a communist and allied Ethiopia with the Soviet Union, China, and Cuba. Heeding the student cry of "land to the tiller," he launched a grandiose land reform scheme, but it lacked planning and failed badly. To make matters worse, he continued the emperor's disastrous war to prevent the secession of Eritrea.

The rise of Mengistu and the length of his military rule has led many outsiders to attribute the fall of the emperor to the rebellion in his army. But as Paulos Milkias, a professor of political science at Concordia University in Montreal and a former Ethiopian student leader, put it in a recent book, "Careful analysis shows that Haile Selassie was not overthrown by the military . . . . Rather, the crucial and decisive deathblow that crushed the Haile Selassie regime emanated from the methodical forays of the students and teachers who were the products of the modern school system." Volunteer teachers played a role—perhaps a significant role—in this. But once the program closed down, there is no evidence that the Peace Corps tried to analyze the impact of the Volunteers on the revolutionaries who brought down the emperor. The cruelty of the aftermath was too horrible to attract that kind of research. Peace Corps officials were pleased to be free from the turmoil of Ethiopia and kept their attention on their other programs.

A POSTSCRIPT

Peace Corps programs in Africa were often battered during the 1960s and 1970s by war, political turmoil, and caprice. In a bizarre and senseless retaliation, Guinea threw out its sixty-two Volunteers in November 1966 after Ghanian police arrested a group of Guinean officials and took them off a Pan-American Airways flight that had stopped in Accra. Guinea blamed Pan-Am for the incident and, mistakenly assuming that the airline was a U.S. government agency, decided to wreak its vengeance on another U.S. government agency—the Peace Corps. In a similar escapade, President Omar Bongo of Gabon, insulted by the low-ranking representation the United States had sent to the funeral of his predecessor and influenced by French advisors who did not like the Peace Corps, satisfied his anger by throwing out the fifty-seven Volunteers of the Peace Corps in December 1967.

After coups in 1969, the new military governments of Libya and Somalia expelled the Peace Corps, evidently feeling that the Volunteers were too identified with the old regime. In Malawi, on the other hand, President Hastings Kamuzu Banda decided not to replace the 141 Volunteers who departed in 1971 because he thought too many sympathized with the illegal opposition.

U.S. foreign policy hampered the Peace Corps elsewhere in Africa. Mauritania expelled its twelve Volunteers after breaking relations with the United States in 1967 because of U.S. support of Israel in the Six-Day War. In Tanzania, President Julius Nyerere decided not to replace the 394 Volunteers after their tours expired in 1968. He was angered by the war in Vietnam, and he was trying to fashion a new African school system that would break the mold of British colonial education and believed that the Volunteers would not fit in.

The Peace Corps itself decided to withdrew all its 105 Volunteers from Uganda in September and October 1972 after unruly soldiers shot and killed a trainee, Louis Morton of Houston, at a roadblock. The soldiers, poorly trained and undisciplined, were upset by an invasion of Ugandan exiles in an abortive attempt to overthrow President Idi Amin. The Peace Corps, fearful of enraging Amin, did not announce the evacuation; it withdrew the Volunteers in small groups and asked each Volunteer to lie that he or she had made a personal, individual decision to quit.

The Nigerian civil war also crippled the Peace Corps program, which was the largest in Africa at that time. Peace Corps officials pulled the Volunteers out of all battleground and potential battleground areas. As a result, the program, which comprised 719 Volunteers in 1967, dwindled to 66 Volunteers in 1970.

Despite such problems, work in Africa remained one of the main-stays of the Peace Corps. The developmental problems of Africa were so great that there were always need for some Volunteers somewhere on the continent.

CHAPTER ELEVEN

The Militant Sam Brown

After the nightmare of the Nixon years and the election of Jimmy Carter as president in 1976, the Peace Corps community felt relief and renewed expectation. They were sure the Democratic president would lift the organization from its doldrums. After all, Carter's own mother, known by all as "Miss Lillian," had served in the Peace Corps as a nurse in India in her late sixties when her son was governor of Georgia. Carter satisfied the Peace Corps staff when he announced that their new leader would be the celebrated antiwar militant Sam Brown. But there was some puzzlement as well. Brown was not named director of the Peace Corps. He was named director of ACTION. Carter was going to maintain the Nixon umbrella organization that kept the Peace Corps in shadows.

Brown was only thirty-three when Carter was elected president, but he was already a familiar figure on television, with his lush head of hair and bushy moustache. He was best known for organizing and serving as the main spokesman of the Vietnam Moratorium, a protest demonstration against the war held in 1969. It was called a *moratorium* because Brown and his colleagues thought the word *strike* would sound too harsh to most American ears. The euphemism seemed to work, for 2 million Americans showed up in the streets throughout the country on October 15 to protest against the war. About 250,000 marched in Washington, D.C., in a follow-up demonstration on November 15.

Although a fervent opponent of the war, Brown, unlike some other young antiwar militants, was not a radical intent on tearing down the system. Brown always worked within it instead. *Washington Post* political writer David Broder once described the suppression of a Brown editorial in a student newspaper in college days as a "radicalizing" experience for him, but added parenthetically, "if one can use that term for a political organizer as circumscribed by convention as Brown is." In 1968, Brown was the youth coordinator of Senator Gene McCarthy's failed but romantic campaign for the Democratic nomination for president. Eight years later, however, when McCarthy ran as an independent, Brown switched to Carter, the Democratic candidate.

Brown grew up in Iowa where his father owned Brown's Better Shoes, a group of shoe stores. At Abraham Lincoln High School in Council Bluffs, Brown won accolades as an outstanding ROTC cadet. He became involved in student politics at the University of Redlands, beginning as a leader of the young Republicans there. He received a master's degree from Rutgers University and was continuing graduate work at Harvard Divinity School when he began to work for the Gene McCarthy campaign. After the Vietnam War started to wind down, he joined his father's company. In 1975, he ran successfully for the post of treasurer of the state of Colorado, giving it up when Carter named him director of ACTION.

There was a good deal of enthusiasm over the appointment. "We would have stood on our heads if that's what he wanted," an ACTION official told the *Washington Monthly*. "This place was euphoric, absolutely overjoyed, about the appointment. We all thought he was going to be our savior." But disappointment would soon set in, especially at the Peace Corps.

As chief of ACTION, Brown did not intend to let the Peace Corps go its own way. He had several grand ideas for change and no hesitation about ordering the Peace Corps staff to carry them out swiftly. It took him nine months to find a suitable director of the Peace Corps: Carolyn Payton, a professor of psychology at Howard University and the head of the counseling service there. She had been involved in selecting and assessing Volunteers under Sargent Shriver and the country director of the eastern Caribbean islands under Jack Hood Vaughn. She was the first woman and the first African American to head the Peace Corps during its first fifty years. Like many others who knew the Peace Corps well, she found the strictures of Brown too sweeping and impractical, and they were soon embroiled in conflict.

Brown insisted that the Peace Corps should wean itself from its large teaching programs in Africa. The school systems, created in colonial days, turned out hordes of elitist graduates who refused to work with their hands and instead sought office and administrative jobs more fitting with their self-image. Since white-collar jobs were few, the streets of African towns filled with unemployed and aimless youths. Instead of bolstering such school systems, the Volunteers, in Brown's view, should concentrate on helping to take care of "basic human needs" in such fields as health, irrigation, agriculture, and fisheries.

Brown also believed that the Peace Corps should concentrate on the poorest of the poor. He wanted to phase out of countries such as South Korea, Malaysia, Brazil, and the Ivory Coast that, in his view, did not need Volunteers as much as poorer countries did. Arguments that a country like Brazil, despite its relative wealth, had masses of poverty and misery did not sway Brown.

Brown's ideas were influenced by theories of Third World development that had been embraced by President Julius Nyerere of Tanzania. Nyerere was a saintly figure in Africa, for unlike most leaders there, he showed no signs of greed or hunger for power. He lived simply, tolerated no corruption, and pondered the problems of African poverty.

The intellectual Nyerere read deeply into the latest treatises on development and churned out thoughtful papers of his own about the needs of Africa. He was an admirer of René Dumont, the French agronomist who had caused a sensation in French-speaking Africa with his book *L'Afrique Noire est mal partie* (published in English under the title *False Start in Africa*). Dumont mocked the colonial school systems that produced useless elitists while their countries needed technicians who could make small changes in agriculture that would enable their economies to take off. Nyerere invited Dumont in the 1960s to assess Tanzanian agriculture and received a scathing report from the agronomist about its primitive state.

Nyerere's sense of justice persuaded him that his government was obliged to use its meager funds to help the poorest areas of Tanzania first. In doing so, he defied a tenet of most economists who advised it made most sense to help the richest of the poor first, for they needed only a small nudge to make great progress.

During the height of the Vietnam War, Nyerere had phased out the Peace Corps, partly as a protest against the war, partly because the Volunteers were mainly teachers in a school system that he wanted to overhaul. On a trip to the United States in August 1977, he had met Brown and discussed the possibility of inviting the Peace Corps back. Brown visited Nyerere five months later at the president's country house in Boutiama, Tanzania, and the president, dressed in gardening clothes and with his hands muddied from planting trees, told the ACTION director that he needed Volunteers trained in fisheries, agriculture, mechanics, and desert prevention. But he did not want teachers because the teaching of English was "a stage of development that has gone by."

Nyerere's ideas, always seductive on paper, usually proved impractical in real life and, in fact, did not work in Tanzania. His lieutenants were ham-handed in trying to carry them out, and most Tanzanians did not understand what was expected of them, either. Moreover, Nyerere tried to achieve his goals through the forced organization of village communities that many people resisted.

These ideas, when interpreted and proclaimed by Brown, did not work in the Peace Corps either. Many Peace Corps officials had long been sympathetic to the theories of Dumont and Nyerere but thought it ridiculous to adopt them wholesale. Most of all, the Peace Corps did not want to abandon the school systems. Most countries other than Tanzania maintained these systems, and Peace Corps officials believed that a good Volunteer teacher could play a vital role in imperfect schools by reducing elitism, eliminating rote learning, and encouraging creativity. The Peace Corps also looked on the English language as an important resource in the modern interrelated world and thought it short-sighted for a country like Tanzania to give up English teachers.

Brown dismissed resistance to his changes as nostalgic, a hanging on to a Peace Corps past. "It [the Peace Corps] is one of the few remaining symbols of our innocence," he said. "But in the minds of many nations that is an era that has past. We can't use the Peace Corps as a way to grab back a mood that is no longer prevalent." What Brown called nostalgia, however, was regarded by the Peace Corps as experience based on fifteen years of trial and error. In the view of his detractors, Brown was turning his back on the achievements and evidence of tens of thousands of Volunteers.

Payton and other Peace Corps officials were reluctant to carry out the orders of Brown. In African countries like Ghana that wanted American teachers, the Peace Corps tried to keep supplying them even as it opened new programs in "basic human needs." "The governments were always asking us for teachers, teachers, teachers," said Reginald Petty, the

Peace Corps director in Swaziland and later Kenya. "Sam Brown just didn't understand the value of knowing English in these countries." To satisfy both Brown and the governments, Peace Corps officials overseas resorted to artful programming. "I used to tell the government ministers, 'If you let me bring in five skill-trained Volunteers, I'll get you ten more English teachers,'" Petty told the writer Karen Schwarz. But the Peace Corps could not save programs in the countries that Brown wanted to leave. By 1981, the Peace Corps had departed from Brazil, South Korea, and the Ivory Coast. Two years later, it was gone from Malaysia.

Aside from their arguments over policy, Brown and Payton seemed caught in a clash of cultures, of genders, and of generations. Although his deputy was a woman, Brown was often accompanied by male aides in their early thirties, many wearing cowboy boots. Payton was fifty-two, a generation older, and, in the eyes of Brown and his cohorts, she drew much of her support within the Peace Corps from other women. When Brown and Payton met privately, according to Payton, he would show up with his agenda typed on a piece of paper. "The funny thing is," said Payton, "he would never look at me directly." It was rare for Brown and Payton to see eye to eye about anything, and both were stubborn about their views.

The tension burst into open conflict in 1977 when Brown proposed sending 200 unemployed youths from Oakland, California, to the Caribbean island of Jamaica. Brown wanted his "Jamaica Brigade" to work at land terracing or some similar activity for three months and then apply their new skill back in the United States as members of VISTA, the other large volunteer program in the ACTION agency portfolio.

The project, according to Brown, would attract a new kind of Peace Corps Volunteer (namely inner-city blacks), would foster a new relationship between the Peace Corps and VISTA, and would involve the Peace Corps in a new kind of short-term project. "The world has changed drastically since the 1960s," he said, "and if the Peace Corps is going to make sense, it has to stay on top of where the world is and stop wishing it could go back to where it was fifteen years ago."

But Payton dismissed the Jamaica Brigade as one of Brown's "crackpot ideas." Jamaica did not need an influx of unemployed Americans; it had tens of thousands of its own unemployed. A skill like land terracing would have no relevance back in the inner city. And, most important, Peace Corps officials had always avoided short-term do-gooder projects. They were more like tourism than development. When the Peace Corps began, Shriver and his lieutenants wanted Volunteers who would commit themselves to at least two years of meaningful work. There seemed to be no point in changing this now just to satisfy Sam Brown's obsession with change.

Vehement opposition from Payton and her director in Jamaica, Loretta Carter-Miller, forced Brown to abandon the Jamaica Brigade. Carter-Miller, in fact, resigned during the bureaucratic infighting. "I just decided that Sam wasn't going to use me to use those kids to make some kind of splash," Carter-Miller told the *Washington Post*. "Then, when the shit hit the fan because of this dumb idea, I was going to have to be the lady to hang around and clean it up. I got tired of fighting with him, so I quit."

The feud between Payton and Brown reached a bitter climax at a meeting of the directors of Peace Corps programs in North Africa, the Middle East, Asia, and the Pacific in November 1978. They met in Morocco in a Mediterranean resort between Rabat and Casablanca called Mohammedia. Brown believed that Payton, for two months before the conference began, "was on the phone every day trying to undercut me in every way possible." Payton believed that Brown had ignored her during the conference and tried to take it over. His strategy, she felt, "obviously was 'Get Carolyn.'" She was also upset that, in her view, Brown was budgeting too little for the Peace Corps. The two continually contradicted each other in front of the country directors.

After one day's session of the conference, Brown phoned her in her hotel room after midnight. Several of her associates, including Ruth Saxe, the deputy director of the Peace Corps, and Ellen Yaffe, the executive officer in charge of the budget, were in the room with her and could hear his loud, angry voice. "Carolyn, why the fuck don't you get out of here?" he said. She hung up, and Brown showed up fifteen minutes later, banging on her door.

The noise was so great, Yaffe recalls, that "you would probably call the police if you were somewhere else." "The voice was angry," she says. "The banging was angry. Who knew what he was going to do? He might have intended to fire her on the spot." But Payton refused to open the door. [Brown acknowledged knocking on the door but told the *Wall Street Journal* he had not banged on it.]

After they returned to Washington, Brown demanded Payton's resignation. At first, Payton agreed, saying she would resign "in the best interests of the Peace Corps." But she soon changed her mind. She would resign only if President Carter asked her to do so, she said. The White House then backed Brown, asking for the resignation, and Payton resigned.

Brown won the battle against Payton but soon lost the Peace Corps itself. Within four months, Brown asked forty-one-year-old Richard F. Celeste, the former lieutenant governor (and future governor) of Ohio, to serve as the new director of the Peace Corps. Celeste knew the Peace Corps well. He had worked in the Washington headquarters of the agency in 1963, and later, as a special assistant to Ambassador Chester Bowles in India, he had watched the Volunteers in action. He was too wise a political operator to accept a job that would subject him to the whims of Sam Brown. He agreed to take the job but only on condition that the Peace Corps have renewed autonomy.

That was not what Brown had in mind, but he accepted the condition. "It was not a slam dunk," says Celeste. "We negotiated it." Bill Josephson, Shriver's old general counsel, took time off from his private practice to help Celeste and Brown work out the details. President Carter soon signed an executive order that gave the Peace Corps complete autonomy even while keeping it in ACTION. Brown's umbrella agency would support the Peace Corps with payroll services, public relations, and recruitment campaigns, but in all other matters "the Peace Corps director will direct and control the operations of the Peace Corps."

Vice President Walter Mondale swore in Celeste at a White House ceremony on May 23, 1979. Sargent Shriver attended, his gesture of support for the return of Peace Corps autonomy. President Carter was supposed to be busy elsewhere, but he made a surprise appearance. "Today, the Peace Corps has resumed its priority in our government," Mondale said. "President Carter has rekindled the dream of Hubert Humphrey and President Kennedy."

That was a blatant exaggeration—there was not enough time left to rekindle anything. President Carter, who would be defeated for reelection a year and a half later, had already wasted his opportunity. By keeping the Peace Corps within ACTION at the beginning of his term and allowing a territorial war between Sam Brown and Carolyn Payton to paralyze the agency, President Carter had ensured that the Peace Corps would remain for the rest of his term in the minor place to which it had been shunted by Richard Nixon.

CHAPTER TWELVE

Mayhem and Illness

From the beginning, Peace Corps staff knew they would have to deal with death. There surely would be bus accidents, jeep crashes, motorbike mishaps, and drownings. But the nature of some of the deaths surprised the staff. During the first fifteen years, for example, two Volunteers died in an earthquake, one was killed by a crocodile, two succumbed to malaria, five died of gastrointestinal disease, one died of rabies, nine killed themselves, and four were murdered. On top of this, there were two sensational trials, one in Tanzania, the other in Tonga, of Volunteers accused of murdering other Volunteers. Both trials unsettled and confused the Peace Corps.

On Sunday, March 27, 1966, twenty-four-year-old Bill Haywood Kinsey and his twenty-three-year-old wife, Peverley Dennet Kinsey, both Volunteer teachers at the Binza junior high school in Maswa, bicycled out of the town until they found a shady and rocky hill that looked ideal for their lunch. The picnic spot, like their school, was in the region of Shinyanga near Lake Victoria in northern Tanzania. The couple had met at Syracuse University, where Peverley, from Riverside, Connecticut, was training for Tanzania and Bill, from Washington, North Carolina, for Malawi. Bill quickly obtained a transfer to the Tanzania program and married Peverley at the end of training. They had now been married a year and a half.

Villagers, watching from afar, were shocked that Sunday to see what looked like a scene of terrible violence: Bill pounding his wife as she lay sprawled amid the rocks on the hill. As he rushed away, the villagers grabbed him and held him for the police.

Bill protested that the villagers were mistaken. Peverley, he said, had fallen onto the rocks from a cliff twenty feet above. When he scampered down to her, he found her flailing her arms in hysteria. Fearful that she would hurt herself more, he had held her down until she stopped flailing. He had rushed away, not to escape, but to seek help. When the police arrived, they found it was too late to help Peverley. She was dead. They arrested Bill and charged him with murder.

Peace Corps Volunteers have no diplomatic immunity. There are no extraterritorial agreements that allow Volunteers to be tried by U.S. courts if accused of committing a crime. Volunteers are subject to the laws and customs of the lands in which they serve.

This limited what the Peace Corps could do for Bill Kinsey. Under the law setting up the Peace Corps, it could not pay for his defense, but it could arrange for his family to hire the most highly regarded defense lawyer in East Africa. As Paul Sack, director of the program in Tanzania, wrote to the Volunteers, "Peace Corps is taking every step possible to help Bill with assistance in securing legal counsel, providing medical attention and support while under detention, maintaining contact with his family and—most important—ensuring protection of all his rights."

Tanzanian officials were proud of their judicial system, which developed under British colonialism, and they resented any hint of what they regarded as Peace Corps interference. Mark Bomani, the Tanzanian attorney general, showed his annoyance when he thought a Peace Corps official was raising the issue of bail for Kinsey even after it had been denied. The official quickly pleaded that he was misunderstood. The Peace Corps, as Sack put it in a letter to Washington, was trying to demonstrate to the Tanzanians "that the Government of the United States is not interfering in the judicial process here."

Some Volunteers felt the Peace Corps was limiting itself too much. "When we joined the Peace Corps," a twenty-two-year-old Volunteer told the Associated Press, "we didn't realize that if we got into trouble, we were on our own. We thought the American government would do something for us." He proposed that an indicted Volunteer like Kinsey should face trial in a U.S. court. But that, of course, would show contempt for foreign justice, an attitude that would mock what the Peace Corps was all about.

The Peace Corps staff and Volunteers acted throughout as if sure Bill were innocent. Justice would be served, in their view, only if a court acquitted him. But the evidence at the trial, which began after Bill had spent almost six months in prison, was not as clear cut. British-born Judge Harold Platt called the evidence "intriguingly elusive" and admitted that his verdict rested "upon a narrow margin of circumstances."

The judge tended to discount the testimony of the eyewitnesses who claimed to have seen Kinsey beating his wife. Their accounts were too inconsistent and unreliable. Yet police found a metal pipe and a stone at the scene covered in blood and bits of hair. They could have been used to hit Peverley, or they could have been stained by Peverley falling and bleeding on them.

Kinsey had copied into his journal passages from a novel that the prosecution insisted proved he believed his wife was unfaithful. According to the prosecution, he intended to confront her with his suspicions, as the copied passages put it, "about the 27th of the month"—the date of the picnic. But the judge dismissed the importance of this; it was normal, the judge said, for a student of literature to copy passages of literary value. Moreover, Peverley's mother testified that her daughter had told her there were no problems in the marriage. The judge, in the end, was most impressed by medical testimony that Peverley's wounds were more consistent with a fall than with blows to the head by a metal pipe and a stone.

A sort of jury of two assessors—one American, the other Tanzanian—sat through the trial and found Kinsey not guilty. Under Tanzanian law, however, their verdict was only advisory. The only verdict that mattered was that of the judge.

In his concluding statement, Judge Platt scolded the Tanzanian police and prosecution for a slipshod performance. If they had been more thorough and careful, he said, they might have come up with conclusive evidence proving Kinsey's guilt or innocence. Absent this, the judge went on, "the weight of the evidence seems to me to be fairly evenly divided." That, of course, worked in Kinsey's favor since the prosecution had to prove his guilt beyond a reasonable doubt.

"While the accused must, therefore, carry with him the suspicion that he may have been responsible for his wife's death," Judge Platt ruled, "he must, in justice, be acquitted and set free . . . ." The Peace Corps welcomed the verdict. It would have been a nightmare for the Peace Corps if a Volunteer had been sentenced to hanging or a long prison term in Africa while some Americans back home clamored for his release.

Kinsey was assigned to headquarters in Washington, where he

worked for a few months before returning home to North Carolina. Peverley was listed as the twenty-third Volunteer fatality in the history of the Peace Corps, killed by an accidental fall.

The second murder trial took place in Tonga, a South Pacific island kingdom with a population of 100,000 or so. In this case, there was little dispute about the evidence. Dennis Priven, twenty-four, a Volunteer science teacher from Brooklyn, New York, stabbed twenty-three-year-old Deborah Gardner, a fellow Volunteer science teacher from Tacoma, Washington, twenty-two times with his long knife on the evening of October 14, 1976.

The Peace Corps reacted in a disconcerting manner, evidently caring more about protecting the murderer than seeking justice. The full shame was hidden in Peace Corps files until journalist Philip Weiss's remarkable book about the case, *American Taboo: A Murder in the Peace Corps,* was published almost thirty years later. Weiss recreated the atmosphere and events in meticulous detail.

The Peace Corps assigned more than eighty Volunteers to Tonga, mostly as teachers and mostly clustered in and around the capital, Nuku'alofa. The Tongan translation of *Peace Corps* was *Kau Ng_ue 'Ofa,* literally "They work for love." The Volunteers worked hard in their schools but had lots of free time to socialize with each other. Volunteer life in this South Pacific paradise featured lots of Peace Corps parties, dinners, card games, movie excursions, couplings, and de-couplings, mostly among the Volunteers themselves.

Deborah, beautiful and vivacious, was one of the most popular women, and she had fallen in and out of love with two or three of her fellow Volunteers in her little more than a year on Tonga. Dennis was one of her suitors, but not a successful one. He pestered her so much that she went out with him on occasion but allowed no intimacy to develop. His frustration reached explosive heights when he believed that a good friend of his was having a sexual affair with her. He arrived in Deborah's hut with his knife and a jar of cyanide, evidently intent on killing her and then himself.

The evidence against Dennis was overwhelming. Tongans had seen him struggling with Deborah and slashing her at the door of the hut. When Tongans rushed Deborah to the hospital, she told them that Dennis had stabbed her. The murder weapon was his. He had rushed by bicycle from the scene, leaving the cyanide behind but later making a half-hearted attempt to cut his wrists. He hid while police searched for him. He finally turned himself in after midnight. But he would not acknowledge his guilt or, in fact, say anything else about Deborah to the police.

Despite the evidence, Mary George, the Peace Corps director in Tonga, persisted in believing Dennis was innocent. George, a model who had run the Barbizon School of Modeling and a lobbyist with good Republican contacts, was also a born-again Christian. According to Weiss, she experienced a vision in church one Sunday that persuaded her that a Tongan had murdered Deborah and the Tongans were framing Dennis for the murder.

But this was a lonely opinion. Peace Corps officials in Washington had no doubt that Dennis had killed Deborah, but they felt an obligation to make sure Dennis received proper representation and a fair trial. Legislation had changed since the Kinsey trial, and the Peace Corps was now required to pay for the defense of a Volunteer in a court trial. The prime concern of Washington officials, however, was to make sure that the murder and the trial hurt the Peace Corps as little as possible.

As a Washington agency, the Peace Corps was weak and lackluster at that time. The Peace Corps was barely visible within ACTION and had survived only because President Richard Nixon became too busy with Watergate and his resignation to worry about getting rid of Kennedy's Peace Corps. Nixon's successor, Gerald Ford, was defeated by Jimmy Carter a few weeks after the murder, and many top Peace Corps officials were more worried about their jobs than about a trial in Tonga.

Although the Volunteers were horrified by the killing, a small group decided they could not turn their backs on Dennis. Nothing could be done for Deborah, they reasoned. But Dennis was alive, and something should be done to salvage or rehabilitate him. These Volunteers, whose thinking paralleled that of officials in Washington, brought him food and visited him often in the weeks before the trial.

The Peace Corps hired the best-known Tongan lawyer to defend Dennis. Faced with the damning evidence, the lawyer, who often practiced in New Zealand, soon decided that the best defense was a plea of insanity. The Peace Corps paid for a psychiatrist to come from Hawaii. He interviewed Dennis and pronounced him a schizophrenic for most of his life. Recent stress had led to depression, the psychiatrist testified, that caused "a breakdown, a state of acute paranoid schizophrenia."

Tonga had been a British protectorate, and its trial procedures were familiar to the Peace Corps. The judge was British-born but, unlike his counterpart in Tanzania, he did not have final say. A jury of seven Tongans would render the verdict. It did not take them very long to agree that Dennis was not guilty because "he was insane at the time when he did the act." The judge recommended "long-term, if not permanent" incarceration.

The Tongans expected that Dennis would now spend many years in confinement, but they did not have suitable medical facilities for the criminally insane. So the Tongan government agreed to turn Dennis over to the United States for incarceration there.

The United States handed several letters to the Tongan government. The most important, approved by the Peace Corps in Washington and signed by Robert Flanegin, the U.S. Consul General in Fiji, who had responsibility for Tonga, pledged that Dennis would be sent to Sibley Hospital in Washington "for detention and treatment . . . until Mr. Priven is declared by competent medical authority that he is no longer a threat to the community and himself."

The Tonga government was also assured, "All relevant jurisdictions in the United States, including Washington, New York, and Maryland, have involuntary commitment procedures. And Mr. Priven's parents would file necessary commitment papers in the event Dennis refused voluntary commitment." A handwritten aerogram from the parents said, "Please be assured that in the event Dennis does not voluntarily sign himself in to be treated, we, the family, will so sign."

The assurances proved worthless, if not bogus. Sibley was not a mental hospital, but a general hospital to which the Peace Corps sent its Volunteers with medical problems. Dennis, in fact, refused to go to Sibley at first, and the Peace Corps did not have the power to force him. Dennis finally bowed to all the cajoling and entered the hospital. He was interviewed by the head of the psychiatry department for many hours. This psychiatrist decided that Dennis was not psychotic at all. He had exploded in Tonga out of frustration over a love that seemed close but always lay beyond his reach. He was not now a danger to himself or others. The psychiatrist had no authority to commit him anywhere.

Neither did the Peace Corps. All its assurances to the Tongans about "involuntary commitment" were blather. So was the promise of the family to commit him to a hospital even if he didn't want to go there. They did not have the authority. Dennis was an adult, not a child. He had no intention of allowing himself to be confined in a mental institution. Dennis drew out his last paycheck, received a certificate for completing his Peace Corps service, and left Washington.

The Peace Corps had told Deborah's family that Dennis would be committed to a mental hospital. But the family was never told this had not happened. For years, they believed the killer of their daughter was languishing in an institution. They discovered the truth only when Weiss, the author of the book, came to interview them. Weiss found Dennis in Brooklyn more than twenty-five years after the killing of Deborah. He was working as a computer specialist for the Social Security administration.

From 1961 to 2009, twenty-two Volunteers were victims of homicide. Since the Tonga trial, however, there was no other case in which one Volunteer was accused of murdering another. Despite the drama of the Tanzania and Tonga trials and the exotic nature of some other deaths, the Peace Corps did not look on safety and illness as debilitating problems in the early days. I do not recall a single Volunteer complaining about safety during my many trips overseas as an evaluator. Only a handful expressed worries about tropical diseases.

Parents, of course, did fret about disease and crime in unknown developing countries. But the Peace Corps medical office would try to reassure them with periodic statements that "incidence of serious illness or death in the Peace Corps has been no greater than that of a comparable age group in the U.S."

The Peace Corps seemed to grow complacent over the issues. It was not until 1990, in fact, that the Peace Corps started compiling annual records on the numbers of rapes, assaults, and robberies suffered by Volunteers—victims of nationals of the countries the Peace Corps was trying to help. And it was not until more recent years that some critics derided the Peace Corps for alleged inadequacies in caring for the safety of Volunteers.

The first rebuke came from the General Accounting Office (GAO), an investigative arm of Congress, in July 2002. It noted an increase in the incidence of major physical assaults against Volunteers from eight per thousand Volunteers in 1991, to seventeen per thousand in 2000. While the incidence of rapes and other major sexual assaults actually decreased from ten per thousand in 1991, to eight per thousand in 2000, the GAO also noted that a 1998 survey revealed that women were not reporting 60 percent of rape cases to the Peace Corps.

The GAO rebuked Peace Corps staff for failing to ensure that all houses supplied by the overseas governments were secure before assigning Volunteers to them. The staff was also criticized for failing to verify that real jobs existed before new Volunteers arrived. An idle Volunteer was in more danger of criminal attack than a Volunteer busily at work.

The GAO attributed a large part of the staff failures to the five-year rule that harked back to the days of Sargent Shriver. Under this rule, now part of the legislation, most staffers had to leave the Peace Corps after working there five years. This caused a good deal of staff turnover every year, and it meant that staffers in their fifth year of work spent much of their time seeking another job outside the agency.

In response to the report, Peace Corps Director Gaddi Vasquez agreed to hire several new officers who would concentrate on safety problems and would not be subject to the five-year rule. But the rule itself, designed to prevent the Peace Corps from becoming an ossified bureaucracy, was too sacrosanct to give up.

The Peace Corps was castigated in much harsher tones more than a year later when the *Dayton Daily News* in Ohio published a weeklong series of articles detailing murders, suicides, rapes, and other mayhem in the Peace Corps. The writers of the series, Pulitzer Prize winner Russell Carollo and Mei-Ling Hopgood, culled examples from more than forty years of Peace Corps history. By stringing many of these tales together, the *Dayton Daily News* left readers with a lurid, frightening, and surely exaggerated picture of the dangers of serving overseas for the Peace Corps.

The articles, which were also carried or summarized by other newspapers, accused the Peace Corps of unwisely placing Volunteers in remote and dangerous villages, failing to make sure Volunteer housing and other living conditions were safe, understating the numbers of crimes committed against Volunteers, and refusing to reveal all details about the circumstances of some deaths. In short, according to the *Dayton Daily News,* the Peace Corps was both incompetent and obsessed with preserving its image.

The *Dayton Daily News* bolstered its accusations with a long series of dramatic case histories. In 1999, for example, the body of Brian Krow, twenty-seven, of Fremont, California, was found on a path seventy-five feet beneath a footbridge in Cherkassy, Ukraine. The Peace Corps listed the death as an "unintentional accident."

But the writers implied it should have been ruled a suicide. No one had ever accidentally fallen off the bridge before. Krow, a trainee, had received a letter from the Peace Corps threatening him with expulsion. He was accused of talking about drugs and seeking Ukrainian women. On top of this, his hosts, the Ukrainian family with whom he lived, had caught him masturbating.

The Peace Corps, which has no police powers, insisted that it had to rely on local authorities for determining the cause of death, and they ruled Krow's death an accident. But Okeksandr Bachysche, the local prosecutor, told the *Dayton Daily News* that he had not been informed by the Peace Corps about the expulsion letter. "Taking into consideration the new information you told me," he said, "I think he committed suicide."

On the night of Christmas 1996, according to another typical story in the series, Diana Gilmour and two other women Volunteers from Guatemala were visiting Volunteer Tom Luben in El Salvador. He was stationed in Agua Fría, a tiny village near the Pacific resort of El Cuco. The four were savoring the breezes of the beach in the moonlight when they were accosted by a gang of armed men. While one held Gilmour back with a pistol and others pinned Luben to the ground, the two other women were gang-raped. Then one of the men raped Gilmour. The gang herded their victims to some high grassland, evidently intent on killing them. But another Volunteer approached, swinging a flashlight, and the rapists fled.

Salvadorean police later arrested six men in the case. Three were convicted of rape and sentenced to thirty years imprisonment. But Gilmour believed the Peace Corps bore a good deal of guilt as well. She said the El Cuco area was a known hotbed of criminal activity, and the Peace Corps should neither have stationed Luben there nor allowed the women to visit him.

"We told them we were going to Tom Luben's site," she told the *Dayton Daily News*. "They knew where we were going. You have to fill out an itinerary . . . . Of course none of us had any clue as to how dangerous it was. We were never warned about going to El Salvador . . . . It should never have happened."

The *Dayton Daily News* articles received some support in the Peace

Corps community. John Hale, who had served as assistant inspector general from 1991 to 1993, insisted, "While zealots may continue to defend the status quo . . . the *Daily News* has said what an adult looking at the facts would say." Unfortunately, he wrote, the Peace Corps had too many personnel "who dismiss unpleasant facts when they contradict Peace Corps myth."

But the series angered many former Peace Corps Volunteers, who found it misleading and exaggerated. "I find the authors of this series verging on irresponsibility for their failure to provide readers a fair or even knowledgeable context for the charges they seem to be leveling," wrote Peggy Anderson. Anderson, a former Volunteer in Togo and a former evaluator, was the author of two distinguished books on medical practices in the United States: *Nurse* and *Children's Hospital*.

"What most astounds me," she went on, "is that they fault the Peace Corps for providing precisely what most people—all putatively adults—join it for: the adventure of going off the beaten path, the opportunity to develop one's own resourcefulness toward a larger good in settings where resourcefulness and the sincere application of it can be useful to recipients."

The Peace Corps was so worried about the series that even before the articles came out, it issued a press release castigating Carollo. The Peace Corps said that, based on its conversations with Carollo, "we believe the upcoming series . . . will provide a misleading picture of the Peace Corps and Peace Corps Volunteer service, particularly with respect to safety and security." The press release also said the Peace Corps had "great concerns about the intentions of" Carollo, accusing him of asserting that he was interested only in the problems of the Peace Corps, not its positive achievements.

The series did amount to a relentless attack on the Peace Corps, but its impact was diminished by its obvious exaggerations, the spirited defense of the Peace Corps by many Volunteers and former Volunteers, and the failure of more prominent newspapers like the *New York Times* and the *Washington Post* to follow through with articles of their own.

In later years, the Peace Corps began issuing detailed annual reports on the safety and the health of Volunteers, and these statistics and analyses revealed a more realistic picture than the sensational series in the *Dayton Daily News*. From 1961 through 2008, 274 Volunteers died while serving in the Peace Corps. More than a third died in traffic accidents. The other major causes of death, in order of frequency, were drownings, accidents from falls and other mishaps, murders, cardiovascular diseases, suicides, and plane crashes.

The death tolls varied from year to year. In some years, there were none. But there were spikes of fourteen dead in both 1966 and 1970 and thirteen dead in 1971, 1972, 1976, 1978, and 1981. The death rate since 1990 remained at the lowest in Peace Corps history. There were only three deaths in 2006, four in 2007, and two in 2008. The Peace Corps experience was so different that it was difficult to compare its mortality rate with that of other Americans. But, on average, the Peace Corps numbers of deaths per thousand Volunteers was about the same as the rate for other young Americans.

The numbers of women Volunteers expanded continually over the years, and this forced the staff to focus on the problem of rape. In 2007, the 4,794 women Volunteers made up 59 percent of the total Peace Corps. There were seventeen reported incidents of rape that year, one less than the previous year. The percentage of women reporting rape remained more or less the same for a decade.

The Peace Corps believed that the statistics understated the problem. Volunteers filled out an anonymous survey every two years about life in the Peace Corps. In the 2008 survey, nineteen Volunteers said they had been raped. Of these, only six said they had reported the rape to the Peace Corps. Six said they had not reported the crime, and seven did not reply whether they had reported the rape or not.

Yet the vast majority of Volunteers insisted safety was not a major problem. According to the 2008 survey, 94 percent felt safe where they worked, 92 percent felt safe where they lived, 82 percent felt safe traveling in the countryside, and 79 percent felt safe visiting the capital—the site of Peace Corps headquarters.

While it could be argued that a Volunteer faced no greater criminal threat in the Peace Corps than elsewhere, there was no doubt that service exposed many to tropical illnesses they would probably not encounter in the United States. In 2007, for example, the Peace Corps reported 5,605 cases of diarrhea and other gastrointestinal illnesses (a significant decrease from the previous year), 195 cases of malaria (a decrease), 152 cases of mosquito-borne dengue fever (a significant increase), and 43 cases of either bilharzia disease or bilharzia infection (an increase).

To deal with these and other medical problems, the Peace Corps contracted with at least one medical officer—usually a local nurse or doctor—to work in each country. If an illness or injury could not be handled by the medical facilities in the country or in a nearby country, the Peace Corps sent the Volunteer back to the United States for further treatment. There were 150 medical evacuations to the United States in 2007.

The statistics underscored the issues. Security was a problem, though surely an exaggerated one. Getting mugged in Guatemala may sound worse to some ears than getting mugged in Boston. But it really isn't. On the other hand, the medical statistics could not be shaken away. Life in the Peace Corps was far different from life elsewhere, and that life entailed medical risks, many unpleasant, some awful. But most Volunteers, who had listened often in training to lectures on minimizing security and health problems, understood and accepted the risks.

CHAPTER THIRTEEN

The Rich Lady in
Her First Job for Pay

The announcement from the White House in 1981 made many admirers of the Peace Corps cringe. Ronald Reagan, the new president, had nominated Loret Miller Ruppe, a wealthy brewery heiress who had never held a full-time job for pay in her life, as the new director of the Peace Corps. Her achievements and connections were all political. As the wife of Philip Ruppe, a former U.S. congressman from Michigan, she was close to Vice President George H. W. Bush and his wife, Barbara. She had chaired Bush's campaign in Michigan for the Republican presidential nomination. When Bush lost but accepted the vice-presidential nomination, she then chaired the Reagan-Bush campaign in Michigan.

The White House tried hard to stretch the credentials of the forty-five-year-old nominee. The announcement said that Ruppe "has spent most of her life in volunteer efforts." That, of course, evoked the unfortunate image for the Peace Corps of a rich society woman setting aside a portion of her time for charity fundraisers and visits to orphanages. Ruppe, the White House went on, "has traveled extensively and shared ideals with past Peace Corps Volunteers in many countries." It did not make clear what this sharing of ideals meant or how it took place.

Ruppe, of course, had a strong Republican allegiance. Philip Ruppe, a Republican, was elected to Congress in 1966, the same year that George H. W. Bush was elected to the House of Representatives. Barbara Bush organized an informal group of the wives of eleven new members of the House and Senate that year, and the Ruppes and Bushes became close friends. Bush served in the House for only two terms, but Ruppe was reelected five times before retiring in 1978. After Loret's work in the 1980 presidential campaign, Bush persuaded Reagan to name her Peace Corps director.

Loret Ruppe's resume, which did not seem to qualify her for the job at all, reinforced the fears of many in the Peace Corps family about the new Republican president, who they saw as even more conservative than Richard Nixon, the Republican president who had buried the Peace Corps ten years earlier. But the fears would prove exaggerated. Many conservatives in the Reagan entourage were suspicious of the Peace Corps, but Reagan himself did not share the contempt for the Kennedy-bred organization that had seethed in Nixon. And neither did his nominee.

Loret Ruppe, in fact, would prove an exciting surprise. It did not take her long to change the mood—and the minds—of the Peace Corps staff. A bureaucratic infighter, she protected the Peace Corps with determination and love. She looked on the idea of the Peace Corps with so much understanding and clear-minded insight that she worked doggedly to keep it out of partisan politics. She would ascend in the eyes of present and former Volunteers and staff until they acclaimed her as the most beloved and inspiring of all Peace Corps directors since Sargent Shriver.

Her associates still talk about her with glowing respect. She listened carefully and quietly to advisers before making decisions. She laughed often and told good-natured stories. She thoroughly enjoyed traveling to impoverished countries to meet her Volunteers. She remembered those she met from one year to the next. She was fearless in the face of snarls from right-wing ideologues. In the end, she proved to be no dilettante— in fact, she served as director for eight years, longer than any other in the history of the Peace Corps.

"She embodied in herself what Peace Corps was," says Jody Olsen, one of Ruppe's regional directors and a future deputy director of the Peace Corps. "She devoted all her time and effort to the Peace Corps. She was personable and charismatic. She inspired others to do the best they could."

When Ruppe's nomination was announced, Peace Corps officials scurried to find out more about her. Her lineage through her father was easily traced. Her father, Frederick C. Miller, who died in a small plane crash in 1954, had run the Miller Brewing Company, which his grandfather founded in Milwaukee in the nineteenth century. Ruppe's father also was a well-known local sports figure, for he had captained the Notre Dame football team in his youth and later helped bring the Boston Braves to Milwaukee.

The background of her mother, Adele Kaualey Miller, was less well known. But as the Peace Corps would discover in the next few years, Adele was an outspoken woman who regarded herself as a social activist and a militant leftist. She embraced radical causes with a passion. The closeness of the Republican director and her "socialist" mother became a kind of running Peace Corps joke in those days.

Loret would sometimes lunch with her mother and a few of her mother's liberal friends on Capitol Hill. To prevent anyone from the White House from spotting her, she told one Peace Corps staffer, "I ought to wear a bag over my head." Carroll Bouchard, the director of the Africa region, recalls lunching with Loret one day and finding her shaking her head. She had just received a phone call from her mother. Adele was down in Fort Benning, Georgia, with a band of protesters picketing the U.S. army's School of the Americas. She and other militants insisted that the army trained Latin American military and police officers at the school in the techniques of repressing their people.

Ruppe took over a Peace Corps in difficulty. Some outsiders called it "the Peace Corpse." The Carter administration had failed to revive it after the nightmare of the Nixon years. The number of Volunteers had dipped below 6,000. Its budget was so paltry that Ruppe found the total listed in the federal budget under "Miscellaneous." More money was set aside for U.S. military marching bands than the Peace Corps. The agency was so insignificant that no one at the State Department caught a typographical error before issuing a document that referred to it as "the Peach Corps."

On her first visit to the White House to meet the staff person assigned as liaison to the Peace Corps, she was kept waiting forty-five minutes. When the liaison finally showed up, he boasted that he had recommended doing away with the Peace Corps. She shook his hand and said, "I guess I'll have to request another liaison." She did, and he was replaced.

She battled early with the White House over personnel. Sargent Shriver's rule limiting Peace Corps officials to five years of service (with a year or two of extensions in some cases) was a boon then to any White House looking for openings to place the party faithful. Every year, a score or more appealing jobs opened at the Peace Corps.

When Ruppe took over, she found ten applicants, selected by Richard Celeste, her Democratic predecessor, waiting for final approval as country directors. Instead of rejecting them and giving in to the White House demand for Republican substitutes, she appointed all ten. She also retained William Sykes, a Democrat, as her deputy director. When Sykes later left to join the staff of Celeste, the newly elected governor of Ohio, he thanked the Peace Corps staff for contributing to Celeste's campaign. This infuriated the Reagan White House.

But Ruppe was proud of her nonpartisanship. At her request, Congress later passed legislation that prohibited political appointments of country directors. The White House could no longer send over lists of party loyalists for the jobs. "We took Peace Corps out of the pit of politics and made it nonpartisan," she boasted several years later. "It must always signify Americans pulling together for peace."

When Ruppe took charge, the Peace Corps, despite a great deal of autonomy, was still part of ACTION. This led to a crisis when the White House nominated Thomas J. Pauken as the new director of ACTION. Pauken had served as an army intelligence officer during the Vietnam War, and his appointment shattered a vital Peace Corps tradition.

From the beginning, Shriver knew that many foreigners would assume that the Peace Corps was a convenient channel for the CIA to spread its spies into developing countries. To counter this image, Shriver exacted a public promise from the CIA that it would never attempt to infiltrate the Peace Corps. And to avoid any embarrassing disclosures in the future, Shriver decreed that no one with any background in the CIA could serve as a Volunteer or staff member of the Peace Corps. This also applied to anyone who had served as an intelligence specialist for any other U.S. agency within the past ten years. The prohibitions remained throughout the history of the Peace Corps.

In short, Pauken's nomination meant that the Peace Corps would be subject to supervision by an official who was ineligible to serve in the organization. His presence, moreover, could stain the image of the Peace Corps. Ruppe objected to the nomination on these grounds, but the Senate confirmed Pauken anyway.

Senator Alan Cranston, a Democrat from California, then came to the rescue of Ruppe and the Peace Corps. Before his election to the Senate, Cranston, a journalist in his youth, had evaluated the Peace Corps program in Ghana for Charlie Peters in the 1960s. He returned from Africa brimming with praise for the Volunteers and later acted as one of the Peace Corps's most enthusiastic boosters in Congress. After the squabble over Pauken, he introduced legislation that would separate the Peace Corps completely from ACTION. It would thus no longer matter to the Peace Corps who was head of ACTION.

The White House opposed the bill, and Ruppe, unwilling to defy Reagan, said in public that she saw no need for the legislation. The right-wing Heritage Foundation, however, accused Ruppe of conducting "a successful behind-the-scenes lobbying campaign against the White House position." Congress passed the bill, and the Peace Corps regained the complete autonomy that had been taken away by Richard Nixon.

Another personnel crisis erupted in August 1982, when President Reagan appointed Edward A. Curran as the new deputy director of the Peace Corps. Curran, the former headmaster of the all-girls National Cathedral School in Washington, had just been fired by Secretary of Education T. H. Bell from his post as director of the National Institute of Education, the research arm of the Department of Education. When the Reaganites came to power in 1981, they were determined to abolish the department. They looked on it as an instrument for spreading leftist, socialist ideas into U.S. schools. The worst offender of the department, in their view, was the National Institute of Education.

Bell was a bitter disappointment to the ideologues. They looked on him as a traitor. He had no intention of leading his department into oblivion; worse, he encouraged social science research. Curran, one of the disappointed ideologues, wrote a letter to President Reagan urging him to abolish the National Institute of Education. The letter, however, arrived at the White House while Reagan was overseas, and an aide automatically forwarded it to Secretary Bell. Bell, incensed at Curran for going behind his back to seek White House intervention in the department, fired him immediately.

Ruppe could hardly be expected to feel pleased when Curran then showed up on her doorstep. She took it as a slap in the face. As far as she was concerned, Curran was a right-wing ideologue appointed by the White House to spy on her, and his actions supported that impression. Curran started to question Ruppe's appointment of country directors who did not qualify as true Reaganites. Curran, according to the Heritage Foundation, also proposed programs to "combat socialism in Third World countries." On top of this, Ruppe suspected him of feeding gossip to the right-wing *Washington Times* to fuel unflattering stories about herself and the Peace Corps.

After a little more than six months, an exasperated Ruppe decided that she had had enough of Curran. She cut down his duties, reduced his staff, barred him from senior staff meetings, and refused to let him serve as acting director when she traveled overseas. When the White House insisted she had no right to do this, she called Curran into her office and secretly tape-recorded their conversation, evidently trying to trap him into saying something disloyal, embarrassing, or stupid. The incident reportedly attracted enough White House notice for Fred Fielding, the presidential counsel, to rule that the taping, though a violation of federal regulations, was not illegal.

The Ruppe-Curran feud grew intense enough finally for the White House to withdraw Curran and nominate him as the new chairman of the National Endowment for the Humanities. The outcry from the academic world was so great, however, that the Senate rejected the nomination.

In December 1984, a month after President Reagan's reelection, the Heritage Foundation issued a report entitled, "The Peace Corps: Out of Step with Reagan." The report, written by a freelance writer named Mark Huber, listed all Ruppe's "sins," especially her campaigns against Pauken and Curran, and concluded:

> Now, on the eve of Reagan's second term, the Peace Corps still largely ignores the Reagan Agenda. Not only have the agency and its director snubbed Reagan policy, they have actually fought against it on Capitol Hill. In numerous ways, the Peace Corps has been an annoying thorn in Reagan's side, disregarding White House directives, making personnel appointments without proper White House clearance, and dragging its heels on vital foreign policy initiatives. As a result, many opportunities have been missed for extending the Reagan mandate to the Peace Corps.

The Peace Corps community, of course, read the report with pride and excitement. By testimony of the influential, right-wing Heritage Foundation, their wonderful director, a Reagan appointee, had proven a thorn in his side and had protected the Peace Corps from succumbing to the Reagan mandate. Every complaint in the report was treated like a medal of honor by the Peace Corps. The report, however, helped persuade Ruppe to act with slightly more caution and far less controversy in her second four-year term.

The report obviously amounted to a call for her removal, but Ruppe was able to withstand any campaign against her because President Reagan liked her, and personality usually counted far more with him than ideology. Ruppe often told the story of the state visit in 1983 of Prime Minister Ratu Mara of Fiji. The White House invited Ruppe to join a meeting of Mara and his delegation with Reagan, Vice President Bush, the cabinet, and other officials.

While seated around an enormous table, Ruppe recalled, "They talked about world conditions, sugar quotas, nuclear-free zones. The president then asked the prime minister to make his presentation. A very distinguished gentleman, he drew himself up and said, 'President Reagan, I bring you today the sincere thanks of my government and my people...' Everyone held their breath, and there was total silence. '... for the men and women of the Peace Corps who go out into our villages, who live with our people.' He went on and on. I beamed. Vice President Bush leaned over afterwards and whispered, 'What did you pay that man to say that?'"

A week later, Ruppe said, Reagan received a copy of the budget with a proposed cut for the Peace Corps. But Reagan refused it. "Don't cut the Peace Corps," Reagan said. "It's the only thing I got thanked for last week" during the Fiji state visit. The cut was restored.

Despite her spirited nonpartisanship and the admiration she attracted and merited, Ruppe also had her share of mistakes. The most significant flaw during her tenure was her embrace of Central America. In many ways, this mistake was understandable. Ruppe wanted the Peace Corps to be relevant, to be noticed by the White House and Congress, to play a vital role in the economic development of the Third World.

But relevance can be a trap. Many politicians have tended to look on the Peace Corps as relevant only when it lined up and assumed a supportive role in U.S. foreign policy. The Reagan administration was obsessed with Central America, intent on overthrowing the Sandinista-led regime in Nicaragua and preventing leftist insurgencies from triumphing elsewhere, and Ruppe fell into the trap of trying to make the Peace Corps relevant within this political cauldron.

The Reaganites came to office bristling with anger at President Jimmy Carter for his failure to prevent the Sandinistas from overthrowing the stalwart anti-communist (though dictatorial) regime of President Anastasio Somoza in Nicaragua. The Sandinista victory was regarded by the new administration as a major defeat in the Cold War. In its new

Central American strategy, the Reagan administration engaged in two main belligerent adventures—sponsoring the anti-Sandinista contras, who used Honduran bases to fight a civil war in Nicaragua, and accelerating military aid to a Salvadoran government guilty of atrocities and human rights abuses while battling a leftist insurgency.

With the Vietnam War still a troubling memory, many news commentators and Democratic members of Congress grew restive over these involvements in Central American wars. In response, President Reagan appointed a bipartisan commission headed by former secretary of state Henry Kissinger in 1983 to recommend long-term U.S. policies toward Central America "that will best respond to the challenges of social, economic, and democratic development in the region, and to internal and external threats to its security and stability."

Ruppe asked the commission to recognize the potential of the Peace Corps in this endeavor. She testified that the Peace Corps, with "the lasting friendships, understanding, and respect created by the Peace Corps Volunteers, not only with the people but also with their country's leaders, is of paramount importance to our long-term foreign policy objectives." The commissioners heeded her plea. In its report in January 1984, the Kissinger Commission urged "a dramatic expansion of [Peace Corps] volunteers in the region from the current 600 to a figure five or six times as great, largely in education."

But the Kissinger Commission report brimmed with Cold War cant. While it called for "greatly expanded support for economic growth and social reform," it also advocated "a significantly larger program of military assistance." The commission accepted the Reagan administration's questionable thesis that the insurgencies depended on Cuba and the Soviet Union, and the report warned that "there are circumstances in which the use of force, by the United States or by others, could become necessary as a last resort."

The Reagan administration treated the Kissinger Commission report as a green light for the expansion of its military programs in Central America. This led to a significant increase in economic aid as well. The Reagan administration knew that Congress would not appropriate funds for military assistance unless even more was requested for economic assistance.

Honduras became one of the largest recipients of U.S. foreign aid in Latin America. Only El Salvador, in fact, received more. The United

States provided Honduras with ten times more aid in 1981–1985 than it had in 1975–1980. A quarter of the aid in the 1980s was direct military spending. By 1985, U.S. funds paid for 76 percent of the Honduran military budget. The outpouring of U.S. money did not reflect an outpouring of generosity. It is hard to see it as anything else but payment by the Reagan administration for allowing an estimated 15,000 contra troops to operate out of Honduras under U.S. training and supervision.

A small portion of the increased foreign assistance covered an increase in the Peace Corps programming. Although one of the poorest countries in Latin America, Honduras had not usually hosted large Peace Corps programs. In 1970, it had only the twentieth-largest Peace Corps in the world, with 128 Volunteers. The Honduran program grew as more U.S. attention turned to Central America in the late 1970s. By 1979, it was the fifth-largest, with 193 Volunteers. This accelerated with the contra war until 1986, when Honduras became the largest Peace Corps program in the world with 310 Volunteers. For the rest of the decade, Honduras either remained in first place or found itself eclipsed only by the Philippines, a country with twelve times the population.

The Peace Corps, by associating itself with the Nicaraguan obsession of the Reagan administration, troubled many friends. In *What You Can Do for Your Country,* her extraordinary 1991 collection of Peace Corps oral histories, Karen Schwarz wrote that "many Volunteers took it for granted that they had been dispatched to Honduras to serve as 'the smile button' on the lapel of United States foreign policy."

Francine Dionne, speaking for the Returned Peace Corps Volunteers Committee on Central America, insisted, "They have declared the Peace Corps an instrument of U.S. foreign policy and a tool of the Reagan administration." Chuck Geisler, an assistant professor of sociology at Cornell and a former Volunteer, told the *New York Times,* "I'm very much against expanding our Peace Corps operations and expanding our military operations simultaneously. It's just a tragedy to give this mixed message and to make Volunteers in the field feel like they're part of a mopping-up operation."

The confusion of roles upset Ron Holcomb and his wife, Kathy McCann, while they were in training in Honduras in 1986. "We . . . came to the conclusion that we wouldn't be able to ignore our being representatives of the U.S. government, which had no business meddling in Honduras's internal affairs," Holcomb told Schwarz. "The Peace Corps appeared to be a piece of the puzzle, and even though it may have been a very small piece, we didn't want to have anything to do with it." Both Holcomb and McCann quit the Peace Corps just before the end of training.

The hurried race to outperform supposed communists led, in one case, to a mediocre project. With Peace Corps encouragement and U.S. funding, Honduras launched Plan Alfa, a campaign to teach illiterate Honduran peasants to read and write. This was an obvious attempt to match the successful Sandinista literacy program in Nicaragua. The Volunteers were assigned to supervise and train literacy teachers and prepare reading materials.

But the program foundered. It had not been planned well. The Honduran government fell behind in its salary payments to teachers. In addition, there were delays in the delivery of materials. Hard-working farmers found it difficult to give up an hour every weekday to a literacy class. Attendance dwindled.

Yet there were great needs in impoverished Honduras, and most Peace Corps Volunteers found satisfying work in agricultural production, tree planting, freshwater fisheries development, soil conservation, public health communication, elementary school teaching, and other projects. For the most part, they set aside concerns about the political role of the Peace Corps.

When Bill Mabie was in training in Honduras in 1985, he blurted out his concern during a lecture, asking from the back of the hall whether the Peace Corps had become just "window dressing for intervention." "Who said that?" the lecturer demanded. "I shrunk down in my seat so he couldn't see me," Mabie recalled more than twenty years later. "I didn't want to get tossed out." The lecturer dismissed the question as cynical.

Mabie was trained to help Hondurans build fishponds as a source of food. The Peace Corps assigned him to the town of Danli, in the province of El Paraiso in southeastern Honduras. He was in contra staging territory, barely twelve miles from the Nicaraguan border.

"When things would heat up on the border," says Mabie, "the U.S. military would roll into Danli. They would occupy a local restaurant a half block from my house as a command post. I tried to walk in once. They were reading a big map spread out on a dining table. A soldier shooed me away."

During the Easter Holy Week of 1986, the contras launched a major offensive but were swiftly repulsed by the Nicaraguan army. The Nicaraguans did not stop at the border but pursued the contras to a town just east of Danli. Soon, as Mabie puts it, "the war went into high gear . . . . I started hearing military convoys rumbling through and around Danli at night. During the day, groups of U.S. Chinook helicopters would fly overhead with artillery guns or jeeps hanging below them. This was no longer a proxy war; the U.S. was now overtly engaged." The Peace Corps pulled Mabie out of Danli.

Mabie was reassigned to a barrio in the town of Trujillo on the northern Caribbean coast. But that did not provide an escape from the contra war. In May 1987, the United States and Honduras staged a military exercise in the north, practicing how to turn back a Nicaraguan invasion if it came by sea. The exercise involved 3,000 Honduran soldiers and 7,000 U.S. troops.

"I literally had [U.S.] soldiers crawling up the beach into my little barrio," Mabie recalls. "That night, some of them got into fights with locals which I had to break up. There was quite a bit of drama about a Navy SEAL's wristwatch that had gone missing during his visit to the local bordello. The SEAL stormed through my barrio chasing a little boy, demanding his watch. Again I had to intervene to protect the kid, who eventually returned the watch . . . . During all of this, I couldn't help but fear that all the goodwill I had been developing with the locals was being erased by a two-day military exercise."

The goodwill did not dissipate. "I established wonderful relationships with Hondurans," Mabie, who was now the chief of staff of a California state senator, said in 2009. "I really enjoyed the experience. It . . . had a huge impact on my life in a variety of ways. And I believe that my service had a positive impact on the little corner of Honduras I called home . . . . My service was very tangible. I built a hatchery. Every day was an adventure. It was the best job I ever had."

Carole Levin and her husband, Andy, were assigned to La Libertad in central Honduras, located about two hours by bus on a gravel road from the provincial capital of Comayagua. Although helicopters from a U.S. air base sometime flew over La Libertad, the town was not caught in the war. Carole worked with a cooperative that supplied loans, equipment, and training to farmers to start aviaries for the production of honey.

"I had a great experience and felt that I really made a difference," says Carole. "These farmers were dirt poor, and they could have cared less what my government was doing. . . . While I was not happy with what my government was doing, it did not interfere with my work."

Similar testimony came from Steve Lenzo, who worked as a forester helping communities protect and reforest the watersheds surrounding the springs and creeks that supplied water. He was assigned to Agua Caliente de Linaca in the south the first year and to Morazán in the north the second year. "It was extremely rewarding and a worthwhile effort and much appreciated," he recalled recently, "regardless of the politics that brought so many of us to Honduras."

Honduras proved so hospitable and worthwhile that it continued to be one of the largest Peace Corps programs in the world long after the contra war, the Reagan administration, and the Cold War came to an end. Yet the satisfying and useful experiences of the Volunteers there did not alter the fact that the Peace Corps, by rushing more Volunteers into Honduras alongside Reagan's troops in the mid-1980s, had allowed more chipping away of the Peace Corps's aura of independence.

Even such a distinguished and admired Peace Corps director as Loret Ruppe did not understand this. She was obviously surprised and puzzled over the criticism that the organization received for its activities in Central America. Jody Olsen, the future deputy director, said recently that Ruppe's puzzlement did not stem from naivete.

"She would have been so surprised because her feeling for Peace Corps was so strong," Olsen said. "It was a feeling that we can make it happen . . . . Knowing that the Peace Corps could do well became consuming." And, of course, the Peace Corps Volunteers did do well in Honduras.

CHAPTER FOURTEEN

200,000 Stories

Jody Olsen, the deputy director of the Peace Corps from 2001 to 2009, insists that the work of the Peace Corps defies labeling because "we are upwards of 200,000 stories. That is what we are," she says. There is hyperbole in her description, but not much. A case can be made, for example, that the experiences of many of the high school teachers in former British Africa were similar enough to invite labeling. But, by and large, the experience of most Volunteers tended to be unique. This became more obvious after the first two decades. As the Peace Corps matured and diminished in size, it began placing more and more Volunteers alone in remote villages. Each one had a separate story to tell.

The stories have not been hidden. Scores of memoirs and novels based on Peace Corps experience have been published. This phenomenon has been celebrated and encouraged by the work of John Coyne and Marian Haley Beil, two Volunteers who served in the first program in Ethiopia. In 1989, they began producing their extraordinary newsletter *RPCV [Returned Peace Corps Volunteer] Writers & Readers,* with Beil as publisher and Coyne as editor. The newsletter publicized the memoirs, novels, short stories, poetry, and essays of former Volunteers, featuring reviews of the works and interviews with the authors. The exchanges encouraged other former Volunteers to seek out agents and publishers. The newsletter went online as Peace Corps Writers in 1997 and then became part of a new Beil-Coyne Web site, Peace Corps Worldwide, in 2009.

There was thus a great deal of written testimony about the Peace Corps experience, and a herald, first in print and later online, to guide us into it. This testimony was essential in understanding the history of the

Peace Corps. Much of the history, of course, involved machinations and politics in Washington. But it was the individual experiences overseas that kept the Peace Corps going, whether the decisions in Washington were wise or foolish. That, in fact, was the genius of the Peace Corps idea: No matter what, the individual Volunteers always powered and ennobled the Peace Corps.

A discussion of three of the memoirs may help an outsider fathom this heart of the Peace Corps better. Mike Tidwell worked in south central Zaire (later the Democratic Republic of the Congo) in 1985 and 1986 as an extension agent for the government's Projet Pisciculture Familiale (Family Fish Project). After training at the University of Oklahoma, he was assigned by the Peace Corps to the village of Lulenga, located alongside the Lubilashi River, a tributary of the Congo River. From Lulenga, he would travel throughout the Kalambayi area by motorcycle six days a week helping the Congolese build, stock, and harvest fishponds. "If you give a man a fish, he eats today," he was told in training. "But if you teach a man how to raise fish, he eats forever."

Tidwell set down his adventures in *The Ponds of Kalambayi,* published in 1990. The job is very frustrating. He must communicate in Tshiluba, the local language. The roads have been neglected for so long that some are impassable, even for his motorcycle. Villagers are reluctant to dig fishponds because they fear that Tidwell, like most whites before him, will keep most profits for himself. Birds ravage the ponds until he finally rigs up scarecrows to keep them away. The river overflows and floods ponds. Yet he perseveres and counts notable successes.

But he cannot escape loneliness. "Yet even as my village friendships improved," he writes, ". . . the lonely times in Kalambayi never left me. There were a lot of them, times when I felt utterly by myself and close to bursting from the pressure of uncommunicated feelings."

When he hears news on his short-wave radio about the *Challenger* space shuttle explosion in January 1986, "I ran to my door and looked out, searching for someone, anyone, with whom to share the news. All I saw, though, were women loaded down with manioc like burros and dirty children eating sugarcane outside boxlike houses . . . . I went back to my chair and nearly exploded like the spacecraft, streaking and whistling. With whom could I discuss the space shuttle, much less more subtle matters like the frustrations, longings, and loneliness that called on me in this remote place?"

Tidwell immerses himself in Kalambayi life in a way that would have enthralled Sargent Shriver in the early days. He chances upon an old blind man by a riverside one afternoon, and they chat.

The whole time we talked, nothing he said suggested he knew I was white and from another continent. We were just two travelers pausing at a riverbank in Africa, speaking Tshiluba. To pull this off, to become this immersed in culture and language, had been one of my goals in coming to Africa. As I talked to the old man, clucking at his descriptions of hardship, guffawing at his jokes, offering my own, there spread through me a feeling of having walked a long way and reached the circled endpoint on a map. For every child my white skin had pumped with horror, for every fried grasshopper I had eaten, sure it would kill me, for every line of Tshiluba I had mangled to the chuckles of those around me, here now was my glory.

Near the end of his tour, Tidwell receives a letter from Brian Steinwand, the Peace Corps director in Kinshasa, asking him to stay on for another year. Some diplomatic squabble has provoked the mercurial Zaire government to withhold visas for incoming Volunteers. It is not clear when anyone can replace him.

"I agreed with him that it would be a shame to leave the post empty," writes Tidwell. "Kalambayi was now one of the top fish farming regions in the country, and there was still room for expansion to the east."

But he has a problem: too much tshitshampa, the local alcoholic brew, distilled from corn. Whenever he enters the home of his neighbors and clients, they serve him tshitshampa. Lately, he has also started drinking tshitshampa on his own, to wipe out feelings of despair.

"I looked around after two years and was terrified by the fact that a majority of the people I cared most about in this world had ten cents in their pocket on a good day and could expect to live, on average, no more than forty-five years," he writes. "And what had I done for them really? What had I changed? The fish farmers had built more than one hundred ponds, and that was a lot. Fresh tilapia were entering village markets at a rate of two metric tons per year. I was proud of that fact. I was proud that, where before they had stood still, several dozen farmers were now walking a course out of absolute poverty. But it was a slow, hard, grinding course. Even with their ponds, the men were poorer than anything I could call acceptable."

If he stays, he will have to rely on even more tshitshampa to fight his dark moods. He fears alcoholism and decides it is time for him to leave Africa and return home.

After the Peace Corps, Tidwell achieved success as a travel writer and environmental leader, founding and running the Chesapeake Climate Action Network, a nonprofit organization dedicated to fighting global warming. His prescient 2003 book, *Bayou Farewell: The Rich Life and Tragic Death of Louisiana's Cajun Coast,* warned that the levee system around New Orleans was causing the loss of coastal land. He insisted that the land behind the levees was sinking and the barrier islands in the Mississippi disappearing, leaving the area without protection against a hurricane. The book was published two years before the terrible devastation of Hurricane Katrina.

Ellen Urbani, a graduate of the University of Alabama, arrived in Guatemala in the spring of 1992, destined in the eyes of her fellow trainees for failure. They called her "China Doll." Urbani understood why they thought she was out of place. "A sorority girl, fresh from college in the refined Deep South, with her Laura Ashley dresses and long, beribboned tresses, should be hosting tea at the country club," she writes.

But Urbani completed her full tour of two years, two months, and eight days while most of her fellow Volunteers felt forced to leave early. Guatemala was a dark and difficult country then, cruelly torn by civil war, unstable government, violence against leftists, and repression of Indians. Volunteers worked in enervating tension. The work for women Volunteers, especially those assigned to sites alone, was even more tense because of the contemptuous machismo of Guatemalan men.

The Peace Corps experience was so fraught with fear that Urbani did not want to talk or write about it for years. Her memoir, *When I Was Elena,* written under her married name, Ellen Urbani Hiltebrand, was not published until 2006, more than ten years after she left Guatemala.

Urbani's writing differs from Tidwell's because she incorporates fiction into the work, interspersing the shortened memoirs of seven other women, including another Volunteer, with her own story. These interludes are evidence of Urbani's empathy, but they are fiction nevertheless.

In the book, the Peace Corps first assigns Urbani to work with the ministry of youth in a small town, San Marquesa de Trójillonada, but the mood sours when her Guatemalan partner begins harassing her, showing up drunk at her house at night, pounding on the door. When the teacher at a nearby mountain village school breaks his leg, Urbani quickly applies to take his place and moves to the village. He returns the next year, and Urbani is reassigned to work with the ministry of youth in Zataquepeque, a town in the Indian highlands. There she hikes to five different schools, spending an afternoon at each working with children, trying to help them think differently, think creatively.

Guatemala will mature her. "At twenty-three . . . I was still too fresh, too new to her shores, for Guatemala to have yet stolen from me my native idealism," she writes. "She would rob me soon; grab hold of me, give me a good flailing, wrench from my embrace the sense of personal omnipotence fueling the perception that a single person can make a difference. Oh, how I grew to hate Guatemala for that!"

The menace of Guatemalan men hangs over the memoir. She tries hard not "to allow this tale to digress and then degrade into a scathing denouement belittling and chastising the Hispanic male." But, throughout her two years, she sleeps with a butcher knife under the pillow, a lead pipe under the bed, and her German shepherd, Cali, on the bed. Four of her fellow Volunteers were raped during the two years.

An ordinary walk through town is always an unpleasant obstacle course. Women would often touch her harmlessly. "Only the men loitering on the streets meant disrespect, not just touching my hair and skin to test their reality but lunging for my crotch or my breasts to taunt me," she writes. "The less ballsy ones, but nonetheless still crude, would call to me sick sexualisms as I strolled down the street. Once, in an effort to gauge the precise frequency with which this occurred, I counted the tally of crude gestures in a seven-block round trip to the store. Fourteen different men assaulted me either verbally or physically."

She describes herself frolicking with her friend Luci and Luci's children at dusk one evening. "Multiply in your mind," she writes, "the beauty of this evening and spread it out over the course of the years. Do not let the robberies and the rapes and the assaults dull the sound of these children laughing or chill the warmth of their hands slipped into mine . . . . After leaving, I recall that the bad overshadowed the good for far too long, and I can find no way to tell the full truth without letting those sentiments creep back in."

She is attacked during her last week in Guatemala. First she finds a warning scrawled in red on the wall of her house. "Gringa bitch, I'll fuck you or I'll kill you," it says. At night, she hears the footsteps of an intruder on the porch. He then smashes down the door and rushes toward her bed. She is so paralyzed with fear that she is unable to reach for her knife or pipe or even scream. All she can do is admonish herself continually to breathe so she does not faint. But Cali, growling, snarling, biting, snapping, scratching, fights off the assailant, who runs away.

"My bond with Guatemala unraveled in those last few weeks, tore clear through that last night," she writes. "The invader did me a favor, though; he filled me with fury and fear and a righteous indignation which swifted me home without regret."

Yet years later, she goes on, "time has softened and tempered my thoughts of her. Guatemala gave to me more than she took, and I would live it all over again, no second thoughts .... Guatemala made me *me,* and if she hurt me, the cicatrix is too much part of what I am to ever relieve myself of it. It is my battle wound, my numbered tattoo, my Purple Heart that says I *thrived.*"

After leaving Guatemala, Urbani married a fellow Volunteer and settled in Portland, Oregon. She had to be treated for tuberculosis, which she contracted in the Peace Corps. After receiving an MA in art therapy, she began designing art programs for cancer patients. Her work became a subject of a well-received documentary, *Paint Me a Future,* by David Kaminsky. Now the mother of two small children, she told John Coyne in an interview in 2007, "I have more books in me, but heaven knows when I'll have time to write them."

Barbara E. Joe arrived in Honduras with forty-eight other trainees in the summer of 2000. She was in a definite minority, the only one over the age of sixty. Despite all the Peace Corps propaganda about its quest for older Volunteers, only 7 percent of its Volunteers throughout the world were older than fifty. Most of the trainees with Barbara were younger than her own children.

Peace Corps lore was rife with stories of older Volunteers who did not make it. Many staffers insisted the older Volunteers were inflexible, weak at foreign languages, often homesick, and squeamish over the primitive living conditions. A male friend predicted to sixty-two-year-old Barbara that she would be out and home by Christmas.

But Barbara persisted, even extended for a third year, and wrote a memoir that flattens all the clichéd objections to older Volunteers in the Peace Corps. The book, *Triumph and Hope: Golden Years with the*

Peace Corps in Honduras, which she published herself, was selected by the Peace Corps Writers Web site as the best Peace Corps memoir of 2009.

Barbara had toyed with the idea of joining the Peace Corps for many years. She was a graduate student at the University of California at Berkeley when Kennedy was inaugurated. She might have answered his call earlier, but education, marriage, career, and children always seemed more important. Many years later, the underpinnings of her life were shaken by divorce, a job loss, and the deaths of a son and a foster child, and she decided the time had come for the Peace Corps.

As might be expected, Barbara came into the Peace Corps with a record of achievement far longer than that of most Volunteers. She was fluent in Spanish, a language she used as a teenager in Colombia when her father worked there for the Organization of American States. A member of Amnesty International, she had served as an election monitor in Chile, Nicaragua, Haiti, and the Dominican Republic, and, on vacations, had taken part in refugee and health projects in Guatemala, El Salvador, Nicaragua, and Colombia. A former social worker, she had worked for many years for the American Occupational Therapy Association. Barbara had even visited Honduras before, when she accompanied her father, a Canadian-born architect, to an archeological project at the Mayan ruins of Copán. She was less than three years old then.

The title of her book comes from the two villages in which she served: El Triunfo (Triumph), where for two years as a health worker she tried to inculcate good sanitation and health habits, and La Esperanza (Hope), where for one year she served as an aide to the staff in a Peace Corps regional office.

In the memoir, Barbara often discusses her relationship with younger Volunteers. In training, she writes, "I soon found myself acting as mother confessor to young trainees missing their own parents, or perhaps finding it easier to talk with me than with contemporaries . . . . A few expressed condescending admiration for my 'bravery' for joining the Corps in my dotage, though I considered myself better prepared than they for what actually lay ahead."

She feels that older Volunteers are "less vulnerable than many younger Volunteers to loneliness and depression," and that their expectations, "tempered by experience . . . were more realistic." In a visit to a maternity wing of a hospital, she notices that her young associates are uneasy about the women in labor for they, unlike herself, had never given birth.

But she is not condescending about their youth. "I was blown away by my fellow trainees, all in their twenties, who made up for lack of experience with touching sincerity and boundless energy," she writes.

Most memoirs by returned Volunteers tend to be introspective, almost self-indulgent in the way they devote lavish space to the discovery of new sensations and ideas that they experience in their first brush with an unfamiliar culture in a distant and impoverished land. Everything is new; everything is a wonder; everything churns out fresh feelings and thoughts.

But Barbara's memoir is different. It is not that she is jaded or bored, but rather that she is matter-of-fact and reportorial in her description of her experiences. Nothing fazes her; nothing drives her to despair; nothing sends her into raptures of wonder.

In El Triunfo, she rents a space in a hut in the crowded compound of eighty-six-year-old Doña Marina. Her space is only twelve by fifteen feet, with a partition separating a living room and a bedroom. Barbara sizes up the pros and cons calmly. "Doña Marina's compound provided me with a welcome status, sense of belonging, and margin of safety," she writes. "But the loyalty cut both ways, preventing me from ever moving elsewhere lest she suffer a huge loss of face. I also had to live with virtually no privacy."

She shows neither sentimentality nor despair as she analyzes the difficulty of her work. "If condoms are unavailable," she writes, "it's futile to recommend their use. If daily brushing protects teeth, toothbrushes are needed. A balanced diet requires access to a variety of foods. Our conundrum as PCVs was educating people who often lacked the means to follow through."

After her fellow Volunteer, a young man, leaves El Triunfo at the end of the first year, Barbara becomes even more immersed in the culture and begins to think like a Honduran. Her tone is even-handed as she discusses the lack of modern conveniences in her village. "Americans often recoil when I mention using an outhouse or bathing bucket, but where that's customary, it's really no big deal and has been the norm throughout human history," she writes. "On vacation visits to the States, I view hot water and flush toilets as terrible extravagances. Honduran peasants would welcome electricity and running water, but their lack is not felt as a daily deprivation."

When her Peace Corps assignment ends, she finds that her readjustment "proves more unsettling than leaving the U.S. in the first place." "There *is* life after the Peace Corps," she writes, "but it's not the same. I really miss Honduras."

These memoirs by returned Volunteers raised some issues about placing Volunteers alone in isolated sites. There is no doubt that each Volunteer was far more enmeshed in a foreign culture than they would have been if they had another American nearby to support them. But the cost was incipient alcoholism in Zaire and trauma over an attempted rape in Guatemala. Only Barbara, the older Volunteer in Honduras, flourished in her isolation (and she had another younger Volunteer in her village for one year). As its fiftieth anniversary approached, the Peace Corps was resisting pressure—like that of the *Dayton Daily News* series discussed in chapter 12—to change its policy of assigning most of the Volunteers to posts by themselves.

The memoirs reflected a changing Peace Corps. By the 1980s, the Peace Corps had become an elite institution of Americans working in remote sites, often alone, coping with poverty and inertia, doing the best they could to change what little they could. They were better trained than Volunteers of the 1960s and 1970s and, most important, were better versed in language. They also escaped the great clusters of Volunteers that drained Peace Corps programs in the past. All in all, based on the evidence in these memoirs, the more recent Volunteers struck an old evaluator like myself as a heroic band.

CHAPTER FIFTEEN

A New Name and a New World

Paul D. Coverdell, a fifty-year-old Georgia politician appointed by President George H. W. Bush to succeed Loret Ruppe as director in 1989, could not fathom why the Peace Corps was not known as the "U.S. Peace Corps." The U.S. government, after all, paid to send the Volunteers overseas and supervise their work. "I do not believe we should hide the name of the country that has sponsored the wonderful things we have done around the world," he told the *Washington Post*. So, in less than a year, he changed the name, emblazoning "U.S. Peace Corps" on letterheads, posters, walls, and the facade of the headquarters, then on K Street in Washington.

Several veteran Peace Corps staffers tried to talk him out of it. When they approached his office, Jody Olsen, his chief of staff, told them, "Don't try, because you won't succeed." He was adamant. Their arguments made no headway.

Without realizing it, Coverdell was turning the agency's history on its head. The law creating the agency called it a Peace Corps, not a U.S. Peace Corps, and made it clear that the Volunteers were working as private citizens. Except for a few administrative details like assistance in voting, the Peace Corps Act said, the Volunteers "shall not be deemed officers or employees or otherwise in the service or employment of, or holding office under, the United States for any purpose."

Coverdell's nomenclature damaged the tradition—albeit a tradition that was often buffeted—that the Peace Corps was not an instrument of U.S. foreign policy. John Coyne, then a director of the National Council of Returned Peace Corps Volunteers, called the name change "a breach of the original intention of the Peace Corps." Senator Alan Cranston wrote Coverdell, "I think you are sending exactly the wrong message to volunteers, prospective volunteers, and other Americans by actively stressing an association of the Peace Corps with the U.S. government or with U.S. foreign policy interests in some fashion." On top of this, Cranston went on, "I cannot imagine any commercial venture that had a name as good and effective and with as much positive connotation as the 'Peace Corps' fiddling around with its name."

But Coverdell never budged: he kept the name "U.S. Peace Corps." That lasted throughout the administration of the first President Bush and then disappeared after Bill Clinton was elected president in 1992. The controversy over the name did not arouse much excitement. It was not front-page news. An account appeared on page 17 of the *Washington Post*. The Peace Corps was now a small agency that attracted little attention. Its director attracted no more attention.

Coverdell began a procession of eight directors who have lead the Peace Corps in the last twenty years. Although he clearly did not understand the fuss kicked up by his foolish name change, he was a warm and creditable administrator with affection and enthusiasm for the Peace Corps and the Volunteers. Friends describe him as an unpretentious, gregarious man with a wide smile and a folksy manner. He liked to unwind over a drink or two before dinner. "He seldom spoke about himself," recalled David Lamb, a longtime friend and a foreign and national correspondent of the *Los Angeles Times*, "but loved talking about the direction he hoped to take the Peace Corps."

Coverdell's two-and-a-half-year administration coincided with dramatic upheavals in Eastern Europe. In 1989, Solidarity came to power in Poland, the Velvet Revolution brought down the government in Czechoslovakia, and the East Germans crumbled the Soviet-built wall that separated them from West Berlin. Unlike his predecessors, who suppressed democratic rebellions in 1956 and 1968, Mikhail Gorbachev, the Soviet leader, did not interfere. The Cold War was soon at an end.

It was natural for these new democratic countries to embrace as many Western European and U.S. institutions as they could. They wanted to feel part of the real Europe and part of what Americans liked to call the Free World. The East Europeans wanted membership in the European Union and the North Atlantic Treaty Organization. Word came to Washington from U.S. ambassadors in Europe that countries like Poland

and Hungary would even welcome Peace Corps Volunteers. There was hesitation among some Peace Corps officials about trying to fulfill these unusual requests. But Coverdell did not hesitate.

Coverdell and President Bush generated an excitement that mimicked those heady early days of Sargent Shriver and President John F. Kennedy. The new director rushed off to several Eastern European countries, leading Peace Corps delegations that promised Volunteers. A traveling President Bush told the students and faculty of Karl Marx University in Budapest that the Peace Corps would soon send sixty teachers to Hungary. While President Vaclav Havel was visiting Washington, he and Bush announced that Peace Corps Volunteers were coming to Czechoslovakia.

On the eve of their departure, the first Volunteers to Poland and Hungary were greeted by President Bush in the White House Rose Garden just the way Volunteers were once saluted by President Kennedy. With Coverdell at his side, Bush told the new Volunteers, "Paul says that in many ways it as if the Peace Corps had been in training for this historical moment. It shows that our mission, our desire for peace, knows no political or geographic boundaries."

When the Soviet Union disintegrated in 1990, the Peace Corps also began sending Volunteers to the former Soviet socialist republics that were now independent states. By 1995, the Peace Corps had Volunteers in the former Eastern Bloc countries of Albania, Bulgaria, the Czech Republic, Hungary, Poland, Romania, and the Slovak Republic; the former Soviet Union republics of Armenia, Estonia, Latvia, Lithuania, Kazakhstan, Kyrgyzstan, Moldova, Turkmenistan, the Ukraine, and Uzbekistan; and Russia itself. Most Volunteers were involved in the teaching of English and the development of small business. The Peace Corps was imparting capitalism and the language of capitalism to what was once the world's most powerful communist region.

Unfortunately, the Peace Corps's frenzied drive to rush Volunteers to Eastern Europe in 1989 and the early 1990s caused some of the same problems that the frenzied drive to rush Volunteers anywhere in the world had created when the Peace Corps began in 1961. The hurry hampered programming. None of the early lessons were heeded.

After a study of the Peace Corps in Poland, Bulgaria, Uzbekistan, and Russia, the General Accounting Office reported to Congress in 1994, "Many of the steps necessary to introduce effective programs were rushed, done superficially, or not done at all. Consequently, many of the new programs we examined were poorly designed and faced a host of other problems, including the lack of qualified staff, the assignment of volunteers to inappropriate or underdeveloped projects, insufficient volunteer training, and volunteer support systems that did not work. These problems frustrated many volunteers who had joined the Peace Corps to contribute to the region's development and contributed to a relatively high resignation rate among the volunteers."

The staffing was inadequate. "Many of the staff we met," the GAO report said, "told us they had little knowledge of the local language and culture before they arrived, which they said significantly hindered their effectiveness." Country directors resigned or were pulled out within the first year in half the eighteen Peace Corps countries in the region. Bulgaria alone had four directors and one acting director in a twenty-month period. In Poland, the staff work was so inadequate that half the small-business Volunteers had to be moved to new sites. "Volunteers assigned to teach English in secondary schools told us that their schools had large numbers of skilled English teachers and that it was hard to justify their continued presence in the schools," the GAO said.

Peace Corps officials knew little about operating in a former communist country. Transferring funds, for example, became a major problem. On a trip to Vladivostok on the far eastern coast of Russia, Ellen Yaffe, then a consultant, recalls, "I was carrying forty thousand dollars in cash on my body under my coat."

Programming had its cowboy antics. When Tim Carroll took up his post as the first country director in Poland in 1961, he planned on the arrival of sixty Volunteer teachers of English. He was soon told to expect twice that number. It seems that Edward Piszek, a Philadelphia industrialist of Polish descent, was disappointed with the original number. So he solicited funds from friends, added $1.2 million of his own, and sent it off to the Peace Corps to finance another sixty Volunteers. This was a rather bizarre way for the Peace Corps to allocate and assign Volunteers.

The push into the former communist countries raised an important question about the mission of the Peace Corps. Was it neglecting, or at least diminishing, its original goal of helping the impoverished Third World? Gerard A. Roy, the agency's inspector-general, reported that "as Peace Corps expanded into new major programs in Eastern Europe, some of the existing Peace Corps programs in Africa, Asia, and Latin

America underwent actual budget cuts, while others received increases that nevertheless failed to keep pace with local inflation." As a result, Roy wrote, there was "evidence of strain, confusion, and chaos" within the Peace Corps.

Some in the Peace Corps feared that the new assignments would lack the traditional rigors of working in the Third World. This attitude was derided recently by Carroll, who directed programs in Poland and later in Russia. Carroll, who had served as a Volunteer in Nigeria in the 1960s, said, "I suggest that standing in line for a public latrine in subzero weather in Ukraine will match any 'suffering' the Third World had to offer our hearty crew."

Yet the Peace Corps in the Ukraine bore no resemblance to the traditional Peace Corps in Nigeria. In 1994, Meg Small, a thirty-nine-year-old Volunteer in Kiev, was flying continually to Paris, Frankfurt, Brussels, and other western European cities to negotiate contracts for a new MBA program in the Ukraine. Jerry Dutkewych, the country director, told his Volunteers they needed suits and business cards. In 2009, Volunteer Claire St. Amant, a recent college graduate teaching English in the Ukrainian town of Tysmentsya, wrote that "many of my colleagues in Ukraine could be my grandparents; they include academics and former business executives." By then, the Ukraine, with 247 Volunteers, was the largest Peace Corps country in the world.

Coverdell cannot be faulted for thinking beyond the Third World, however. The term *Third World,* in fact, was a relic of the past. It had been coined by French demographer Alfred Sauvy in 1952 to describe the underdeveloped nations who were not aligned with either of two powerful and antagonistic worlds—the NATO alliance of the United States and Western Europe and the communist bloc of the Soviet Union and Eastern Europe. But, more than thirty-five years later, with the world of capitalism and the world of communism no longer at war, the term *Third World* had lost its meaning.

The Peace Corps's push beyond the Third World into Eastern Europe and the former Soviet Union was indiscriminate. It surely made sense for the Peace Corps to work in countries like Moldova and Uzbekistan, which were ranked by the UN Development Programme on the same level of development as traditional Peace Corps countries like Honduras and Guatemala. But the rationale for bringing the Peace Corps to countries such as Poland, Hungary, and the Czech Republic was far more questionable. All three were European countries with literate, skilled populations that probably needed investment far more than they needed Peace Corps Volunteers.

Despite questions about the wisdom of the new programs, many Volunteers tended to have satisfying experiences. "I don't think it was totally necessary for the Peace Corps to be in Poland," Amy Utzinger, who taught in Olesno in southern Poland, wrote recently. "After all, it is an industrialized nation with a good education system. But I do think it was helpful for the Peace Corps to be in Poland."

"In some ways it was a typical Peace Corps experience," she went on, "although in other ways it wasn't. I mean, although I had access to electricity and running water, when I first arrived in Poland, there were food shortages. I never went hungry, but I ate the same thing for breakfast, lunch, and dinner for month after month. Lots of potatoes . . . And once when I went into a grocery store, the only thing on the shelf was vinegar."

But, most important, she said, "I know I had an impact on my students . . . . I brought fresh ideas and modern teaching methods, which were greatly appreciated by the students. I didn't 'save' anyone from hunger or disease or ignorance, but I taught them about the world, which they had been denied knowledge of by the Soviet system."

Eventually, both the Peace Corps and the host countries recognized the anomaly of assigning Volunteers to industrialized nations. Faced with a budget cut in the mid-1990s and the need to open new programs in poorer counties, Peace Corps director Mark Gearan reexamined the rationale for the Eastern European commitment. "How do we remain in Prague and not serve in Haiti?" Gearan, recalling his thinking at the time, said recently. "How can we be in Warsaw and not in Bangladesh? How can we not accept Peace Corps Volunteers for Jordan and South Africa and stay in Budapest?"

Gearan ended the programs in Hungary and the Czech Republic in 1997 and set in motion the end of the Peace Corps in Poland four years later. By 2002, the Peace Corps had left the Slovak Republic and the Baltic Countries as well. A year later, President Vladimir Putin ended the Peace Corps program in Russia. The Peace Corps continued only in those Eastern European countries and former Soviet republics that resembled those of the Third World.

Despite all his travel overseas, Coverdell began to attract attention for his trips to his home state of Georgia. This travel, if it were personal travel paid in full by Coverdell, was somewhat understandable since his wife, Nancy, an airline stewardess, had never moved to Washington. She maintained the family home in Atlanta. But according to records obtained by the *Washington Post* under the Freedom of Information Act, the Peace Corps had paid, in full or in part, for twenty-six trips to Georgia during Coverdell's first eighteen months as director—an average of more than once a month. *Post* reporter Al Kamen, a former Volunteer, wrote there was "widespread speculation in the agency that the veteran Georgia politician intends to run for office in Georgia."

Coverdell, while not ruling out a future run for office, insisted that his Georgia travel was prompted by recruiting; he was trying to drum up interest in the Peace Corps among southerners and non-whites, two groups underrepresented among Volunteers. He said Atlanta was an obvious target "because it is the home seat of so much of the minority population of the country."

Coverdell was soon excoriated by *Washington Post* columnist Colman McCarthy both for the Georgia trips and for the rush into Eastern Europe. McCarthy derided Coverdell as "a self-promoter keeping himself visible to the home folk for the day when he jumps back into Georgia politics." The columnist also accused Coverdell of making the Peace Corps "an arm of Bush Administration foreign policy." Third World programs should not be shunted aside, McCarthy said, "because Bush officials now see Eastern Europe as the politically fashionable place to be."

Nine months after the article about his trips to Georgia, Coverdell announced his resignation as director of the Peace Corps and his candidacy for the Republican nomination for a U.S. Senate seat from Georgia. The announcement, in the eyes of his critics, confirmed their suspicion that he had used the Peace Corps as a launching pad for his ambitions. Coverdell won the seat in a close election that required a runoff, and he remained in the Senate until he died of a cerebral hemorrhage in 2000 at the age of sixty-one.

Coverdell had proven a quiet though influential senator. "In a time of rising partisan rancor," *Washington Post* columnist David Broder wrote after the senator's shocking death, "Coverdell chose the role of mediator or facilitator . . . . He was admired and cherished." Senator Olympia Snowe, Republican of Maine, described Coverdell as a model of those who look on public service as a noble calling. "People like Paul Coverdell exist in the world—good, honorable, trustworthy people who call us to our better nature," she told the Senate.

The wave of emotion over the death of a fellow legislator did not dissipate in the Senate, and several Senators came up with the idea a few months later of naming the Peace Corps headquarters after him. It seemed like a logical move to the senators: Coverdell had served as a Peace Corps director and championed the Peace Corps in the Senate. The sponsors, mostly Republicans, knew little about Peace Corps history and would not have cared even if they had known.

But many former Volunteers felt insulted by the idea. In their view, Coverdell had served as director for only two and a half years, challenged tradition by sticking "U.S." in front of the Peace Corps name, rushed heedlessly into Eastern Europe, and used the Peace Corps shamelessly as a springboard to the Senate. If the headquarters were to be named after anyone, it ought to be Sargent Shriver. Or, if a Republican-controlled Congress had to find a Republican to honor, it ought to be Loret Ruppe.

Barbara Ferris, an official of the National Peace Corps Association, the organization of returned Volunteers, tried to whip up a letter-writing campaign to Congress against the legislation. She wrote former Volunteers, "I personally am disgusted by the thoughtlessness of this idea, the political posturing and the insult to all of us who have chosen to serve . . . . Paul Coverdell may have been a nice guy, but he was also a very controversial director."

But it was a hopeless battle against a determined, Republican-controlled Congress. Opponents had to be careful not to insult the memory of Coverdell. Senator Christopher Dodd, a Democrat from Connecticut and the only former Volunteer in the Senate, urged his colleagues to act more deliberately in attaching a name to Peace Corps headquarters. "The concerns I raised . . . have nothing whatsoever to do with my admiration and respect for Paul Coverdell," Dodd said during the Senate debate. "They have to do with an institution with which I have been closely identified and affiliated for forty years, the Peace Corps."

Dodd said that the Peace Corps community had never believed in naming itself or its headquarters after anyone. Too many people had contributed to its strength to single anyone out. "Over the years," he said, "we have talked about the Peace Corps not as John Kennedy's Peace Corps or Hubert Humphrey's Peace Corps or Sargent Shriver's Peace Corps or Loret Ruppe's Peace Corps or my Peace Corps; it has been the nation's."

He chided the senators for perpetuating a process in which they were always "sort of racing to the finish line as to who gets to put a label on some building or monument."

Dodd's plea was unheeded. The Senate passed the bill on a voice vote, and the House passed it by a margin of 330 to 61. President George W. Bush signed it into law at a ceremony in the ornate Indian Treaty Room on July 26, 2001, a year after the death of Coverdell. The law proclaimed that the headquarters of the Peace Corps, no matter where it was housed, would be known from then onwards as the "Paul D. Coverdell Peace Corps Headquarters." The name would remain a permanent irritant.

CHAPTER SIXTEEN

The Expansive Mood
of the Clinton Years

The election of Bill Clinton as president in 1992 ushered in eight straight years of Democratic rule in the White House. The Peace Corps had not experienced that many consecutive years of Democratic rule since the early years of the John Kennedy and Lyndon Johnson administrations. Of course, the fortunes of the Peace Corps did not always depend on the fortunes of the political parties. Although created by Democrats, the Peace Corps did fairly well during the Republican administration of Ronald Reagan, thanks to the protective care of Loret Ruppe, and fared poorly during the Democratic administration of Jimmy Carter, thanks to the confrontations with Sam Brown. Nevertheless, the Peace Corps was in an expectant and expansive mood when Clinton took office.

Loret Ruppe had often called for an expansion of the Peace Corps, but her calls were heeded by neither the White House nor Congress. There was hope that this mood would change under Clinton, but there was another dividend as well. Clinton had pledged during the campaign to appoint a former Volunteer as director of the Peace Corps. This campaign promise was fulfilled, though it took several months to persuade Clinton's choice, Carol Bellamy, the former president of the New York City Council, to take the job.

Bellamy came out of those euphoric first years of the Peace Corps. One night in 1962, she had fallen asleep while studying in the stacks of the library of Gettysburg College in Pennsylvania. When she awoke, she found the library closed and locked—she literally could not leave. Whiling away the hours, she came upon a brochure about President Kennedy's new agency, the Peace Corps. She had heard about the Peace Corps, of course, but she knew little about it. The brochure was persuasive. By the time the librarians arrived to open the doors that morning, she had resolved to apply.

The Peace Corps invited Bellamy to train for work in Guatemala after graduation. She arrived in Guatemala in 1963 among the first batches of Volunteers ever assigned there. Based in the town of Santa Elena, in the isolated northern province of Peten, as a community development worker, she ran a school lunch program, raised chickens, and broadcast a daily Spanish-language program on radio called "The Housewife's Hour," full of suggestions for good health and a wholesome diet.

The Peace Corps, she told the *New York Times*, taught her that "there's a whole big world out there and you ought to give it a try." It also taught her how to deal with failure. "What I took out of the Peace Corps," she said, "was that you need to be willing to try a lot of different things and actually fail in some things. You get up and wipe your bloody nose, and head forward."

After the Peace Corps, Bellamy entered New York University law school, intent on working some day for AID, which she regarded as "a Peace Corps with flush toilets." But she found herself more interested in courses on contracts and corporations. Moreover, by the time she received her law degree in 1968, the anger over the Vietnam War had intensified, and young idealistic Americans like herself found it unseemly to apply for work in the federal government.

After a few years practicing law, Bellamy, who grew up in Plainfield, New Jersey, across the Hudson River from New York City, embroiled herself in New York state and city politics, achieving a notable run of electoral successes for more than a decade. She was elected three times to represent a Brooklyn district in the New York State Assembly and then was elected in a runoff to be president of the City Council in New York—the first woman to hold that job.

But electoral failures mounted afterwards. She lost a bid for the Democratic nomination for mayor and then, in a major disappointment, she failed by three percentage points to oust the incumbent Republican state comptroller, one of the highest statewide positions, in 1990.

During the 1992 presidential campaign, while Bellamy was working as an investment banker, Bill Clinton made his pledge to put the Peace

Corps in the hands of a former Volunteer. After his election, Bellamy, one of the most prominent former Volunteers, seemed a logical choice.

Two former Volunteers—Donna Shalala, the new Secretary of Health and Human Services, and Senator Christopher Dodd of Connecticut—and Harold Ickes, an old friend of Bellamy and a member of the White House staff, urged Bellamy to take the Peace Corps job. But she had other plans that had nothing to do with the Clinton administration.

A couple of weeks after Clinton's inauguration, state comptroller Edward V. Regan, the Republican who had narrowly defeated Bellamy two years earlier, announced that he was resigning to head an economic institute. Under New York law, the two houses of the state legislature would meet to choose someone to complete the final two years of Regan's term. Bellamy put herself forward once more as a candidate for the post.

Taking over the Peace Corps "had not been in my game plan," she told the *New York Times* later. "My game plan was that I run for the state comptroller's position."

New York politics, in any case, attracted her more than national politics. "I know there's a pecking order out there where people think that really smart people are in the federal government, and the kind of mezzo-mezzo people and real idiots are at the state and local level," she said. "But my whole life I happen to believe it's the other way around. So Washington government just never really turned me on."

But Gov. Mario Cuomo and other leading Democrats supported another candidate, H. Carl McCall, and the Democratic-controlled legislature followed their lead in the special election in May, inflicting another major defeat on Bellamy. "It left the worst taste of any campaign I've been involved in," she said.

The Peace Corps directorship was still open, and Bellamy, no longer reluctant, accepted the offer this time. "It's like someone said to me," she told the *New York Times*, "Sometimes when windows close, doors open."

For the most part, former Volunteers were pleased that one of their own had been chosen. "We're thrilled that after all this time, there is a returned Peace Corps Volunteer who has been named to head the agency," said Charles F. Dambaugh, the executive director of the National Council of Returned Peace Corps Volunteers (which later became the National Peace Corps Association). Not only was she the first former Volunteer to head the Peace Corps, but as a prominent politician in New York City, the media capital of the United States, she was the best-known appointee to take the job since Sargent Shriver.

But her renown troubled some former Volunteers, who feared that she would mimic Coverdell and use the Peace Corps as a convenient channel back into state politics. In a related concern, John Coyne, the editor of the *Peace Corps Writers* newsletter, observed, "It remains to be seen if, after a lifetime of politics in New York, she still has the heart of a Volunteer."

Bellamy proclaimed her enthusiasm. "I'm ready to shout from the rooftops about the Peace Corps," she said. "I want to get on the road at once, not only overseas but in this country as well. I want people to know that the Peace Corps is alive and well."

Bellamy never fit the fuzzy image that some in the public had of former Volunteers as soft-hearted do-gooders wearing their idealism on their sleeves. Instead, she proved a hard-working, tough, intelligent taskmaster who expected her staff to measure up to her high standards.

"She was a workaholic," said one of her staff, an admirer. "She was manic. She would send e-mails at 1:00 a.m. She was action-oriented. She wanted everyone to move, move, move. She was a micromanager. No detail was too small for her to check." Ellen Yaffe, who was Bellamy's chief financial officer, said, "She was a good director, but she was a tough cookie. She didn't suffer fools gladly. If she thought they weren't up to the job, she was all over them like a cheap suit."

But she was admired by the Volunteers overseas. Coyne, who was working on the Washington staff during Bellamy's reign, said she could talk with the Volunteers in the field and acted as their advocate in all staff and congressional discussions in Washington. He described her as cautious, not warm, but a "good person," and concluded that, despite his earlier worries, "she did have the heart of a Volunteer."

But he, like many others, was disappointed by the brevity of her term as director. In a year and five months, she resigned to become executive director of the United Nations Children's Fund (UNICEF), the most glamorous agency in the U.N. system. Her surprise appointment was evidently a by-product of the continual feuding at the United Nations between U.S. ambassador Madeleine Albright and U.N. secretary-general Boutros Boutros-Ghali.

By tradition, an American was always appointed head of UNICEF. But when James P. Grant, the popular American executive director, died in January 1994, Boutros-Ghali indicated that he might break that tradition. Partly he was responding to pressure from European governments that felt it was Europe's turn to head the agency. In addition, the Europeans pointed out that Europe now contributed twice as much to the UNICEF budget as did the United States.

But the controversy played out against the background of the antipathy between the U.S. ambassador and the U.N. secretary-general. Boutros-Ghali found Albright aggressive and undiplomatic. She found him stubborn, continually ignoring the wishes of the United States. Albright proposed Dr. William H. Foege, a former director of the Centers for Disease Control and Prevention for the job. But Boutros-Ghali announced it was time for a woman to take over UNICEF, and he indicated that he probably would appoint the European candidate, Elizabeth Rehn, a former defense minister of Finland. So Albright quickly withdrew Dr. Foege's candidacy and came up with a list of a few American women. Bellamy was the most prominent of these candidates, and Boutros-Ghali, finally giving in to the U.S. pressure, chose her.

In one of her final interviews as Peace Corps director, Bellamy told the *Los Angeles Times* that she did not feel it was a tremendous advantage for a director to come from the Volunteer ranks. "I think we've had some terrific directors of the Peace Corps who had no past connections with [it]," she said, "but, like all of us, have learned to love it and still do .... Nevertheless, I hoped that, at least as I visited Volunteers in the field, I could bring kind of a simpatico for both the highs and the lows, the joys and the sorrows, the difficult moments, the lonely moments and yet the wonderful exhilarating moments that Volunteers experience. I think it's important to be out there and reach out and touch those Volunteers .... I don't think you have to be a returned Volunteer to be the director, but I hope I brought it something a little different."

Bellamy set a kind of precedent. Although she was succeeded by Mark Gearan, the White House communications director, who had not served in the Peace Corps, three of the four directors after Gearan were former Volunteers. The presidents of the twenty-first century found it difficult to resist the pressure from the Peace Corps community and reach outside the organization for a director.

When Bellamy left the Peace Corps in 1994, there were 6,745 Volunteers serving throughout the world. There was nothing unusual about that. Since 1970, the Peace Corps had remained small, mainly in the

6,000s, reaching a high for that twenty-five-year period of 7,341 in 1973 and dropping to a low of 5,219 in 1987.

Sargent Shriver found this situation intolerable. "If you ask me what I think," he told an oral history interviewer for the Lyndon B. Johnson Library in 1990, "I can tell you that the Peace Corps ought to be at least three times bigger than it is today, maybe four or five times bigger. It's only a third as big as when I left there in 1965 . . . . I think that's a disgrace." When Shriver left, the Peace Corps Volunteers numbered 13,248; a year later, under Jack Vaughn, the total was 15,556, the highest ever.

Preaident Clinton appointed Gearan, his thirty-nine-year-old director of communications, to succeed Bellamy. There was some grumbling. Although Gearan was youthful enough to resemble some of the Volunteers, he had never been one. This lack disappointed many former Volunteers, but Donna Shalala came to his rescue. "We have worked closely together for the past two and a half years," she told the annual meeting of the National Peace Corps Association. "He is a decent, thoughtful, energetic and caring man . . . [and] will do a great job for all of us. Please support him."

Gearan possessed a keen sense of public relations and an intelligence open to new ideas. His creation of a Crisis Corps was a significant innovation—a program that rushed former Volunteers on temporary duty to areas in emergency need. After the devastation of the Indian Ocean tsunami on the day after Christmas in 2004, the Crisis Corps sent twenty-seven former Volunteers to Thailand and twenty-five to Sri Lanka to such assignments as constructing a water treatment plant and providing education and research for homeless people forced to live in camps. The Crisis Corps also sent 272 former Volunteers to the U.S. Gulf Coast after hurricanes Katrina and Rita in 2005. (The name "Crisis Corps" was changed by Peace Corps officials during the George W. Bush administration to the prosaic and bureaucratic "Peace Corps Response.")

Gearan, reviving an old proposal of Loret Ruppe, persuaded Clinton to support a spirited campaign in 1998 and 1999 to expand the Peace Corps. Clinton, in one of his weekly radio talks, called on Congress to augment the budget enough to increase the number of Volunteers to 10,000 by the year 2000.

There was a good deal of bipartisan support for the bill in Congress. At a hearing of the House Committee on International Relations, for example, Representative Benjamin Gilman of New York, the Republican chairman, said, "Rarely in our public service has there been a government program as effective, cost efficient, or as popular as our Peace Corps."

A half-dozen members of Congress who were former Volunteers testified in favor of the bill. They included Senator Christopher Dodd, who served in the Dominican Republic; Representative Sam Farr of California, a Democrat who served in Colombia; Representative Tony P. Hall of Ohio, a Democrat who served in Thailand; Representative Thomas E. Petri of Wisconsin, a Republican who served in Somalia; Representative Christopher Shays of Connecticut, a Republican who served in Fiji; and Representative James T. Walsh of New York, a Republican who served in Nepal.

Shays began his testimony with a greeting in Fijian, and Walsh did the same with a greeting in Nepalese. "I am a city kid from Syracuse, New York," Walsh, mocking himself a little, told the committee, "and I drew upon my vast agricultural background of cutting the lawn and trimming the hedges to going to Nepal and teaching people how to grow rice, but it was a marvelous experience."

Another prominent Republican, Senator Paul Coverdell of Georgia, the former Peace Corps director, also testified in favor of the bill. After the testimony, a member of the Peace Corps staff told the *Los Angeles Times*, "We used to criticize Coverdell when he was director for spending all that time in Georgia looking for votes. Now we're glad he was elected."

Further support came from Secretary Shalala. Shalala, born in Cleveland to Lebanese immigrant parents, charmed the committee with the story of her family's reluctance to let her join the Peace Corps. "My father offered me a car as a bribe to keep me from joining the Peace Corps," she said. "However, my Lebanese grandmother settled the situation. She announced to the family that . . . I would be fine. As I left for the Peace Corps, she gave me a letter. It was in classical Arabic addressed to the head man of the village I was going to visit. I presented the letter to the mullah of the village and found out later that my grandmother had written, 'This is to introduce the daughter of a great sheikh in Cleveland, Ohio. Please put her under your protection.'"

All these good feelings led Congress to pass legislation in 1999 that authorized the 50 percent increase, with the goal of increasing the number of Volunteers past 10,000. The target, however, was delayed to 2003. The legislation was nevertheless looked at as a Peace Corps victory. Clinton's signing of the law on May 24, 1999, is still listed as a significant moment in Peace Corps history on the agency's Web site.

The Web site, however, fails to mention that Congress never appropriated the funds that were authorized, and that the total number of Volunteers never even reached 8,000. The Peace Corps was a victim of what Gearan calls the annual "political appropriations saga." The appropriations committees of the House and Senate, usually more conservative than Congress as a whole, often vote to provide fewer funds for an agency than authorized.

Mark Schneider, a former Volunteer who succeeded Gearan as director during the Clinton administration, says that it is always difficult for the Peace Corps to persuade Congress to increase its appropriation because the Peace Corps lacks a "constituency." In other words, there is no large mass of voters ready to pressure Congress on its behalf. Clearly, the 200,000 or so former Volunteers, who come from fifty different states, cannot pressure enough on their own. And the Peace Corps no longer generates the dazzling appeal it had for most Americans during the Kennedy years.

In any case, there are members of the Peace Corps community who are wary of campaigns to increase the size of the Peace Corps. Their fear is that the drive to fulfill the campaign goals—moving higher than 10,000 Volunteers or, more recently, doubling the Peace Corps by its fiftieth anniversary—would renew the old numbers game that weakened the Peace Corps in the early years. Many ailments of the Peace Corps in the Shriver and Vaughn years—huge clusters of Volunteers in the capitals, poor evaluation of jobs by harried and hurried staff, too many Volunteers with little to do—could be attributed to unthinking drives to expand the numbers of Volunteers.

Carol Bellamy is among those who dislike expansion campaigns. In a recent phone interview, she explained that she did not oppose expansion, but she felt that it should be guided by the needs of the countries overseas, not by the demands of a campaign in the United States.

"There should be more attention to what the countries want," she noted. "It doesn't make sense to have Volunteers crawling all over themselves. I don't think you should put more Volunteers out there just to put Volunteers out there . . . . To me, the critical component is that the country must sign on."

The sloganeers, of course, insist that they too oppose wild, chaotic growth and that they would increase the size of the Peace Corps in the orderly manner set down by Bellamy. But the experience of the Peace Corps in both the early years and in the later rush into Eastern Europe indicates that sloppiness and confusion usually seep in whenever Peace Corps planners have numbers on their minds.

CHAPTER SEVENTEEN

The Quiet Bush Years

Christiane Amanpour, chief foreign correspondent of CNN, took part, in March 2008, in a George Washington University panel discussion on America's role in the world. While discussing how the United States' standing had fallen, Amanpour mentioned some of the factors that had contributed to American popularity in earlier days. "There *was* a Peace Corps," she said as an example.

After the session, Jon Keeton, a former Volunteer in Thailand and a former country director in South Korea, rushed to the lectern and told Amanpour, "There still *is* a Peace Corps." Amanpour blushed but pointed out that there must be something wrong if someone like herself did not realize the Peace Corps still existed.

Perhaps Amanpour's ignorance was understandable. The early years of the twenty-first century were quiet ones for the Peace Corps. News about the agency rarely made headlines, and almost never onto a front page.

But there were flurries of controversy. President George W. Bush provoked a bit of a fuss at the beginning when he nominated a disgraced California politician as the new director of the Peace Corps. This was taken by the Peace Corps community as a gross insult.

The nominee, Gaddi Vasquez, was once regarded as a rising star in the Republican party. As a member of the Board of Supervisors of Orange County, he was the highest-ranking elected Republican Hispanic in California. His story was appealing. As a young boy, he and the family had moved continually in a trailer, for his father was a migrant farm worker. Then they had settled in Orange County when his father obtained work in a furniture factory and later became pastor of the Apostolic Church there. Vasquez, the first college graduate in his family, had started his career as a policeman before entering politics. In 1988, he excited the Republican National Convention with a rousing speech that mocked Democratic presidential candidate Michael Dukakis and his facility with the Spanish language. "The Democratic candidate may speak Spanish," Vasquez told cheering Republicans. "But he doesn't speak our language."

But in 1994, a disastrous scandal astounded Orange County and clouded Vasquez's future. Robert Citron, the county treasurer, revealed that he had invested the county's funds in risky enterprises that had now plunged in value, for a loss of more than $1.5 billion. Orange County, one of the richest counties in the United States, declared itself bankrupt. The treasurer pleaded guilty to six felony counts, paid a fine of $100,00, and was sentenced to almost a year of house arrest.

The supervisors were not charged with criminal wrongdoing, but they were accused of negligence for failing to monitor the treasurer's investments and failing to keep the public informed about the nature of the investments. Angry voters began filing papers demanding the ouster of the supervisors in recall elections. Three weeks after he was served with recall papers in 1995, Vasquez, by then chairman of the board, announced his resignation. The *Los Angeles Times* wrote that "Vasquez's once-promising career has come to an abrupt end, at least temporarily."

Vasquez slipped into the private sector easily, however, and soon was heading the public affairs department of Southern California Edison, the electric utility company. He still possessed a campaign war chest that he had filled when he was a supervisor, and, during the 2000 presidential election, he transferred $106,216 of these funds to the Republican party. In a biting column, Judy Mann of the *Washington Post*, who described Vasquez as "a discredited California party hack," said his gift to Bush's campaign "bought him a ticket to Washington."

Many returned Volunteers and former staff mounted a campaign to persuade the Senate to reject the nomination. Joan Borsten, a Californian who had served in Panama, echoed many when she said the nomination "demonstrates that the president does not understand what the Peace Corps is about." Roni Love, a former Volunteer in Malaysia, called the nomination "very insulting to those of us who have served this country, as it should be to all Americans." Jack Vaughn, the former director of the Peace Corps and still a registered Republican, told his hometown newspaper, the *Tucson Citizen*, "It's clearly a political payoff, and it would be a shame to see him approved." Before the Senate Foreign Relations Committee, Vaughn testified that Vasquez "does not possess the qualifications, leadership tools, or the demonstrated financial management skills to head a large federal agency."

Newspaper editorials scorned the nomination, too. The *New York Times* said, "It is distressing that Mr. Bush views the Peace Corps directorship as a place to park generous donors with mediocre resumes." The *Los Angeles Times* said that the Bush administration "has demeaned the high purpose of an agency that requires vision, diplomatic skill and even bravery at the helm."

But the campaign against Vasquez fizzled, largely because he had the support of many Hispanic organizations and of the two senators from California, Barbara Boxer and Dianne Feinstein, both Democrats. The Foreign Relations Committee approved the nomination by a vote of 13 to 4. Even Senator Christopher Dodd of Connecticut, a Democrat and the only former Volunteer in the Senate, voted for Vasquez. Dodd called the nomination troublesome but said he wanted to give Vasquez a chance. There was no roll call vote in the Senate. Vasquez was one of forty presidential nominations passed without objection on January 25, 2002.

President Bush tried to open the Vasquez era with some fanfare. In his 2002 State of the Union address, he announced plans to double the size of the Peace Corps to 15,000. At the Vasquez swearing-in ceremony a month later, Bush talked about his hopes for a program of Volunteers working in the reconstruction of war-ravaged Afghanistan. Neither goal was met. The size of the Peace Corps, much as before, never even reached 8,000 during the Bush administration. And the war in Afghanistan never subsided enough to allow Volunteers to work there.

Vasquez underwent open-heart surgery in June 2001, shortly before his nomination. Yet he proved an energetic director. When a group of Orange County officials visited him in his office during his first months on the job, he told them, "I traveled in two and a half weeks from the United States to Kabul, Afghanistan, to Islamabad, Pakistan, to Beijing, China, to Chengdu, China, and then Lima, Peru, to sign a bilateral agreement to reenter Peru. I was on such a high I never got tired."

Despite his enthusiasm, Vasquez issued a series of confusing announcements in 2003 that smacked of the old Jimmy Durante routine,

"Did you ever have the feeling that you wanted to go and still have the feeling that you wanted to stay?" In late October, he suddenly announced that he was resigning, effective November 14. He would be leaving after only twenty-one months on the job. He told the staff and Volunteers that his resignation came with "mixed emotions," and he thanked President Bush "for the high honor and confidence he had in nominating me to serve." The White House praised his "tremendous leadership." Vasquez told reporters that he needed to take care of his aging parents back in Orange County.

But Vasquez was still working in his office on November 15. He said that he had postponed his departure to take care of some important matters, like the signing of an agreement with Mexico to send Volunteers there. The Peace Corps announced it was now uncertain when he would leave.

A little over a month later, Vasquez had a new announcement. He explained that he had resigned earlier because "I was facing difficult challenges that prolonged medical issues can impose on a family." He did not say that he and his family had successfully dealt with these issues. But he said, "In light of my continued desire to serve, and with the concurrence and support of my family, I intend to remain in my present role as director of the Peace Corps through the end of the current term."

There was immediate speculation that this odd vacillation had nothing to do with aging parents. Patrick McGreevy of the *Los Angeles Times* suggested that Vasquez, much like Coverdell more than ten years earlier, had kept his eye on home state politics. Vasquez had announced his resignation just after the election of Republican Arnold Schwarzenegger as governor of California in a special recall election to unseat Democrat Gray Davis. Vasquez, as a prominent Republican Hispanic, according to this theory, anticipated a significant appointment in the new administration. "One wonders," McGreevy wrote, "whether perhaps Vasquez concluded that the job picture in California wasn't as rosy as he thought it was."

While Vasquez was making up his mind about whether he wanted to go or wanted to stay, the *Dayton Daily News* in Ohio published its long series of articles about murders, accidental deaths, rapes, assaults, and other dangers in the Peace Corps, as described in Chapter 12. Vasquez stayed on the job as director for almost five years, resigning in September 2006 to accept a rather plush appointment as ambassador to the U.N.

Food and Agriculture Organization in Rome. Ronald Tschetter, an investment broker who, along with his wife, had served in India as Volunteers in the 1960s, was named director by President George W. Bush and served for the rest of the administration.

In 2007, while Tschetter was director, the *Washington Post* revealed that Vasquez had not been able to overcome his Republican loyalties while he ran the Peace Corps. He had allowed the White House to send a deputy of political adviser Karl Rove to brief two dozen staffers at the Peace Corps about the party's prospects after the 2002 congressional elections. The session, though not compulsory and open only to political appointees, appeared to be a violation of the Hatch Act, which prohibited government employees engaging in politics. Vasquez was not alone in allowing such electioneering. The White House held similar briefings at the State Department, AID, and another dozen agencies.

Tschetter had to face withering questions about this from Senator Dodd and other members of the Senate Foreign Relations Committee. Dodd, insisting that "the good reputation the Peace Corps has built over forty years has been soiled," warned he would "have heads" if the incident was repeated. Senator Bob Corker, a Republican from Tennessee, asked Tschetter to make sure the "Peace Corps is still the gold standard in nonpartisanship."

Much like the Volunteers of the late 1960s and early 1970s, the Volunteers of the George W. Bush era lived through a war that turned more and more unpopular among the American public. But the Peace Corps did not have to worry as much about embarrassing protests as it had worried, to the point of distraction, during the war in Vietnam.

There were several reasons for the less frequent outbursts of Volunteer militancy against the war in Iraq. Perhaps most important, the draft was gone. In the early years of the Peace Corps, most of the Volunteers were young men whose service overseas deferred them from the draft but did not exempt them. They faced the grim possibility of completing their Peace Corps duty only to be rushed back overseas to face possible death in Vietnam. The draft pressed them like a nightmare and made them cry out against a war they feared and hated. That immediacy did not exist in the 2000s.

There also was a large difference in the mood of generations. The 1960s had spawned a militancy that struck out at more than the war in Vietnam. Young Americans joined the campaigns to register blacks in the

South, and young students seized administrative buildings on campuses with demands that authorities make curriculums relevant. This kind of militancy was alien to Peace Corps Volunteers during the war in Iraq.

The diminished numbers of the Peace Corps also made antiwar demonstrations harder to organize. There were no longer large clusters of Volunteers in the major cities. Assembling a substantial number of Volunteers in front of U.S. embassies was a difficult task in the twenty-first century, especially in large countries with rutted dirt roads.

Would-be protesters in the twenty-first century also had to face what amounted to a Peace Corps zero-tolerance policy, at least in principle. As discussed in Chapter 8, the Peace Corps, after losing the Bruce Murray case in federal court, allowed criticism of U.S. policy in Vietnam so long as the Volunteer, while exercising a U.S. citizen's right to free speech, refrained from harming the Peace Corps or interfering in the local politics of the host country. That policy remained in the Peace Corps manual, but the Peace Corps, after the U.S. invasion of Iraq, chose to interpret protest against the U.S. action as interference in local politics.

In the Dominican Republic, for example, Volunteers Aaron Drendel and Aaron Kauffman, even before the Iraq invasion began, planned a protest demonstration by Americans in the capital of Santo Domingo. The issue was still being debated at the United Nations, but there was little doubt that President George W. Bush intended to invade. Drendel and Kauffman expected sixty Volunteers to join their protest. They did not plan to identify themselves as Peace Corps Volunteers. "We didn't want to do anything that would bring the Peace Corps in," says Kauffman. But they wanted to show Dominicans that some Americans opposed the impending invasion.

At first, local Peace Corps staffers said they had no objection so long as the demonstration was not identified as a Peace Corps protest and the Volunteers broke no Dominican laws in staging it. But the mood changed when the invasion of Iraq actually took place and word about the planned demonstration reached Peace Corps headquarters in Washington.

Under pressure from Washington, the local Peace Corps staff changed its stance and warned all Volunteers in the Dominican Republic that they could be thrown out of the Peace Corps if they took part in the demonstration. The Peace Corps insisted that the invasion of Iraq had become a local political issue because the president of the Dominican Republic "has taken a formal stand in supporting the U.S. against Iraq."

In an e-mail to the Volunteers that was also posted on the bulletin board at Peace Corps headquarters in Santo Domingo, the local staff told the Volunteers that "one of the compelling reasons the Peace Corps has been so well accepted in this country and in more than 136 countries throughout the world over the past 42 years has been that it scrupulously avoids any political involvement." The staff said the effectiveness of the Peace Corps has become impaired whenever "we have become publicly involved in political matters of local concern." "Why should a small group of Volunteers," the staff went on, "have the right to compromise the non-political nature and autonomy of our agency as a whole?"

Quoting from the Peace Corps manual, the staff therefore warned anyone planning to take part in the demonstration that a Volunteer's words or actions involving local political controversies "may be grounds for administrative separation or other disciplinary action." Faced with this threat, most Volunteers stayed away. Drendel, who was married and planned on working for the U.S. government after his Peace Corps experience, pulled out, fearful of jeopardizing his future career and livelihood.

Kauffman was already in Santo Domingo when he read the Peace Corps admonition. He had only two weeks before the end of his Peace Corps tour, but he knew that dismissal would stain his record. Nevertheless, he intended to defy the Peace Corps. He headed back to his village by bus, gathered up his belongings, made his farewells to Dominican friends and colleagues, and returned to the capital. He was sure he would soon be dismissed.

Only three people showed up at the Parque Colon in downtown Santo Domingo to demonstrate: Kauffman, a second Volunteer who had already left the Peace Corps for another reason, and a French Canadian working in a different foreign assistance project. Drendel was there as well, but only to photograph the demonstrators as a friendly witness. A Dominican journalist arrived, and Kauffman handed him a short statement explaining their opposition to the war. The statement did not mention the Peace Corps.

The trio of protesters and their photographer walked from the Parque Colon in downtown Santo Domingo about a mile and half to the U.S. embassy. Kauffman carried a pair of signs in Spanish, one quoting Martin Luther King, Jr.: "Peace is not just the absence of war but the presence of justice," the other quoting Mahatma Gandhi: "An eye for an eye, and the whole world goes blind." They did not shout slogans. They stopped at a corner facing the embassy and held their protest signs aloft. They stood there for five minutes and walked away. In all, their protest march and demonstration had lasted about an hour.

The Peace Corps, despite its threats, decided not to discipline Kauffman. It is not clear why, but Kauffman's father, a retired lawyer, had discussed his son's legal rights with the Peace Corps's general counsel office in Washington. Perhaps the Peace Corps did not want to risk a lawsuit like the one it lost during the Vietnam War. In any case, the Peace Corps's tough policy had accomplished its main goal. The threats had shut down an antiwar demonstration by sixty Volunteers that would have embarrassed the Peace Corps.

The Peace Corps was upset in 2008 by a barrage of criticism from one of its own, the former director of the program in Cameroon who had served in Liberia as a Volunteer. The critic, Robert L. Strauss, managed to vent his complaints in two prestigious publications, the *New York Times* and *Foreign Policy* magazine. This was far more publicity than the Peace Corps attracted for any of its achievements in the new century.

Strauss's *Times* article, an op-ed piece, repeated the hoary notion that the Peace Corps needed older and more skilled Volunteers. Too often, Strauss said, "young volunteers lack the maturity and professional experience to be effective development workers in the 21st century." Strauss disparaged the work of present Volunteers. In his view, "an objective assessment of its impact would reveal that while volunteers generate good will for the United States, they do little or nothing to actually aid development in poor countries."

The *Foreign Policy* article, published a few months later, offered a grab bag of complaints. Strauss insisted that most foreigners do not realize the Volunteers are American; that both Volunteers and staff are often mediocre, with Volunteers sometimes seeking "a chance to escape a humdrum life" and staff sometimes made up of "minor political underlings who get parked at the Peace Corps"; that the Peace Corps keeps sending Volunteers back to the same countries year after year, whether or not they are still needed; that the Peace Corps is not really a development organization; that Volunteers are sometimes resented where they live because "the Peace Corps has its share of deadbeats, philanderers, parasites, gamblers, and alcoholics."

Strauss concluded, "The Peace Corps remains a Peter Pan organization, afraid to grow up, yet also afraid to question the thinking of its founding fathers." To change all this, Strauss called on the Peace Corps to "avoid goodwill-generating window dressing and concentrate its resources in a limited number of countries that are truly interested in the development of their people."

Strauss's proposals would tear the heart out of the Peace Corps and reconstitute it as an elite agency of older, highly skilled Volunteers working under harsh conditions in a few countries. In many ways, his views were old-hat and impractical, and his assessment of the young Volunteers unfairly dismissive of their great energy and enthusiasm, but the prestige of the two publications that harbored him demanded that the Peace Corps engage his arguments.

Tschetter, the director, chose not to do so. In his letter to *Foreign Policy,* he called Strauss's article "an insult to every volunteer who has ever served in the Peace Corps . . . . I can tell you each of his arguments is false, and with all certainty, our agency is thriving." But, as evidence, Tschetter could come up only with a testimonial from someone unlikely to influence the readers of the two publications. President George W. Bush, Tschetter boasted, had recently said the Peace Corps "really is the best foreign policy America could possibly have."

Many current and former Volunteers filled the breach left by Tschetter's perfunctory defense. They rushed letters to both the *Times* and *Foreign Policy,* arguing against Strauss's points and defending the Peace Corps. While some acknowledged staff deficiencies in planning, organizing, and managing programs, many more had no use for the kind of Peace Corps advocated by Strauss.

Emily Armitage, a Volunteer in Bulgaria, saw little value in a Peace Corps of older and more skilled Volunteers. "Older Volunteers often have difficulty learning the language, which can limit their contacts within the community," she wrote. She also pointed out that older Volunteers find it hard "to spend two years of their lives in difficult, sometimes primitive conditions." "While older Volunteers have more life experiences," she went on, "many younger Volunteers possess knowledge of technology, web design, e-mail, and the Internet—integral skills for the developing world."

Others like Blair Reeves, who was a Volunteer in Cameroon while Strauss was director, challenged the notion that the Peace Corps was ineffective in development. Reeves wrote that "no matter what Robert thinks, genuine, sustainable, long-term development is accomplished by individual Volunteers on a local basis—just ask the village of Okong, where I helped arrange to fund and build two sources of potable water where there were none before."

Many letter writers believed Strauss misunderstood the Peace Corps by failing to rank its cultural goals on the same level as its goal of development. As Senator Dodd put it in a letter to the *New York Times,* "Every American of goodwill we send abroad is another chance to make America known to a world that often fears and suspects us. And every American who returns from that service is a gift: a citizen who strengthens us with firsthand knowledge of the world."

CHAPTER EIGHTEEN

Diplomatic Troubles

When word reached Tanzania in the summer of 2005 that Michael Retzer would arrive soon as the new ambassador, the American professionals on the scene could not hide their apprehension. For almost two years, the U.S. embassy had lacked an ambassador; it was run instead by a senior foreign service officer. The Americans did not know much about Retzer. But his resume made him look like the ultra-stereotype of a political appointee.

President George W. Bush did not appoint Retzer because of his familiarity with Tanzania or Africa, or even with foreign affairs. Retzer was a former national treasurer of the Republican party, and he had served as chairman of the Mississippi Republican Party several times. He owned McDonald's fast-food restaurants in more than twenty towns in Mississippi and was a generous contributor to the Republican Party. He had, for example, personally contributed $60,500 to the party and its candidates and raised more than $200,000 for President Bush's reelection campaign in 2004.

Among the apprehensive Americans was Christine A. Djondo, the Peace Corps country director, who had just arrived in Tanzania herself. The forty-four-year-old Djondo was one of the most experienced staffers in the Peace Corps. A Volunteer in Cameroon and later a supervisor of scholar exchange programs for the Institute of International Education, she had served as Peace Corps country director in Lesotho and Gabon before her assignment in Tanzania. The Peace Corps Act normally limits employment of staff to five years, but the Peace Corps can extend that in exceptional cases. Djondo, married to a Togolese and the mother of two children, was one of those whose tour had been extended.

Although apprehensive, Djondo was less so than the diplomats in the embassy. The Peace Corps, after all, is an independent agency of the federal government. Ambassadors, even the political appointees, usually let the Peace Corps operate without any interference at all.

For the first year, the ambassador, according to Djondo, busied himself with ceremonial duties and with the magnificence of Tanzania's wildlife. But, during his second year, the State Department asked all its posts to reorganize their operations to make them more efficient and less costly. The request energized the ambassador. He was, after all, a very successful entrepreneur. He regarded efficiency and cost cutting as the hallmarks of a skilled manager.

Ambassador Retzer swiftly moved the headquarters of three U.S. agencies—AID, the Centers for Disease Control (CDC), and the President's Emergency Plan for AIDS Relief—into the embassy compound. Not only would this cut down on rental costs, but the agencies could share embassy services, allowing them and the embassy to dismiss some of their support staff.

The ambassador, for example, decided to create a motor pool for the embassy and U.S. agencies so the total number of drivers could be reduced. Djondo felt pressure for the Peace Corps to join, but she resisted. She needed her own special drivers, who knew where all the 130 Volunteers lived and worked, who could leave the capital of Dar es Salaam on a moment's notice, and who could repair a car if it broke down upcountry.

The ambassador did not try to force the Peace Corps into the new embassy motor pool, but its creation left several drivers without jobs, and the ambassador decided to transfer them to the Peace Corps. The ambassador did not think much of Djondo's management of her own drivers, for she had to fire two recently for stealing several hundred dollars worth of fuel. The Peace Corps, which normally employed six drivers, was now down to three (one driver had resigned for a better job elsewhere). The Peace Corps inspector-general, after an investigation, had found no grounds to dismiss these three, but the ambassador regarded them as tainted by the fuel theft and wanted them fired as well to make way for his excess drivers.

Djondo refused to accept the ambassador's drivers. The embassy drivers were used to driving in Dar es Salaam, not upcountry, Djondo says, and lacked training as mechanics. Djondo looked on the ambassador's whole exercise as a backhand way of pushing the Peace Corps into the embassy motor pool. Djondo informed the Peace Corps in Washington of her refusal, and officials there supported her stand.

A dangerous impasse developed. So long as Djondo refused to hire the laid-off embassy drivers, the embassy refused to grant the required security clearance to any driver-mechanic she tried to hire. For a half-year, the Peace Corps had only three drivers for all its tasks, including the delivery of supplies and the escort of staff to Volunteers throughout the vast country.

Finally, David Liner, the chief of staff of the Peace Corps in Washington, negotiated a compromise with the ambassador. The Peace Corps, while not firing any of its own drivers, hired two of the laid-off embassy drivers. The embassy then granted a security clearance to an outside driver-mechanic hired by Djondo. That brought the Peace Corps contingent of drivers back to six.

But the compromise did not assuage the ambassador's anger at Djondo. He soon came up with another demand. The Peace Corps staff included a doctor and a nurse to care for Volunteers. Ambassador Retzer did not like this arrangement. He insisted, according to the Peace Corps, that Volunteers see the U.S. embassy doctor rather than the Peace Corps nurse whenever the Peace Corps doctor was unavailable.

Ambassador Retzer denies this. He says that he simply suggested that the embassy and Peace Corps doctors fill in for each other when one goes on leave. The Peace Corps, however, maintains he proposed far more than that. Some of the correspondence between the ambassador and the Peace Corps does make it clear that the ambassador did not like the idea of the Volunteers seeking treatment from the Peace Corps nurse.

Djondo says that the ambassador wanted her to fire the nurse. He denies this, but the nurse obviously would have had little to do if the Volunteers could see only a doctor. Djondo felt that she could not count on the embassy doctor in case of an upcountry emergency. This doctor, who cared mainly for all official Americans and their families in Dar es Salaam, might not be available to rush out of the capital. Djondo regarded this as a threat to her Volunteers.

Djondo said that Purnell Delly, a foreign service officer who was the deputy chief of mission, warned her that she would be thrown out of Tanzania if she continued to cross the ambassador. But Djondo, with the support of the Peace Corps in Washington, refused to give in.

Peace Corps director Ronald Tschetter wrote Ambassador Retzer that a Memorandum of Understanding between the State Department and the Peace Corps did not allow the kind of "coordinating medical operations" he had in mind.

The ambassador, according to the Peace Corps, dismissed this as a sample of "Washington turf battles." He wrote Tschetter that "there is no substitute for seeing a physician if one is available," and he warned, "I hold Peace Corps directly responsible should your policy result in lasting injury or death to a Volunteer."

Retzer was clearly infuriated. In April 2007, he called in Djondo and offered her a choice. She could resign quietly or be expelled publicly. Ambassadors have the power to approve or reject all U.S. officials serving in a country (except for soldiers serving under a military commander).

Djondo told the ambassador that she would not resign and that only the Peace Corps director had the right to hire and fire her. Ambassador Retzer then withdrew his approval for her to remain as a U.S. official in Tanzania, agreeing, however, to delay the order until June so her children could complete their schooling for that academic year. As Retzer acknowledged a couple of years later, his status as a political appointee allowed him to take so dramatic a step. "Career ambassadors, God bless their hearts, they don't ordinarily make waves," he said.

Retzer's ouster of Djondo provoked a blistering cable from Tschetter to the ambassador. Tschetter warned that he would have to reduce the number of incoming Volunteers unless the ambassador rescinded his order. "Unfortunately, such a reduction in numbers will have a disturbingly negative impact on Tanzanian government officials, as well as the Tanzanian people," he wrote. Tschetter added that Djondo's departure "will also have a powerful and negative influence on the morale of Peace Corps staff members and Volunteers in Tanzania."

The Peace Corps director was unstinting in his praise of Djondo. "The strength and vitality of the Peace Corps program in Tanzania," he wrote, "is directly attributable to the outstanding leadership of Ms. Djondo." He described "a pronounced increase in Volunteer satisfaction" with their work and staff support under her leadership.

Tschetter called on the ambassador to allow Djondo to remain on the job, but the Peace Corps director added, in biting tones, "I question your commitment to supporting the Peace Corps program in Tanzania, and without full support, the Peace Corps program is potentially at risk." But the ambassador would not give in.

As soon as news of the ouster spread, support for Djondo intensified. In a letter to Volunteers and staff in Tanzania, Tschetter praised "her vigorous defense of the integrity and independence of the Peace Corps program in Tanzania." Peace Corps press chief Amanda Host issued a news release that made it clear the Peace Corps "strongly disagree[d]" with Retzer and had "full confidence" in Djondo. Volunteers in both Gabon and Tanzania signed petitions of protest and wrote many letters of support.

In the midst of this brouhaha, the White House announced that Ambassador Retzer had resigned and would be replaced by former Representative Mark Green of Wisconsin. This led to speculation that Retzer had resigned under pressure or had grown weary over the controversy. But Retzer insists that he had long ago advised the State Department that he intended to leave after two years on the job.

Green, a Republican who had recently lost the election for governor of Wisconsin, knew Africa well. He was the son of a South African doctor and had taught in Kenya for two years. But confirmation in the Senate was held up by Senator Christopher Dodd of Connecticut. Dodd, the only former Volunteer in the Senate, said he would put a hold on Green's nomination unless the Bush administration either rescinded the ouster of Djondo or sent her a letter of apology.

Faced with this obstacle, Assistant Secretary of State Jeffrey T. Bergner wrote a carefully worded letter to Djondo that amounted to an expression of regret rather than an apology. Bergner praised her as "a highly capable Peace Corps employee" but noted that it had become impossible for her and Ambassador Retzer "to continue working productively together" because of their disagreements. "The Department regrets that this matter unfolded in the way it did," Bergner said. Despite the weakness of the letter, Senator Dodd accepted it as an apology, and Green was confirmed as ambassador.

The controversy did not hurt Djondo's career in the Peace Corps. After six months on the staff in Washington, she was assigned overseas once more, taking over the program in Mozambique in 2008 as country director.

The flare-up in Tanzania was surely the most extreme example, but some tension between embassies and the Peace Corps existed for half a century. The tension was built into the relationship, for the Peace Corps is an independent agency of the U.S. government, yet it is, at least on paper, still subject to some kind of supervision by the ambassador on the scene, who is the representative of the American president.

Relations between the embassies and the Peace Corps were frigid from the beginning. President Kennedy, after all, had mocked the failures of U.S. diplomats in his campaign speech proposing a Peace Corps. Diplomats could hardly feel welcoming to callow youngsters who had arrived to do a better job at befriending locals than themselves. This feeling was aggravated by all the publicity the new Peace Corps generated. Diplomats worked in obscurity, while youngsters selected for Peace Corps training made the front pages of their hometown newspapers.

The Volunteers reciprocated these ill feelings. They believed that they would immerse themselves in a culture in ways never dreamed of by U.S. diplomats. The Volunteers saw themselves as the true ambassadors for the United States even while they asserted their independence. They took pains to try to explain to the people around them that they had nothing to do with the U.S. embassy.

The subject was discussed in the early days at a meeting in the State Department between Sargent Shriver and G. Mennen Williams, the former governor of Michigan appointed by Kennedy as the first assistant secretary of state for African affairs. An account of the meeting survives in the files of the National Archives.

"There is one minor point of irritation, however, that I would like to mention," said Williams. "Our FSOs [foreign service officers] tell us that the Volunteers think they are poison and a bunch of cookie pushers. I want more cordial relations . . . . Do you think your Volunteers should never go near the embassy?"

Shriver was diplomatic in what amounted to a putdown. "We don't say there is anything wrong with the official American community," he said, "but we do say to our Volunteers that the more they work with Americans and the more they enter into American life, the more difficult and less effective their job will be."

Sometimes the tension was ludicrous. In 1965, I called on U.S. ambassador Leland Barrows at his embassy in Yaoundé, the capital of Cameroon, to discuss the work of the Peace Corps. In the midst of our conversation, he burst into a monologue. He had one searing issue on his mind.

"I've heard," the ambassador said, "that a Volunteer has accused some member on the embassy staff of buying forty-four jars of Skippy peanut butter in Victoria [the port of West Cameroon, the English-speaking region where most Volunteers worked]. Now there isn't any Skippy peanut butter for the Volunteers. I suppose Shriver will hear about this soon at one of those big board meetings in Washington. And everyone will be talking about how we bought up the Skippy peanut butter.

"First of all, I want to tell you that it simply is not true. I've checked and no member of my staff bought that peanut butter. But even if he did—do you realize there are fifty-five children on this embassy post? They certainly have a right to Skippy peanut butter ahead of your Volunteers.

"If your Volunteers want peanut butter so badly, why don't they go out and make it? They're Peace Corps Volunteers. I can give them a recipe."

Ambassador Barrows astounded me with the vehemence of his concern for a matter so trivial—an incident, in fact, that not a single Volunteer had mentioned during my four weeks of interviewing in Cameroon. The ambassador's peanut butter outburst, etched with so much sarcasm, came out of a long-simmering resentment with the Peace Corps.

In his fifth year in Cameroon, Ambassador Barrows, a career foreign service officer, was near retirement after many years with both AID and the State Department. In his view, the Peace Corps had a penchant for showy ways that often tried to upstage the embassy.

The Peace Corps, for example, encouraged the staff to live in comfortable but far from ostentatious homes. Shriver wanted Volunteers, who often lived in spare quarters, to feel at ease when they dropped by the home of their country director. While he did not expect staff and their families to be housed in mud huts, he wanted them to live at least a notch or two below the level of the U.S. embassy staff.

It rankled Ambassador Barrows that Larry Williams, the first Peace Corps director, and his wife lived in a modest house close to the center of town rather than a large home farther out. When Williams's tour was over, Shriver proposed Bill Dretzin, a New York businessman, as the replacement. The ambassador cabled his concurrence but warned that the Dretzins, with their three children, would need a larger house. Despite this, the Dretzins upset the ambassador by moving into the Williams house.

Ambassador Barrows was still complaining about Peace Corps staff housing more than five years later when he sat for an interview for the oral history program of the John F. Kennedy Library. "Oh, you'd get this ostentatious virtue, this vicarious austerity and that sort of thing among them," he said, discussing the Peace Corps staff. "You'd have one director who'd insist that he had to have a certain kind of house . . . . Then the next man would find the house a little too fancy, and he wanted to move somewhere else. They were all trying to fit the image."

"I always felt," he went on, "that the Peace Corps, particularly under Shriver, was operated more with the American public in mind than with the needs of the countries that we were helping . . . . I suppose that the general atmosphere that the Peace Corps brought gave me as much feeling of skepticism about the [Kennedy] administration as any other one thing I can think of because it was largely governed by image-making."

Over the years, this kind of resentment eased as the Peace Corps slipped out of the public spotlight, U.S. foreign service officers became more familiar with Peace Corps work, and former Volunteers began entering the ranks of the foreign service. By October 2009, the official Peace Corps Web site listed two assistant secretaries of state and fifteen ambassadors or former ambassadors as ex–Peace Corps Volunteers. Most ambassadors and Peace Corps country directors could work out a relationship of mutual respect that allowed the Peace Corps a great deal of independence.

But there were ambassadors who still chafed over Peace Corps independence. In rare cases, as in the case of Ambassador Retzer, this brought on bitter confrontation. Yet as Deputy Director Jody Olsen and other Peace Corps officials acknowledged, there was an ambiguity over the relationship. Ambassador Retzer did not fashion his authority out of thin air. Like all other ambassadors, he received instructions from the secretary of state about the Peace Corps and instructions from the president about the ambassador's authority, and the two messages differed in tone and substance.

The instructions during Retzer's tenure came in a cable from Secretary of State Condoleezza Rice to all ambassadors that followed the traditional line of the State Department about dealing with the Peace Corps. Rice, in fact, quoted the guiding principle of Dean Rusk, the secretary of state when the Peace Corps was formed in 1961: "The Peace Corps is not an instrument of foreign policy because to make it so would rob it of its contribution to foreign policy."

Rice therefore asked ambassadors "to provide the Peace Corps with as much autonomy and flexibility in its day-to-day operations as possible, so long as this does not conflict with U.S. objectives and policies." Since the Peace Corps, as a grassroots, people-to-people organization, needed to be accessible to the people of the country, Rice told ambassadors to "give favorable consideration to requests from the Peace Corps to maintain its offices at locations separate from the [U.S.] Mission and thus preserve this autonomy."

As far as staffing was concerned, Rice said the selection of a country director was "a decision reserved to the [Peace Corps] director exclusively." The Peace Corps, however, did welcome the ambassador's assessment of the performance of the country director and the rest of the staff, she said.

While the instructions from Secretary Rice contained some loopholes, the cable should have persuaded Ambassador Retzer to leave the Peace Corps motor pool, medical staff, and country director alone. But Retzer, like all other ambassadors, also had a letter of instructions signed by President George W. Bush.

This letter from Bush, following the traditional line of presidential letters to ambassadors, stated clearly, "As Chief of Mission, you have full responsibility for the direction, coordination, and supervision of all United States Government executive branch employees" in Tanzania. No exception was made for the Peace Corps.

"I ask that you review programs, personnel, and funding levels regularly," Bush went on, "and ensure that all agencies attached to your Mission do likewise . . . . In your reviews, should you feel staffing to be either excessive or inadequate to the performance of priority Mission goals and objectives, I urge you to initiate staffing changes in accordance with established procedures."

Ambassador Retzer, a political appointee, obviously decided that the letter from the president was more important than the cable from the secretary of state. Using the presidential letter as his guide, Retzer could justify his concern about the Peace Corps drivers, medical staff, and country director.

Olsen, who was deputy director during the Retzer controversy, says the traditional presidential letter creates "a very ambiguous situation," because the letter "is not in complete harmony" with the understanding that the Peace Corps has with the State Department about its independence.

"Almost all ambassadors respect the normal processes," she says, but "occasionally there is an outlier ambassador who takes the letter too seriously." When that happens, Olsen goes on, "there is only so much that can be done because of the letter." Even the State Department's "hands are tied" by the presidential letter.

This jurisdictional tension between an ambassador and the Peace Corps is just another side to the ambiguity about the place of the Peace Corps in U.S. foreign policy. Although Rusk's dictum about the Peace Corps not taking part in U.S. foreign policy is quoted often, the Peace Corps Act puts it much differently.

Under the Act, the president is authorized "to assure coordination of Peace Corp[s] activities with other activities of the United States Government in each country" and the Secretary of State is authorized to supervise Peace Corps programs to make sure "the foreign policy of the United States is best served thereby."

For the most part, the Peace Corps operated independently throughout its half-century of history. But from time to time, administrations enlisted the Peace Corps into campaigns of foreign policy—the expansion of programs in Latin America to counter the influence of Fidel Castro, the influx of Volunteers into Honduras as compensation for harboring the contras, and the rush into Eastern Europe to spread capitalism are obvious examples. In the case of the Dominican Republic in 1965, foreign policy and Peace Corps independence clashed in bitter confusion when many Volunteers denounced the invasion by U.S. Marines.

Peace Corps programs often faltered when inflated or distorted for foreign policy ends. But there was no way to escape this tension. In a memoir written in 1971, Brent Ashabranner, a former deputy director, proposed that the Peace Corps be run by a foundation financed by Congress but completely independent of the U.S. government. The proposal came out of his concern about Volunteers chafing that they represented a U.S. government fighting an unpopular war in Vietnam.

Ashabranner's idea never attracted support. It is hard to imagine Congress ever appropriating several hundred million dollars for a Peace Corps completely out of the government's control. Faced with this difficulty, even Ashabranner concluded, "Meanwhile, I think that a Peace Corps as part of government is much better than no Peace Corps at all.

A few words about the Central Intelligence Agency: from the beginning, it was clear that the Peace Corps would be dogged by suspicions and accusations that many of its Volunteers were disguised agents of the CIA. This came from communist propagandists and nationalist hotheads. Even American expatriates in the capitals liked to gossip and point fingers of suspicion. The Peace Corps seemed such a logical place to hide an agent.

Sargent Shriver knew that if any cases of infiltration by the CIA were proven and publicized, the Peace Corps would probably be destroyed. Few countries would let Volunteers in if they thought with good reason that some were agents. Shriver therefore solicited and received assurances from President Kennedy, his brother-in-law, that he had instructed the CIA to keep its hands off the Peace Corps.

Neither Kennedy nor Shriver trusted the CIA, though, and both pestered it to make sure it was obeying the president. In 1962, Stanley Grogan, assistant director of the CIA, reported to the White House that "CIA has nothing whatever to do with the Peace Corps." In 1963, Shriver telephoned Kennedy and said he had heard rumors "that some of our friends over in the Central Intelligence Agency might think they're smarter than anyone else and that they're trying to stick fellows in the Peace Corps." The president told Shriver to phone CIA Deputy Director Richard Helms and warn him that the president does not want any CIA agent in the Peace Corps, "and if they are there, let's get them out."

Over the years, the CIA renewed vows of noninterference, and there has not been a single known case of a CIA agent serving as a Peace Corps Volunteer or a member of the Peace Corps staff. At a meeting in Havana, Fidel Castro, discovering that Senator Dodd had once been a Volunteer in the Caribbean, told Dodd that "despite rumors that have flowed from all sources, we never once have had one piece of specific information to link any Peace Corps Volunteer . . . with any foreign intelligence operation."

In 1996, John M. Deutch, the CIA director, told the Senate Intelligence Committee that there never had been a case of the CIA using a Volunteer as an agent. But he still opposed legislation that would have prevented the CIA from using Volunteers, as well as journalists and clergy, if it saw fit. Deutch said that CIA policy was not to use Volunteers, but the agency still wanted the right to waive this policy if necessary. This waiver would occur, he testified, only under even more "circumscribed circumstances" than waivers for the use of journalists and clergy. Congress never passed the legislation.

The Peace Corps has set down several policies to allay suspicions. Since the beginning, the Peace Corps refused to accept any former CIA employee as a Volunteer. Former employees of other U.S. intelligence operations, like army or navy intelligence, were eligible, but only ten years or more after their service there had ended.

The Peace Corps struggled to stamp out any hint of association with the CIA. In the late 1960s, the CIA station chief in Tanzania, a flamboyant and affable man, invited a new Peace Corps staffer to go sailing. The U.S. embassy in Dar es Salaam was an important listening post because southern African guerilla groups headquartered in Tanzania and because the Chinese communists, with whom the United States had no diplomatic relations, ran several important foreign aid projects in the country. During the sailing, the CIA chief did not grill the Peace Corps about anything. But when word of the outing reached Washington, Jack Hood Vaughn, the Peace Corps director at the time, was furious. He phoned the staffer, berated him for the mistake, and made it clear there was no room for that kind of fraternization.

The Tanzanian government in those days did not allow most U.S. diplomats to travel to its southern border, where guerillas were launching raids into the Portuguese colony of Mozambique. Paul Sack, the Peace Corps country director, had no trouble obtaining permission to visit his Volunteers in the area.

Yet he never shared what he found out with the embassy.

Since the Peace Corps insisted it was not involved in intelligence gathering, he was not going to gather or deliver any. Whenever the question of Mozambique came up at meetings of the ambassador, senior diplomats and the heads of U.S. agencies in Tanzania, Sack recalls, "I kept my mouth shut."

An incident in Bolivia in 2007 illustrated how suspicions can multiply and then be bent for use by both a foreign government and the U.S. government. Relations between the United States and Bolivia had frayed after the 2005 election of President Evo Morales, a leftist ally of Venezuela's anti-American president, Hugo Chávez. While briefing thirty Volunteers in July about safety, the U.S. embassy security officer asked them to report to the embassy if they came across any Cuban or Venezuelan doctors and other workers in Bolivia. Doreen Salazar, the deputy director of the Peace Corps program in Bolivia, interrupted, told the Volunteers not to comply with the request, and then complained to the embassy.

"We made it clear to the embassy that this was an inappropriate request," Salazar told ABC News later, "and they agreed." But their agreement did not muzzle the security officer. Four months later, he made the same request to a Fulbright scholar. Since the Fulbright program has the same policy on intelligence as the Peace Corps, the Fulbright scholar angrily and publicly accused the embassy of trying to persuade him to spy for them. An embarrassed State Department official in Washington said, "We take this very seriously and want to stress that this is not in any way our policy."

It is well known, especially overseas, that two or three CIA agents, including the station chief, are usually hidden in every U.S. embassy as members of the staff. That made it easy for some Bolivians to assume that the intelligence requested from the Peace Corps and the Fulbright scholar was supposed to end up with the CIA. Indeed, the Peace Corps/Fulbright incident was quickly seized on by the Bolivians as evidence of U.S. bad faith. Foreign Minister David Choquehuanca said, "Any U.S. government use of their students or volunteers to provide intelligence represents a grave threat to Bolivia's sovereignty."

But the United States used the incident as well. After opposition rioting erupted against Morales in 2008, the Bolivian president expelled U.S. ambassador Philip Goldberg, accusing him of conspiring with the opposition. The Peace Corps then shut down its programs in Bolivia, transporting all 113 Volunteers out of the country in cargo planes.

Assistant Secretary of State Thomas Shannon said that the Volunteers had been evacuated for their safety. Shannon told the Associated Press, "Remember, the Bolivians . . . said they thought the Peace Corps was part of a larger intelligence network that they thought we had constructed in Bolivia. Those kind of statements we find very worrisome." In short, the United States was saying that the Bolivian reaction to the intelligence gathering brouhaha had forced it to evacuate the Peace Corps.

But several Volunteers believed their programs had been shut down as retaliation for the ouster of Goldberg. "Peace Corps unfortunately has become another weapon in the U.S. diplomatic arsenal," Sarah Nourse wrote in an e-mail to fellow Volunteers.

The most embarrassing cross-pollination of the Peace Corps and the CIA came in a way that Shriver and President Kennedy least expected. Edward Lee Howard, a Volunteer in Colombia in the early 1970s, joined the CIA in 1981. Under its rules, designed to assuage the sensitivities of the Peace Corps, the CIA would hire former Volunteers only after at least five years had elapsed since the end of their Peace Corps service.

Howard rose rapidly in the service. The CIA was preparing to send him to the coveted post of Moscow as a spy. But he failed a lie detector test in 1983, trying to hide some drug use and petty theft in his younger years. Instead of posting him to Moscow, the CIA fired him.

Howard, infuriated over the firing, decided to sell secrets of the CIA operation in Moscow to agents of the Soviet Union. According to one CIA agent, Howard "wiped out Moscow station" with his betrayal. The CIA traced its problems to Howard, and FBI agents descended on his home in New Mexico. But Howard slipped out of the FBI trap in 1985 and showed up a year later in Moscow. The former Peace Corps Volunteer and former CIA employee died there in 2002.

CHAPTER NINETEEN

Obama and the Future

In December 2007, while trolling for support in the Democratic presidential caucuses of Iowa, Senator Barack Obama of Illinois stopped at Cornell College in Mount Vernon to deliver a brief campaign speech on the value of national service. The college, a liberal arts school with only 1,200 students, had an unusual history and curriculum. A woman earned her diploma there in 1858, marking Cornell as the first college in Iowa to graduate a woman. In 1870, the trustees changed its charter to allow the admission of students of all races. In modern days, the school was noted for requiring students to study only one subject at a time, switching to a new course every three and a half weeks.

This was the earliest stage of Obama's presidential campaign, and little attention was devoted nationally to what he said in Iowa. The most influential pundits did not believe he had much chance of upsetting Senator Hillary Rodham Clinton of New York and her well-financed campaign machine.

During the speech, Obama pledged to more than triple AmeriCorps, create a new Classroom Corps, increase the size of the Foreign Service, and encourage high school and college students to devote from fifty to a hundred hours a year to community service. As for the Peace Corps, Obama promised, "We will double the size of the Peace Corps by its fiftieth anniversary, in 2011."

As the campaign progressed, Obama became vaguer about Peace Corps numbers, but his early promise became a slogan for advocates of a bigger Peace Corps. The National Peace Corps Association, the organization of former Volunteers, set up a committee called More Peace Corps to drum up public enthusiasm and lobby Congress for a doubling of the number of Volunteers by the anniversary year.

The committee was headed by young, enthusiastic, and tireless Rajeev K. Goyal. The American-born Goyal, who grew up on Long Island, was the son of immigrants from India. His father, a medical doctor, and his mother, a scholar of Sanskrit, left Rajasthan for the United States in 1973, as Rajeev puts it, "to seek adventures and greater opportunity in America." Rajeev served as a Volunteer in Nepal from 2001 to 2003, working in sixteen rural villages in remote hill country. Since his tour there, Goyal had returned to Nepal ten times, helping to build five schools in traditional Nepalese architecture.

When President Obama took office in January 2009, he faced an enormous budget deficit and the worst economic crisis since the Great Depression of the 1930s. A total of $700 billion had been set aside for bailing out banks and other desperate financial houses, and Obama spent $787 billion to stimulate the economy. Many other matters, including a large increase in the Peace Corps, had to be shelved.

For his 2010 budget, President Obama proposed $373 million for the Peace Corps, an increase of $33 million over the previous year's appropriation. This was a great disappointment to the Peace Corps community. The funds would probably have increased the total number of trainees and Volunteers from 7,600 to a little more than 8,000 in 2011, nowhere near the campaign promise of 15,000 to 16,000.

This did not stop Goyal from lobbying. Although the goal of a doubling by the anniversary year was clearly unattainable, Goyal set out to put the Peace Corps on a path toward comfortable growth. He enlisted the aid of Rep. Sam Farr of California, a former Volunteer in Colombia, who persuaded the House Appropriations Subcommittee on Foreign Operations to increase the appropriation to a substantial $450 million. That was accepted by the House.

But Senator Patrick Leahy of Vermont, the Democratic chair of the Senate Appropriations Subcommittee on Foreign Operations, objected to the increase, and the Senate voted for exactly what President Obama had requested. After a conference committee session worked out a compromise, Congress passed an appropriation of $400 million.

Goyal hailed the vote as a victory. It would provide $60 million more than the previous year, the largest increase in an annual appropriation in the history of the Peace Corps. Figuring it cost $3 million to open a country program and $30,000 to send a single Volunteer overseas, Goyal estimated that the new appropriation would allow the Peace Corps to open operations in five new countries and increase the numbers of Volunteers overseas by 1,500, to more than 9,000 during the anniversary year. That would be a much more manageable increase than the doubling promised by candidate Obama, and it would swell the Peace Corps to its largest size in forty years.

Much of the struggle for funds took place without an Obama appointee as head of the Peace Corps. The president did not nominate a director until six months into the administration. Senate confirmation was swift, but it still took a month, and the new director did not take office until August 24, 2009.

Soon after Obama's inauguration, rumors had spread that he intended to appoint James Arena-DeRosa as director. Arena-DeRosa was head of the Peace Corps's New England recruiting office in Boston. The gossip aroused a good deal of dismay in Peace Corps circles. Arena-DeRosa had never been a Volunteer and had never served overseas in his nine years as a member of the staff. Even though his extensions were legal, some critics even carped about his managing to evade the five-year limit on employment.

Arena-DeRosa, who also taught at Brandeis University, had strong support for the job from Governor Deval Patrick of Massachusetts, a good friend of Obama's. That struck many as a disheartening example of cronyism. There was a great deal of relief when the rumors proved unfounded, perhaps because Peace Corps dismay had persuaded the White House to find someone else. In July 2009, Obama nominated Aaron Williams, a former Volunteer and an experienced hand at overseas development, as the eighteenth director of the Peace Corps.

Williams and his story appealed to Peace Corps enthusiasts. There is no doubt that the Peace Corps had set his life's course. When he arrived in the Dominican Republic in 1967 as a Volunteer, he had never set foot in a foreign country before. He had never even flown in an airplane before. Indeed, he had not even left home to go to college. An African American born in Chicago, he grew up, as he puts it, "in a modest home on the south side . . . never dreaming that one day I would have a career in international development." His father was a supervisor at the post office.

Williams graduated from little-known Chicago State University, majoring in geography and education. He started teaching in the

Chicago school system but, encouraged by his mother and a classmate, soon applied to the Peace Corps. His education degree and brief teaching experience attracted notice. The Peace Corps assigned him to a rural teacher training program in the small town of Monte Plata. He had to reach fifty elementary school teachers in the countryside by motorcycle, horseback, or foot and help them complete high school and improve their teaching skills. "I bonded with these teachers," Williams told television interviewer Tavis Smiley, "and I said, 'My God, what an awesome responsibility. These people are depending on me to deliver on something they need to improve their lives.'"

Williams met his wife, Rosa, a Dominican high school science teacher, while serving as a Volunteer. They were married in the Dominican Republic, and afterward, he stayed on for a third year in the Peace Corps as a professor of education at the Católica Universidad Madre y Maestra in Santiago.

After the Dominican Republic, he was employed as a recruiter for the Peace Corps in Chicago before earning an MBA from the University of Wisconsin. Armed with his business degree, he worked for a pair of multinational corporations, International Multifoods and General Mills, for five years and then joined AID in 1978.

He put together an extraordinary career in his twenty-two years at AID, serving in Honduras, Costa Rica, Haiti, Barbados, and South Africa, among other places. He received both the Presidential Award for Distinguished Service and the AID Distinguished Career Service Award, and he was in charge of AID's $1-billion foreign assistance program in South Africa during the administration of President Nelson Mandela.

After AID, Williams was named executive vice president of the International Youth Foundation, a nonprofit organization that solicits corporate donations to assist young people in the developing world, and later he became vice president for international business development at RTI International, a nonprofit research institute founded by Duke University, the University of North Carolina, and North Carolina State University. He was at RTI International when President Obama nominated him to head the Peace Corps.

Williams had many admirers. They described him as a manager who listens carefully to the views of others but does not hesitate to make a decision when the time comes. He was no ideologue, they said, but a pragmatic actor. Williams was also lauded as professional, efficient, and leavened by a pleasant sense of humor. In an interview, he struck me as genial, unassuming, self-confident, thoughtful and non-dogmatic. So he did not have any difficulty getting the job.

Williams did not come to the Peace Corps determined to turn it upside down. After a few months on the job, he professed three goals: "measured, targeted growth" by entering new countries and by expanding successful projects; creation of an office of innovation to look into new approaches like partnership with international humanitarian organizations overseas; and an increased effort to help Americans understand the Third World.

Despite his impressive credentials and accolades, one significant aspect of Williams's career troubled some former Volunteers and staff—his strong association with AID. AID has long been a creature of U.S. foreign policy. Its own Web site boasts that one of its goals is "furthering America's foreign policy interests." During the George W. Bush administration, it even became part of the State Department. The administrator of AID holds the rank of undersecretary of State.

Throughout its fifty-year history, it has not been easy for Peace Corps directors to resist the frequent pressure from the White House and Congress to step in line with U.S. foreign policy and interests, and some have succumbed. Would Williams, with his strong AID background, allow the independence of the Peace Corps to bend? That was the fear of some in the Peace Corps family.

His AID career posed another question. From time to time, the Peace Corps has placed Volunteers in AID projects or in the projects of contractors funded by AID. Since the Peace Corps has not developed these projects, they sometimes do not allow the kind of person-to-person contact that is one of the main goals of the Peace Corps. Instead of Volunteers fitting into a well-conceived and well-organized Peace Corps experience, they may become no more than cheap labor for AID and its contractors. Skeptics wondered whether Williams would be tempted to engage in too many projects for AID and its contractors.

One skeptic was Hugh Pickens, the former Peru Volunteer who edits *Peace Corps Online* (www.peacecorpsonline.org), an independent news Web site with an extraordinary range of information about the Peace Corps, offering far more detail and far more discussion of controversial issues than carried on the bland official Peace Corps Web site (www.peacecorps.gov).

Reporting on the Williams confirmation hearings by a Senate Foreign Relations subcommittee, Pickens wrote, "There were a couple of issues discussed in the hearings that were a little unsettling. One was the idea that one of the purposes of the Peace Corps is to bolster U.S. foreign policy and that the State Department should take a large role in deciding which countries the Peace Corps should go into.

"Another concern is Williams' many years working with USAID," Pickens went on. "The debate has raged for decades on whether the Peace Corps should work more closely with USAID and the consensus has been that Peace Corps is a people-to people program—not a junior USAID.... We would caution that Williams needs to be careful about applying the USAID model of foreign aid to the Peace Corps."

Pickens's concerns seemed to reflect the tone of the questions of the senators rather than the tone of the replies of Williams. But in his own public statements later, Williams sounded somewhat ambiguous about these issues. In an interview with the *National Journal* in September 2009, Williams was asked why the Peace Corps had programs in countries like Fiji, Vanuatu, and Cape Verde, where "the U.S. has no strategic interests." Williams replied that the Peace Corps needed to look at a couple of things in selecting countries for Peace Corps programs. "First of all, where are there countries that desire Peace Corps Volunteers?" he said. "And also, what about U.S. interests? I'm going to look at both sides of that equation."

Later in the interview, Williams was asked about former senator Harris Wofford's view that linking the Peace Corps "with American foreign policy, no matter how benign, may hurt its credibility around the world." Williams replied, "I think not only is that Senator Wofford's view, it's also Sargent Shriver's view and it was also Kennedy's view, and I stand by that. It's been a successful way of viewing the Peace Corps for nearly fifty years."

His two replies appeared contradictory, as if he had given an AID answer to the first question and a Peace Corps answer to the second. But, in our interview, Williams said he had used the phrase "U.S. interests" in the earlier interview in a very general way. What he was trying to convey, he said, was "you also want to be in a place where you want to develop friendship between American society and the society of that particular country, and that's in America's best interests and it's also in the best interests of those countries."

Williams recognized that his long career in AID might raise concerns about his loyalty to Peace Corps ideals. But, he said, "I'm here because I love the Peace Corps. The Peace Corps changed my life forever."

Most members of the Peace Corps family were clearly pleased with the appointment of Williams. But as the fiftieth anniversary approached, it was still much too soon to assess his impact on the work, idea, and spirit of the Peace Corps.

Does the Peace Corps
Do Any Good?

In 1964, twenty-one-year-old Nancy Deeds, a new Peace Corps Volunteer, hunted for a place to live in a rundown, dirt-poor neighborhood in the fishing port of Chimbote on the Pacific coast of Peru. Joel Meister, another new Volunteer, helped her in the quest. The staff had imbued them with the Peace Corps housing ethos. Nancy needed quarters that brought her close to Peruvians and cost little enough for her meager living allowance.

But poor neighborhoods are overcrowded neighborhoods, and the first few houses had no room for her. The Volunteers encountered a teenager in front of the next house, a polite high school student with dark Indian features wearing black trousers and a white short-sleeved shirt. He listened carefully to their explanations in recently acquired Spanish and, after promising to see what he could do, slipped into the house.

The house was adobe, with no electricity or running water. An open sewer dribbled behind it, and the well lay 150 feet away. Scrawny dogs roamed the unpaved street without leash or supervision. The teenager's father made bricks in the back yard. His mother added to the family income by selling fruit and vegetables out of a front window. The house had only three bedrooms, and all were occupied by the parents and nine children.

The teenager proposed that his reluctant parents rent the little room from which the mother sold fruit and vegetables. The American woman could pay more than the mother earned from her sales. The parents agreed, and Nancy rented the room—known as *La Tiendita,* or "little store"—for 150 *soles* ($7) a month.

The teenager—seventeen-year-old Alejandro Toledo—was the first member of his family to reach as far as high school. He shined shoes and sold snow cones to make up for the loss of family income caused by the time he had to spend in school. Chimbote was a step ahead for the Toledo family. They had come down from the impoverished village of Cabana in the nearby Andes highlands more than ten years earlier. Many other highlanders had joined them in the migration. The Toledos were a large family cut down by poverty, disease, and lack of sanitation. Seven of Alejandro's fifteen brothers and sisters had died as infants.

Alejandro and the Peace Corps Volunteers grew close during the next two years. Joel, who lived two blocks away, and Nancy became counselors to the social and sports club that Alejandro and his friends had organized. Alejandro, in turn, helped the Volunteers with their summer camp, Campamento Atahualpa, and other community development projects.

Alejandro and Nancy would talk in her room, lit by a kerosene lamp. He would ask her questions about the world outside Chimbote. "There's no doubt that I woke up and said, 'Maybe I can go somewhere,'" Alejandro told a reporter more than forty years later.

A year after their arrival, Nancy and Joel Meister married in Chimbote with Alejandro's parents, Anatolio and Margarita, standing in for the absent parents of the Peace Corps Volunteers at the wedding ceremony. Later that year, Alejandro won a small grant from a local civic organization to travel to the United States to study at a university.

That presented difficult problems. He had not been accepted by a university, and he did not have funds to live on while studying. Nancy and Joel, after their Peace Corps tours ended, began graduate work at the University of California at Berkeley and helped Alejandro enroll in a special program for foreign students at the University of San Francisco. They also helped finance the first year.

Although his poor English made studies difficult, Alejando showed a talent for soccer that won him a partial athletic scholarship. With the help of odd jobs like pumping gas at a station at night, he managed to pay his tuition and expenses for the next three years. After his graduation from the University of San Francisco, he won a Ford Foundation fellowship to study at Stanford University, where he earned a master's in education, a master's in economics, and a PhD in economic development and education.

A distinguished career followed. He worked for the United Nations, the World Bank, the Inter-American Development Bank, the Organization for Economic Cooperation and Development, Harvard University, Waseda University in Japan, and the Peruvian government as an economics advisor. He later entered Peruvian politics. Then, in 2000, the teenager who once pleaded with his parents to let a Peace Corps *gringa* live in their crowded home was elected president of Peru.

After that, the Peace Corps community liked to call Toledo "the Peace Corps president." Both Nancy and Joel attended his inauguration. His single term was not a successful one. Governing Peru after the havoc of the years of President Alberto Fujimori proved bitterly difficult, and he steadily grew more and more unpopular. Although Toledo's economic policies improved conditions substantially, his administration was beset by accusations of corruption, sex scandals, and the forging of electoral signatures. Under the Peruvian constitution, Toledo could not succeed himself for a second term.

Toledo did manage to bring the Peace Corps back to Peru. The program had been halted in 1975 by leftist army officers who had taken over the country in an earlier coup. Toledo never forgot his debt. As he said in a lecture to Peace Corps staff and others in Washington, "A large portion of the path that I took—through my education, leaving the shanty town in Chimbote—Peace Corps had a lot to do with . . . . You people are responsible for this president!"

From time to time, some critics—even a few who know the developing world well—dismiss the accomplishments of the Peace Corps. They acknowledge that the Volunteers make a lot of friends overseas but insist they do little or nothing for economic, social, and political development. In his op-ed article in the *New York Times,* Robert L. Strauss, the former Cameroon country director, wrote that the overwhelming majority of Volunteers "lack the maturity and professional experience to be effective development workers in the 21st century." A cynical professor once proposed that the Peace Corps reimburse a Latin American country for the harm wreaked on its economy by the Volunteers. It is worth keeping the Alejandro Toledo story in mind when considering this issue.

For the most part, the numbers of the Volunteers have been too small to have an obvious impact on the countries that host them. In the early days of the Peace Corps, Warren Wiggins, his imagination aflame, envisioned sending 50,000 Volunteers to India, 5,000 to the Philippines, and 5,000 to 10,000 to Nigeria. The Peace Corps never recruited Volunteers in such numbers and, if it had, the programs would have been disastrous. Only in Ethiopia did the numbers of Volunteers have a discernable impact on a country, and the unhappy consequence was not something the Peace Corps recognized as an achievement. The Peace Corps has become a small and elite agency focusing on crucial projects, but a limited number of them.

The Peace Corps tries hard to quantify some of its accomplishments for Congress and the public. In its 2008 annual report, the Peace Corps said that in the past year, its 7,750 Volunteers had worked with 2.1 million people, helped train 126,000 teachers, health workers, and other service providers, and assisted 24,000 government agencies and nongovernmental organizations throughout the world.

In its country-by-country summaries, the Peace Corps report also provided statistics illustrating the achievements of the Volunteers. In Burkina Faso, for example, the Volunteers helped seventy community organizations educate their villages about HIV/AIDS, malaria, polio, tuberculosis, family planning, and other health matters. In Cameroon, they helped farmers establish ninety-one nurseries that produced more than 88,000 tree seedlings and cuttings.

In El Salvador, a Volunteer persuaded a U.S. charity to donate 400 computers for distribution to schools in twenty-seven communities, where Volunteers trained teachers to use them in classroom work. In Ghana, Volunteers taught science, math, computer skills, and visual arts to 7,600 students in rural schools. In Honduras, Volunteers helped build or restore potable water systems to eighty-seven communities for the benefit of more than 50,000 Salvadorans. In Kenya, a Volunteer trained 300 Kenyans in beekeeping and helped redesign a new beehive in a project that enabled the new beekeepers to earn four times the normal income from the sale of honey. These are just a few of the numerous examples.

Yet the numbers never seem fully satisfying. No one can demean a 400 percent increase in the profits from honey or the supply of healthy water to 50,000 poor people or the gentle whirring of 400 new computers in public schools. But much of Peace Corps achievement cannot be measured in numbers.

There is a good deal of testimony and anecdotal evidence about the elusiveness of capturing and measuring the essence of the Peace Corps experience. Some Volunteers simply feel and know that what they are doing helps the people around them. When they evaluate their work, they usually spurn measurements.

In 1977, Debbie Erickson, a Volunteer in Chichigalpa, Nicaragua, told Terence Smith, a reporter for the *New York Times*, "I know some Americans think what we do is patronizing, a form of cultural imperialism. And the Nicaraguans—most of them don't know what in God's name we are doing here. About half think we are CIA agents, and the other half think we are crazy. But I work among these women and children, I see their needs, and that's the only justification I need. If I am able to help them organize themselves and improve their life, then it is worth it as far as I am concerned."

Judy Guskin and her husband, Alan, were among the pioneers of the Peace Corps. Among the first accepted as Volunteers, they taught in the Philippines. After the Guskins returned to the Philippines for a visit, Judy wrote a brief essay on the twenty-fifth anniversary of the Peace Corps. "It is possible to count the number of wells dug or acres sown by Peace Corps Volunteers," she wrote, "but how do you measure the results of teaching? It's hard to measure the impact of a teacher anywhere, and Peace Corps teachers are no exception. What matters for teachers is not only what their students learn, but that they learn to love learning, to have faith in their own abilities, to want to give themselves fully to whatever they do . . . . I think Al and I can say, like most Peace Corps Volunteers, that we affected the lives of a few individuals. For them, we thought, we had somehow made a difference."

One of the most eloquent and sensitive portrayals of the best work of Volunteers came from evaluator Leslie Hanscom after he visited Afghanistan in 1966. Hanscom, a renowned writer for the *Saturday Evening Post* and other magazines, joined *Newsday* after leaving the Peace Corps and served for many years as the New York newspaper's book critic and columnist.

Describing Peace Corps nurses in Afghan hospitals, Hanscom wrote, "To see them work is to be struck by the power that can be exerted by a little common decency. Moreover, it is not just the visiting outsider who is struck, but the local hospital workers who are there to stay."

Even patients are surprised. "There are strong reasons why it has an almost startling effect upon people to see an American girl in a white uniform appearing to take their troubles to heart," Hanscom went on. "They themselves have been conditioned by life to stifle human sympathy in their own natures. Most of them, by the time they are ten years old, have witnessed more misery and disaster than an American would see in several lifetimes."

"The practical instinct to shrink from the suffering of others is fully shared by Afghan nurses," said Hanscom. "Their attitude toward the ill is ironically close to the ancient Oriental attitude toward the leper— 'unclean, don't touch.' Before the advent of the Peace Corps, there was almost nobody to drum it into them that not turning aside from the spectacle of suffering is what their trade is all about.

"From all signs," Hanscom concluded, "the lesson is now taking hold. Afghan nurses see the patients' surging response to the Peace Corps girls, and—out of plain jealousy—try to divert some of this to themselves. That the response exists is unmistakable."

How do you measure the value of the brush of a nurse's fingers against the brow of a patient? Or the success of a teacher's desire to instill the love of learning? Or the worth of bringing women and children together in Nicaragua? How do you measure the power of a young girl's talks by kerosene lamp with a poor boy who will become the president of Peru?

I do not want to suggest that all Peace Corps Volunteers are successful agents of change who do wonderful things beyond measure. The Peace Corps has its share of failure. But the best Volunteers do accomplish a kind of magic that is not caught by the statistics of an annual report.

The least-known side of Peace Corps service is that for many, it never ends. That is why the Volunteers like to call themselves Returned Volunteers, not ex-Volunteers or former Volunteers, when they come home after their tours of overseas duty. Their links with the Peace Corps and fellow Volunteers, and their service to their countries and friends abroad, go on.

There are more than 140 organizations of returned Volunteers, almost all involved in helping the developing world. Half are made up of Volunteers who worked in the same country and bear names like Friends of Liberia, Amigos de Honduras, and the Peace Corps Alumni Foundation for Philippine Development. The others mainly comprise former Volunteers from the same areas of the United States, like the Returned Peace Corps Volunteers of Wisconsin—Madison, the Heart of Texas Peace Corps Association, and the Cincinnati Area Returned Volunteers.

There are also a handful of small national groups—like the Lesbian, Gay and Bisexual Returned Peace Corps Volunteers—and one major national organization, the National Peace Corps Association. The latter has a membership of 30,000. Almost all the various Volunteer groups are affiliated with the National Peace Corps Association, and it usually speaks in the name of the returned Volunteer community.

One of the most successful activities is the annual calendar produced in Madison, Wisconsin. Former Volunteers throughout the United States submit photos of life in Peace Corps countries, and more than fifty members of the Madison group donate their time to produce a calendar brimming with spectacular pictures and miscellaneous facts about the Peace Corps and the countries pictured. There is an array of details, noting, for example, that January 6 is Maroon Day in Jamaica, April 27 is Independence Day in Togo, July 13 is the Jagannath Festival in India, and November 9 is Sargent Shriver's birthday.

Since 1988, sales of the calendars have brought in more than $820,000, all of it spent in giving small grants to the projects of Volunteers throughout the world. In 2008, for example, calendar proceeds were used to buy a mimeograph machine for the Tubman School in Liberia, build fifteen latrines in the Dominican Republic, help train birth attendants in Morocco, sponsor a chess club in Bolivia, and fund parts of sixty-five other small projects.

Similar good works come from other associations. The Peace Corps Alumni Foundation for Philippine Development, for example, has funded scholarships for more than two hundred young Filipinos to study in Filipino universities. The Returned Peace Corps Volunteers of South Florida have worked with the enormous swell of families displaced by the insurrections in Colombia, offering them interest-free micro-loans to start small businesses. The Marafiki wa Tanzania (the name is Swahili for "Friends of Tanzania"), which spends more than $25,000 a year in grants, donated $7,000 over three years to the Mkombozi Vocational and Community Center, located in Moshi near Mount Kilimanjaro, for the vocational training and health education of women and youths.

There also are many examples of individual Volunteers who become so attached to their countries that they go back there to work after their service is over. Matt Marek, a Volunteer in Jacmel in Haiti from 2000 to 2002, joined several fellow Volunteers in founding Haiti Innovation, a nonprofit organization offering advice for development projects in the country.

Marek worked for the National Peace Corps Association in Washington for two years. But when the turmoil of an insurgency drove the Peace Corps out of Haiti in 2004, he set up residence in Haiti once again. He soon joined the American Red Cross as chief of its Haiti operations. When Haiti was devastated by the earthquake of January 2010, Marek, a relief worker on the scene, took on the added role of describing the extent of the horrors to U.S. television news shows and newspapers before their own correspondents could reach Haiti.

Alice O'Grady was part of the first contingent of Peace Corps Volunteers ever to reach their host country. In fact, she did most of the singing when the group of teachers alighted from their plane in Ghana in 1961 and sang an anthem in the Twi language. After her service ended, she returned to Ghana in 1968 to teach science at the Accra Academy for four years. Afterwards, she went back for brief trips to collect material for a children's novel she was writing about the history of Ghana.

In 2008, almost fifty years after Alice first set foot in Ghana, some of her old students at the Accra Academy, now successful doctors and engineers, endowed a scholarship in her name at the school. The donors praised Miss Alice for her "dedication, tirelessness, discipline, and enthusiasm" and said she had "ignited in her students a passion for scientific knowledge." They also paid for her to fly to Accra to present the scholarship to the first winner.

The United States itself has benefitted enormously from the Peace Corps as well. The evidence is overwhelming. Work overseas has fostered qualities of leadership and innovation and commitment that have propelled many Volunteers into positions of influence. In the political world, for example, two U.S. senators were former Volunteers—the late Paul Tsongas of Massachusetts (Ethiopia) and Chris Dodd of Connecticut (the Dominican Republic). The roster of Volunteers in the House of Representatives, from both parties, has included Steve Dreihaus of Ohio (Senegal), Sam Farr of California (Colombia), John Garamendi of California (Ethiopia), Tony Hall of Ohio (Thailand), Mike Honda of California (El Salvador), Thomas Petri of Wisconsin (Somalia), Christopher Shays of Connecticut (Fiji), James Walsh of New York (Nepal), and Mike Ward of Kentucky (Gambia). Governors Jim Doyle of Wisconsin (Tunisia) and Bob Taft of Ohio (Tanzania) were also Volunteers, as were the mayors of Pittsburgh, San Angelo, Texas, and Urbana, Illinois.

Twenty Volunteers have served as ambassadors—an astounding number considering that in the early days, State Department diplomats resented the Peace Corps. The list includes Christopher Hill (Cameroon), who served the George W. Bush administration as the chief nuclear negotiator with North Korea and then became the Obama administration's ambassador to Iraq. Robert Gelbard, a veteran diplomat appointed an assistant secretary of state in 2009, served as ambassador to Bolivia from 1988 to 1991 a little more than twenty years after he had worked there as a Volunteer. During Gelbard's time as ambassador, the Bolivian foreign minister joked to former Peace Corps director Jack Vaughn, "I have no idea if he's speaking for the U.S. government or the Indians of the altiplano. He knows Indian curse words that I have barely heard in my lifetime."

Many Volunteers gravitate to AID. A large number have become mission directors overseas. Richard Greene, a former Volunteer in the Ivory Coast who directed AID's Office of Health, Infectious Diseases, and Nutrition, was selected as Federal Employee of the Year in 2008.

The renowned novelist and travel writer Paul Theroux (Malawi) heads a long list of writers who came out of the Peace Corps. Others include detective novelist Dick Lipez (Ethiopia), who uses the pseudonym Richard Stevenson; novelist John Coyne (Ethiopia); best-selling nonfiction writer Peggy Anderson (Togo); and journalist Peter Hessler (China). Among Volunteer journalists are Chris Matthews of MSNBC (Swaziland), George Packer of the *New Yorker* (Togo), Maureen Orth of *Vanity Fair* (Colombia), Josh Friedman of *Newsday* (Costa Rica), Karen De Witt of ABC News (Ethiopia), Al Kamen of the *Washington Post* (the Dominican Republic), and Loren Jenkins, the foreign editor of National Public Radio's news division (Sierra Leone).

The list of distinguished alumni includes such well-known names as Carol Bellamy (Guatemala), who became executive director of UNICEF after serving as Peace Corps director, and Donna Shalala (Iran), the president of the University of Miami and former secretary of Health and Human Services. Ten other Volunteers have become presidents of universities and colleges.

All fields are represented. The founders of Netflix and the Nature Company and the board chairs of Levi Strauss and the Chicago Bears are former Volunteers. So are sculptor Joel Shapiro (India) and artist Tomas Belsky (Brazil).

There is another important benefit to the United States beyond the lists of influential alumni. The US now has 200,000 citizens who have lived and worked in the developing world and understand it well. This extensive knowledge of Africa, Latin America, Asia, and Eastern Europe is an enormous and vital resource that would not exist without the Peace Corps and its fifty years of service.

ACKNOWLEDGMENTS

I am, of course, indebted to the hundreds of Peace Corps Volunteers and the scores of Peace Corps staffers that I met during my two and a half years with the agency during the 1960s. This wonderful experience came after Charles Peters hired me for his elite evaluation division. I gained many insights into the Peace Corps in those years from members of his crew, including Timothy Adams, Peggy Anderson, Meridan Bennett, Maureen Carroll, Russ Chapell, Phil Cook, Kevin Delany, Richard El-well, Leslie Hanscom, David Hapgood, Richard Lipez, Robert McGuire, Richard Richter, Robert Shogan, and William Tatge. More recently, Pe-ters, Anderson, Delany, Lipez, Richter, and, especially, Carroll spent a good deal of time with me discussing various themes and events for this book.

John Coyne, who has often explored the history of the Peace Corps with his Babbles blog and Peace Corps Writers Web site (both now at www.peacecorpsworldwide.org), suggested that I write this history. John, whom I first met when he was on the Peace Corps staff in Ethiopia, forwarded much vital material to me as I worked on the project.

Several Peace Corps directors agreed to lengthy interviews for the book, either by phone or in person: Jack Hood Vaughn, Joseph Blatch-ford, Richard Celeste, Carol Bellamy, Mark Gearan, Mark Schneider, and Aaron Williams. Jody Olsen, who served as deputy director during the George W. Bush administration and acting director afterward, also spent several hours talking with me.

Many others, most having served the Peace Corps as Volunteers or staffers or both, helped me, usually through interviews or e-mail correspondence. The list includes David E. Apter, Megan Blackburn, Carroll Bouchard, Lewis H. Butler, Tim Carroll, John Demos, Christine A. Djondo, Aaron Drendel, Josef Evans, Jane Fazio-Villeda, Frederick Fox, Mark Gearan, Rajeev K. Goyal, Eric Griffin, David Gurr, Gretchen Handwerger, Andy Hanson, Deborah Harding, Barbara E. Joe, Kirby Jones, William Josephson, James Jouppi, Aaron Kauffman, Susan Klee, Robert Klein, David Lamb, Steve Lenzo, Carole Levin, Adrian Lozano, Bill Mabie, Frank Mankiewicz, Edie Martinez, Eugene B. Mihaly, Lawrence J. O'Brien, Philip B. Olsen, Hugh Pickens, Allison Price, Ross J. Pritchard, Kate Raftery, Daniel Rapoport, William Reese, Michael Retzer, Joan Richter, Janet Romero, Paul Sack, Bob Satin, Ruth Saxe, Bennett Schiff, Michael Schmicker, Theodore C. Sorensen, Robert Steiner, Sal Tedesco, Robert B. Textor, Collin Tong, Amy Utzinger, Theodore M. Vestal, Roberta (B. J.) Warren, Kevin Wheeler, Harris Wofford, and Ellen Yaffe.

The archivists at the National Archives and the Nixon Library, both at College Park, Maryland, were always helpful, as was the staff of the Lyndon B. Johnson Library at the University of Texas in Austin. Senior archivist Regina Greenwell of the LBJ Library saved me countless hours of work by steering me to the pertinent files.

My editor at Beacon Press, Gayatri Patnaik, wielded a gentle but remarkably deft pencil. My agent, Scott Mendel, realized early that Beacon Press was the right home for the book.

I had my usual family cheering section. The book is dedicated to six of them. The others are Julie, Hunter, Sarah, Ronella, Jake, Luke, Claire, John, Ava, Elodie, Solal, Patricia, Sophia, Penelope, and Mallory.

As I have mentioned in previous books, my wife, Elizabeth Fox, does not suffer as I research and write. She simply has too much to do, especially in her work at the U.S. Agency for International Development, where she is, in fact, surrounded by many former Peace Corps Volunteers. It was amazing to watch her take on, without missing a beat, the extra duties that came with the terrible earthquake in Haiti in January 2010. I continue to look on her with love and awe.

TABLE I

Annual Numbers of Volunteers *(at end of fiscal year)*

1962	2,940	1978	7,072	1994	6,745
1963	6,646	1979	6,328	1995	7,218
1964	10,078	1980	5,994	1996	6,910
1965	13,248	1981	5,445	1997	6,660
1966	15,556	1982	5,380	1998	6,719
1967	14,968	1983	5,483	1999	6,989
1968	13,823	1984	5,699	2000	7,164
1969	12,131	1985	6,264	2001	6,643
1970	9,513	1986	5,913	2002	6,636
1971	7,066	1987	5,219	2003	7,533
1972	6,894	1988	5,812	2004	7,733
1973	7,341	1989	6,248	2005	7,810
1974	8,044	1990	5,583	2006	7,628
1975	7,015	1991	5,866	2007	7,896
1976	5,958	1992	5,831	2008	7,876
1977	5,752	1993	6,467	2009	7,671

SOURCES: Elizabeth Cobbs Hoffman, *All You Need is Love: The Peace Corps and the Spirit of the 1960s* (Cambridge, Mass.: Harvard University Press, 1998); Peace Corps.

TABLE II
Directors of the Peace Corps

R. Sargent Shriver, 1961–66

Jack Hood Vaughn, 1966–69

Joseph Blatchford, 1969–71

Kevin O'Donnell, 1971–72*

Donald Hess, 1972–73*

Nicholas Craw, 1973–74*

John Dellenback, 1975–77*

Carolyn R. Payton, 1977–78*

Richard F. Celeste, 1979–81*

Loret Miller Ruppe, 1981–89

Paul D. Coverdell, 1989–91

Elaine Chao, 1991–92

Carol Bellamy, 1993–95

Mark D. Gearan, 1995–99

Mark L. Schneider, 1999–2001

Gaddi H. Vasquez, 2002–6

Ronald A. Tschetter, 2006–9

Aaron S. Williams, 2009–present

* Peace Corps was part of ACTION during these years.

SOURCE: Peace Corps

No history of the Peace Corps can be written without consulting four pioneering books: Gerard T. Rice, *The Bold Experiment: JFK's Peace Corps* (Notre Dame, IN.: University of Notre Dame Press, 1985); Coates Redmon, *Come as You Are: The Peace Corps Story* (New York: Harcourt Brace Jovanovich, 1986); Karen Schwarz, *What You Can Do for Your Country: An Oral History of the Peace Corps* (New York: William Morrow, 1991); and Elizabeth Cobbs Hoffman, *All You Need Is Love: The Peace Corps and the Spirit of the 1960s* (Cambridge, MA.: Harvard University Press, 1998). My debt to them, especially in my discussion of the early years, will be obvious to anyone who knows these books.

I was fortunate enough to benefit as well from the research of the recent biography *Sarge: The Life and Times of Sargent Shriver,* by Scott Stossel (Washington, D.C.: Smithsonian Books, 2004).

Hugh Pickens, a former Volunteer from Peru, has created an extraordinary Web site, www.peacecorpsonline.org, which includes historical documents, news archives, late reports, Volunteer directories, and a host of other Peace Corps information. His Web site was invaluable. So were the commentaries of former Ethiopia Volunteer John Coyne on www.peacecorpsworldwide.org. I have also consulted extensively the archives of three newspapers: the *New York Times, Washington Post,* and *Los Angeles Times.*

Comprehensive tables listing all Peace Corps countries, the numbers of Volunteers who have served in each, and the prominent alumni from each country can be found at www.beacon.org/whentheworldcalls.

SOURCES

Chapter 1. The Challenge from JFK

James MacGregor Burns's *John Kennedy: A Political Profile* (New York: Harcourt Brace, 1960) discusses the campaign problems of Kennedy's attitude toward Joe McCarthy, pp. 131–55, and Kennedy's Catholicism, pp. 237–58. Ted Sorensen's quote on Kennedy and McCarthy is from his memoirs, *Counselor* (New York: HarperCollins, 2008), p. 155. The protest against *The Bicycle Thief* was reported in the *New York Times,* February 16, 1951, in the story, "K. of C. Marches on Movie Theatre; Showing of 'Bicycle Thief' Canceled."

For my analysis of the campaign, I have depended on Theodore H. White, *The Making of the President 1960* (New York: Atheneum, 1961); and Theodore C. Sorensen, *Kennedy* (New York: Harper and Row), pp. 168–210. Transcripts of the televised debates are available on the Web site of the Commission on Presidential Debates, www.debates.org.

For the narrative of the University of Michigan events, I have followed the accounts of James Tobin, "JFK at the Union: The unknown story of the Peace Corps," *Michigan Today,* January 2008 (found on the www.michigantoday.umich.edu Web site); participants who sent comments to the same Web site; Coates Redmon, *Come as You Are: The Peace Corps Story* (New York: Harcourt Brace Jovanovich, 1986), pp. 3–7, 11–14; Karen Schwarz, *What You Can Do for Your Country: An Oral History of the Peace Corps* (New York: William Morrow, 1991), pp. 27–29; Harris Wofford, *Of Kennedys and Kings: Making Sense of the Sixties* (Pittsburgh, PA.: University of Pittsburgh Press, 1980), pp. 244–50; Richard N. Goodwin, *Remembering America: A Voice from the Sixties* (New York: Harper and Row, 1989), pp. 120–21; and Gerard T. Rice, *The Bold Experiment: JFK's Peace Corps* (Notre Dame, IN: University of Notre Dame Press, 1985), pp. 18–22.

The text of Kennedy's remarks to the Michigan students can be found on the Peace Corps Web site, www.peacecorps.gov. Russell Baker's front-page article on the campaign in Michigan appeared with the headline "Kennedy Resumes Whistle-stopping" in the *New York Times,* October 15, 1960.

The text of Kennedy's San Francisco speech can be found on the American Presidency Project Web site of the University of California at Santa Barbara, www.presidency.ucsb.edu. The *New York Times* front-page article "Kennedy Favors U.S. 'Peace Corps' to Work Abroad" was written by Harrison E. Salisbury and published on November 3, 1960. The negative reaction can be found in Wofford, p. 243, and in the Tobin article.

Chapter 2. Sarge's Peace Corps

For details on the early life of Sargent Shriver, I have depended heavily on Scott Stossel, *Sarge: The Life and Times of Sargent Shriver* (Washington, D.C.: Smithsonian Books, 2004), pp. xxi–xxx, 3–139. The quote from Shriver's mother can be found in "The Peace Corps: It Is Almost As Good As Its Intentions," *Time,* July 5, 1963.

Shriver's role in the 1960 campaign, and the phone call to Coretta King, is covered by Wofford, pp. 11–66, and Stossel, pp. 155–69. The Peters quote on Bobby Kennedy is in Stossel, pp. 157–58. White's assessment of the importance of the King phone call can be found in White, p. 323.

The hunt for Kennedy administration talent is described in Stossel, pp. 173–86, and Wofford, pp. 67–99. The Kennedy quotes about talent are from Stossel, p. 174. The David Halberstam quote is from his book *The Best and the Brightest* (Greenwich, CT: Fawcett, 1973), p. 272.

The work of the Peace Corps task force is covered in Stossel, pp. 189–208, and in Wofford, pp. 252–61. The public version of the task force's report can be found on the National Archives Web site at www.arcweb.archives.gov. There is extensive material about "A Towering Task" in the January 1997 issue of *RPCV Writers & Readers*. The Wiggins/Josephson report itself can be found on www.rpcv.org. Wiggins's recollections are from an interview by John Coyne in the January 1997 *RPCV Writers & Readers* issue, p. 15, and from the blog "John Coyne Babbles," March 17, 2008 (which can be found at www.peacecorpsworldwide.org/babbles/). The Donovan McClure quote is from p. 24 of the same issue. Josephson put down his recollections in an e-mail to me on June 16, 2008. The Braestrup quote comes from Stossel, p. 217.

The fight over the independence of the Peace Corps is covered in Stossel, pp. 218–25, in Wofford, pp. 262–67, and in Rice, pp. 60–67. Shriver's April 21, 1961, letter to Labouisse are in the files of the vice president, 1961–63, Box 82, Lyndon B. Johnson (LBJ) Library. Shriver's recollection about receiving the Wiggins cable in New Delhi comes from his oral history, August 20, 1980, LBJ Library.

The Shriver trip to solicit invitations for Peace Corps programs is detailed in Wofford, pp. 268–74. It is also covered in Stossel, pp. 226–32 (the Bayley quote is on p. 231); Rice, pp. 71–73; and the *Peace Corps News,* vol. 1, no. 1, June 1961. The anti–Peace Corps tirade in the *Ghanian Times* is quoted in Robert Klein, "Being First: A Memoir of the First Peace Corps Volunteers, Ghana I 1961," unpublished manuscript, 2001, p. 11.

Re: the Peace Corps talent hunt, the Franklin Williams story is covered in Redmon, pp. 69–70; the Jack Hood Vaughn story comes from "How I Became Director of the Peace Corps," a chapter from his unpublished memoir, "Kill the Gringo"; Vaughn's quote about Shriver and jocks comes from a telephone interview on April 16, 2008; and material on the Bates and Houston hires come from Redmon, pp. 81–84. The Moyers quote comes from Stossel, p. xiii. The Charles Peters quote comes from his memoir, *Tilting at Windmills: An Autobiography* (Reading, MA: Addison-Wesley, 1988), p. 120.

The Maiatico building is described in Stossel, p. 211.

The JFK quote praising Shriver as a lobbyist comes from Peter Braestrup, "Peace Corpsman No. 1—A Progress Report," *New York Times Magazine,* December 17, 1961.

Rep. Frances Bolton's quotes come from the Associated Press (AP) story, "Rep. Bolton Hits Peace Corps Plan," *New York Times,* March 8, 1961. The Daughters of the American Revolution (DAR) resolutions come from Wofford, p. 243; AP, "D.A.R. Move Asks Peace Corps Ban," *New York Times,* April 19, 1961; and United Press International (UPI), "D.A.R. Sends Plea to Congress to Check Reds in the Caribbean," *New York Times,* April 20, 1961.

The five *New Yorker* cartoons ran in the issues of March 25, August 19, September

16, November 25, and December 2, 1961. The Meehan piece of humor ran in the August 26 issue of that same year.

Alyce Ostrow's story comes from an interview with her on April 13, 2008, and an e-mail on July 23, 2008. The quote about Shriver draining people comes from the Braestrup magazine article. Shriver's quote about picking brains comes from the blog John Coyne Babbles, October 9, 2007. Shriver's quote about conflicting points of view comes from Wofford, p. 279.

Chapter 3. The Pioneer Volunteers and the Postcard

The story of the first Ghana Volunteers is fully documented in Klein's unpublished 2001 manuscript. One pioneer Ghana Volunteer, Arnold Zeitlin, wrote a very useful and engaging memoir, *To the Peace Corps, with Love* (New York: Doubleday, 1965).

For the section on Ghana, I have consulted the evaluation reports by Charles Peters, April 1962; Robert Lystad, December 11–20, 1962; and Richard Richter, January 6, 1965, in *Peace Corps Country Program Evaluations 1961–1967,* National Archives, Washington, D.C.

The UCLA training anecdotes come from the Klein manuscript, a follow-up telephone conversation with Klein on July 7, 2008, and a telephone interview with David Apter on June 29, 2008. The quotes from the Apter-Shriver interview and the Apter-Nkrumah phone call were recalled by Apter in that interview. The Nkrumah phone call episode is also described by the Klein manuscript, pp. 28–29. The quote about learning soccer and the creation of the cigarette lighter pun come from comments by John Demos in the *First Annual Peace Corps Report* (Washington, D.C.: Peace Corps, 1962), pp. 36–38.

Shriver's pep talk to the Ghana Volunteers in Washington is covered in the Klein manuscript, p. 35. The White House reception, including the comment by Klein, is covered by Tom Wicker, "Kennedy Praises 74 in Peace Corps," *New York Times,* August 29, 1961. The text of Kennedy's remarks was carried in the *New York Times* the same day under the headline, "President's Talk on Corps." Newell Flather's comment to the president comes from the Klein manuscript, p. 36; Klein describes the Ghana ambassador's party and aftermath on pp. 36–37.

The statistics about the Ghana secondary school system come from the Lystad evaluation. The problem of memorization in African schools was discussed in my article, "Peace Corps Teaching in Africa," *Africa Report,* December 1966. The concept of "chew and pour" is described in the Klein manuscript, pp. 52–53, while the incident about Tom Peterson's Greek classes comes from the same source, p. 51. The problem of misunderstanding accents and meaning is covered in the Klein manuscript, p. 49.

The Peters quote about the role of Volunteer teachers comes from his evaluation report. The goals of the Peace Corps are set down in Sec. 2, Declaration of Purpose, of the Peace Corps Act, Public Law 87–293, which can be found at www.archives.gov/education/lessons/peace-corps/images. This declaration of purpose is usually broken down and simplified in Peace Corps publications as the three goals; see, for example, *First Annual Peace Corps Report,* p. 5.

Volunteer housing is discussed by Demos in the first annual Peace Corps Report, p. 37; Tom Livingston, "A Peace Corps Teacher Writes Home," *Peace Corps News,* January 1962, and the Klein manuscript, p. 45. Klein also discusses the servant situation and the Laura Damon incident on pp. 42 and 68. The summer vacation conflict is covered by the Klein manuscript, pp. 79–81. The ease of involvement in Ghanian life for teachers living off the compound is demonstrated throughout Zeitlin's book.

For the Peace Corps problems with Nkrumah, I have consulted Zeitlin, pp. 145–50; two cables from Ghana Peace Corps director George Carter to Washington on December 3, 1962, *Subject File of the Office of the Director, 1961–66,* Peace Corps files, National Archives; and the Klein manuscript, pp. 76–79. Zeitlin describes the Nkrumah farewell party, pp. 347–50.

Shriver's visit to Ghana was described in the Klein manuscript, pp. 94–96, and in a John Demos phone interview on July 8, 2008. The *Time* photographer/reporter team story comes from Schwarz, p. 42. The living quarters of Livingston were described by him in his article in the *Peace Corps News.*

For the Nigeria postcard episode, I have consulted "The infamous Peace Corps postcard" at www.peacecorpsworldwide.org/pc-writers and the more elaborate version in John Coyne's blogs in ten parts, August 30, 2007–September 11, 2007, which can be found at www.peacecorpsworldwide.org/babbles; Redmon, pp. 118–28; Stossel, pp. 251–55; Brent Ashabranner, *A Moment of History: The First Ten Years of the Peace Corps* (New York: Doubleday, 1971), pp. 81–92; and Rice, pp. 241–44.

The Peters quote about Margery Michelmore comes from Rice, p. 244. The Wiggins quote on the domino theory comes from Redmon, p. 120. All the Timothy Adams quotes come from Redmon, pp. 121–24. Michelmore's quotes come from "Incident 'Blown Up,' Corps Member Says," *New York Times,* October 21, 1961. The recipient of the postcard was identified in "She Had No Idea," *Time,* October 27, 1961. President Kennedy's note to Margery is quoted in Rice, p. 244.

The Eisenhower quotes come from Leo Egan, "Eisenhower, at Rally Here, Derides Kennedy Policies," *New York Times,* October 25, 1961. Sandburg's quotes come from Russell Baker, "Sandburg Is Critical of Eisenhower on the Peace Corps," *New York Times,* October 26, 1961. John Updike's quotes are in "The Talk of the Town," *New Yorker,* October 28, 1961. The musical *Hot Spot* is discussed in John Keating, "'Hot Spot' On Spot," *New York Times,* April 14, 1963; Howard Taubman, "The Theater: 'Hot Spot,' Musical at Majestic Stars Judy Holliday, *New York Times,* April 20, 1963; and "Torpid Trio," *New Yorker,* April 27, 1963.

Aubrey Brown's refusal to eat at the university is described by Redmon, p. 128. Kennedy's admonition to Harris Wofford about postcards comes from Wofford, p. 284. The Ashabranner postcard story comes from Ashabranner, p. 91. The Wiggins quote about the postcard as a vaccination comes from Redmon, p. 128.

Chapter 4. The Battle of Britain

All the Peace Corps country evaluation reports can be found in the National Archives in twenty-six boxes filed under the rubric of *Peace Corps Country Program Evaluations 1961–1967.*

There are histories of the evaluation division in Rice, pp. 110–12; Redmon, pp. 199–218; and Stossel, pp. 255–58. Haddad's quote about the Peace Corps correcting itself before the press starts screaming comes from Redmon, p. 199. The Shriver quote about *Time* magazine comes from Rice, p. 110.

Peters's quotes about Shriver as a lightweight and a great man come from a Peters interview on May 12, 2008. Klein's description of Peters comes from his unpublished 2001 manuscript, p. 23.

The Peters quote about the squandering of idealism in Pakistan comes from his memoir, p. 121. Gelman's descriptions of the woeful Somalia program come from his December 1962 evaluation. The description of the Philippines program is based on an interview with Maureen Carroll on July 17, 2008.

The story of the attempt to get rid of Peters and the evaluation efforts is told in full by Redmon, pp. 205–7. The *Time* cover story, "It Is Almost As Good As Its Intentions," was published in the July 5, 1963 edition. Sargent Shriver's marginal notes are on the copy of the *December 12—17, 1962, Dominican Republic Evaluation* in the National Archives. Rice, p. 110, and Stossel, p. 255, title their sections on Peters, "The Conscience of the Peace Corps."

The Peters quotes about Wiggins's attitude toward evaluation come from a July 27, 2008, telephone interview. The Cook quote about the Battle of Britain comes from Redmon, p. 214.

Peters's views on community development come from his memoirs, p. 123. The views of David Hapgood and Meridan Bennett on the community development program in Peru come from their book, *Agents of Change* (Boston: Little, Brown, 1968), pp. 129–30. The story of the project in Blanquita, Colombia, is on pp. 133–35.

Peters's views on Shriver and expansion and on the attitude of the evaluators toward the numbers game come from the July 28, 2008, telephone interview. Kevin Delany's portrait of the Volunteers moving their livestock across Nepal comes from his *June 26—July 19, 1963, Evaluation Report of Nepal,* pp. 35–37. My portrait of Volunteer Judy Erdmann comes from the *Overseas Evaluation of Cameroon, Distributed January 13, 1966,* pp. c–e.

The information about the Ethiopia program comes from Stanley Meisler and Richard Lipez, *Overseas Evaluation, Ethiopia, Distributed May 24, 1965.* The expansion of the India program is discussed in the evaluation report of Lipez and Meisler, *India, May 20, 1966.* Brent Ashabranner's views on the expansion of India can be found in his memoir, pp. 219–23. The results of the expansion can be found in Allen Bradford, David Hapgood, and J. Richard Starkey, *India Evaluation, July 28, 1967.* The letter to the *Volunteer* magazine is quoted in Ashabranner, pp. 223–24. Ashabranner discusses Micronesia on pp. 217–19 and describes Pritchard's drive to expand on p. 217.

Tom Quimby's comments on evaluation come from Redmon, pp. 209–10. The India staff's reply to the 1967 evaluation is included with the evaluation report in the National Archives.

O'Brien outlined his ideas about evaluation to me in an interview on July 31, 2008.

Chapter 5. Friday, November 22, 1963
The story about Nancy Norton and her roommate in Peru is based on Norton's narrative, *"Tu Presidente Esta Muerte!"* in the *Peace Corps Reader* (Washington, D.C.: Peace Corps Office of Public Affairs, 1968), pp. 94–95. Peggy Anderson's story is based on e-mail messages from her on September 22–23, 2008. Donna Shalala's encounter comes from Schwarz, p. 45. Richard Lipez's account comes from his e-mail messages on August 29 and August 30, 2008. Maureen Carroll wrote of her reaction to the assassination for a round-up of returned Volunteer reactions that appeared under the title "I Was in the Chorus That Answered Him" in *Peace Corps Volunteer,* December 1963. Jack Vaughn's recall of November 22 is quoted in Redmon, p. 393.

Shriver's reaction is described in Redmon, p. 391, and in Stossel, pp. 297–300. Stossel discusses Shriver's relations with Johnson, pp. 301–22. Bobby Kennedy's angry remark to Shriver about the date for the Johnson speech comes from Stossel, p. 316.

The story of Johnson's badgering of the reluctant Shriver to accept the job of czar of the war on poverty is based on Stossel, pp. 345–54; Michael Beschloss, *Taking Charge: The Johnson White House Tapes, 1963–1964* (New York: Touchstone, 1998), pp. 202–5, 208–13; a September 18, 2008, e-mail message from William Josephson that included a copy of his July 12, 2003, letter to Scott Stossel; and the four recorded phone conversations of Johnson and Shriver on February 1, 1964, from Citations 1804, 1807, 1809, and 1815 on WH6402.01 and WH6402.02 on the Web site of the University of Virginia's Miller Center of Public Affairs, http://millercenter.org/academic/presidentialrecordings.

Shriver's attempt to run both the Peace Corps and the War on Poverty, and his decision to resign from the Peace Corps, is covered by Stossel, pp. 447–50.

Chapter 6. U.S. Troops Invade the Dominican Republic
For background on the U.S. intervention, I have depended on Abraham F. Lowenthal, *The Dominican Intervention* (Baltimore, MD: Johns Hopkins University Press, 1995), and Tad Szulc, *Dominican Diary* (New York: Dell, 1966). Szulc describes the Peace Corps nurses on p. 75. The Francisco Caamaño quotes come from Josef Evans, "The Only Americans Welcome," draft 2 of the unpublished manuscript of the play, p. 40.

Frank Mankiewicz's views on community development were expressed in "A Revolutionary Force," his article in *The Peace Corps Reader,* pp. 46–59. Dean Rusk is quoted in Rice, p. 258. Mankiewicz's quote about the Peace Corps not being an instrument against U.S. policy comes from an interview on October 2, 2008. Shriver's resistance to an Algeria program is described in Rice, pp. 266–67. The Peace Corps emphasis on Latin America was covered in Hedrick Smith, "Peace Corps Aims at Latin Nations," *New York Times,* December 3, 1962.

For the story of Charles Kamen, I have depended on the *First Annual Peace Corps Report,* p. 55; an AP article, "Peace Corps Youth Attacked in House," *New York Times,* August 8, 1961; a UPI article, "Draft Appeal Slated," *New York Times,* September 7, 1961; a UPI article, "Kamen Is Rejected," *New York Times,* September 26, 1961; a Daniel Rapoport e-mail on June 23, 2008; a Maureen Carroll interview on July 17, 2008; and a Charles Peters phone interview on August 6, 2008.

The Johnson speech justifying the invasion is covered in "Text of Johnson's Address on U.S. Moves in the Conflict in the Dominican Republic," *New York Times,* May 3, 1965.

Kirby Jones's story is based on his unpublished manuscript, *Journal Written by Kirby Jones, Peace Corps Volunteer in Dominican Republic, 1963–65. Pages 512–609: April 24–July 26, 1965. Period Covering the Dominican Revolution;* an interview on October 1, 2008; an e-mail message from Jones on October 31, 2008; and Schwarz, pp. 77, 79–81.

Bob Satin's adventures were recounted by him on YouTube, October 3, 2007 (www.youtube.com/watch?v=VJEbAOW1bRQ) and in two phone interviews on September 22, 2008, and November 10, 2008. The critique is based on the Jones diary, p. 565, and a phone interview with Roberta (B. J.) Warren on November 1, 2008.

The Alice Meehan quote is cited in "Peace Corps Dilemma," an editorial in the *Washington Post,* May 26, 1965, and in Schwarz, p. 74. The Joan Temple quotes come from Lee Winfrey, "Peace Corps Still Safe in Santo Domingo," a *Chicago Daily News* dispatch in the *Washington Post,* May 16 1965. The Volunteer quote about "pupils scared to work with us" comes from Dan Kurzman, "Warriors' Arrival Ends Peace Corps Welcome," *Washington Post,* May 15, 1965. The Warren quote about being accused of being communist comes from Martin Arnold, "Peace Corps Plea Frees Marines," *New York Times,* May 7, 1965. The *Richmond News Leader* complaint and the *Herald Tribune* reporter's remark about the war corps can be found in the *Fourth Annual Peace Corps Report* (Washington: Peace Corps Office of Public Affairs, 1965), p. 70.

The report of the May 6 White House meeting was reproduced as Document 5 in *Foreign Relations of the United States, 1964–1968, Vol. XXXII,* pp. 133–36. Bill Moyers's quote to Mankiewicz about going down to the Dominican Republic was recalled by Mankiewicz in his oral history interview on April 18, 1969, LBJ Library, p. 44.

The account of the dispatch of Mankiewicz to Santo Domingo, including his quotes, is based on the April 18, 1969, oral history, pp. 41–45, augmented by my October 2, 2008, interview with him.

The story of the Volunteer letter to President Johnson comes mainly from the Kirby Jones diary. The letter is reproduced at the end of the diary. Jones's reporting of Mankiewicz's argument against publishing the letter is set down on pp. 580–81 of the diary. Lynda Edwards's reaction is from Schwarz, p. 82.

The Bundy memorandum is reprinted in *Foreign Relations, 1964–1968, Vol. XXXII* as Document 137, pp. 329–30. The story of Operation 1500 is told in Jack Rosenblum's evaluation of the Dominican Republic program, dated June 3, 1966, and in Kevin Lowther and C. Payne Lucas, *Keeping Kennedy's Promise: The Peace Corps: Unmet Hope of the New Frontier* (Boulder, CO: Westview Press, 1978), pp. 31–33. The Warren quote comes from a phone interview on November 1, 2008.

Johnson's holdup of sending the Volunteers to India is described in Lowther and Lucas, pp. 33–34, and in the evaluation of the India program by Richard Lipez and Stanley Meisler, dated May 20, 1966. Johnson's quote about the Volunteers being "the first ones to jump us" comes from his recorded phone conversation with Bill Moyers at the LBJ ranch on November 9, 1965, and Citation No. 9144 and Tape

WH6511.04 on the Web site of the University of Virginia's Miller Center of Public Affairs, http://millercenter.org/academic/presidentialrecordings.

Chapter 7. Johnny Hood

Background to the U.S.–Panamanian dispute can be found in Tad Szulc, "Reports on Difficulties in Panama Reached the U.S. 48 Hours Late," *New York Times,* January 14, 1964. Bill Moyers's recommendation of Jack Vaughn is in an undated memo in the National Security Files, LBJ Library. Vaughn describes his meeting with Johnson in Senegal both in "How I Became Director of the Peace Corps," a chapter from his unpublished memoir "Kill the Gringo," and in his Oral History interview, LBJ Library, December 4, 1968. Vaughn's reception in Panama is described by Richard Eder, "Panama Irked by U.S. Proposal to Survey for Canal in Colombia," *New York Times,* April 18, 1964.

Johnson's instructions to Vaughn for the Dominican Republic report was made in a recorded telephone conversation on May 3, 1965, Citation No. 7551 and Tape WH6505.03 on the Web site of the University of Virginia's Miller Center of Public Affairs, http://millercenter.org/academic/presidentialrecordings. The account of the task force meeting comes mainly from a telephone interview of Vaughn, April 16, 2008. Johnson's comment about the news media comes from a handwritten note by Jack Valenti, dated May 8, 1965, in the National Security Files of Jack Valenti, Box 13, LBJ Library.

Vaughn's comment about "communist elements" came in a recorded telephone conversation with Johnson, Citation No. 7368, Tape WH6504.06 on the Miller Center Web site. His run-in with Robert Kennedy at an interagency meeting was described by Vaughn in an April 16, 2008, telephone interview.

The account of the Vaughn-Kennedy clash at the State Department briefing is based on the April 16, 2008, Vaughn telephone interview; the Frank Mankiewicz oral history interview on May 1, 1969, LBJ Library; and the Frank Mankiewicz oral history interview on June 26, 1969, John F. Kennedy (JFK) Library.

Shriver's comment on Johnson's refusal to let Moyers return to the Peace Corps comes from the Shriver oral history interview on August 20, 1980, LBJ Library. Johnson's final selection of Vaughn as successor to Shriver is related in both Vaughn's chapter from "Kill the Gringo" and in Redmon, p. 403. The Tom Mann–LBJ phone conversation cited by Vaughn can be found as Citation No. 9511 and Tape WH6601.09 on the Miller Center Web site. The Peters quote on Moyers comes from Redmon, pp. 402–3.

Brent Ashabranner's comparison of Shriver and Vaughn and his quote by Vaughn come from his book, p. 229.

Chapter 8. The Specter of Vietnam

The Peace Corps cable to Saigon can be found in Box 42 of National Security File—Agency File, LBJ Library. Ross Pritchard's comments came in a telephone interview on May 5, 2008. Vaughn's comments on the Vietnam trip and on President Johnson's pressure to send the Peace Corps there came in a telephone interview on April16, 2008.

Johnson's quotes at Vaughn's swearing-in ceremony come from "Excerpts from the President's Remarks on Vietnam," *New York Times*, March 2, 1966.

Gerald Berreman's case against the Peace Corps is described and discussed in Ashabranner, pp. 273–74. The Marlyn Dalsimer quote comes from Schwarz, p. 127.

The Paul Theroux story was detailed in John Coyne's essay "Living on the Edge: Paul Theroux" on www.peacecorpsworldwide.org/pc-writers and in Coyne's analysis of the life and work of Theroux on the independent forum for returned Peace Corps Volunteers, www.peacecorpsonline.org, dated August 15, 2007. The Kirby Jones–Jack Vaughn conflict over a Vietnam protest letter was described by Jones in an October 1, 2008, interview and in Schwarz, pp. 104–5.

For the Bruce Murray case, I have depended on Schwarz, pp. 103–11; Ashabranner, pp. 276–80; John Osborn, "Dissent: Peace Corps On the Line," *The Volunteer,* March–April 1970; "The Bruce Murray Case," *The Volunteer,* March–April 1970; an AP article, "Peace Corps Aide Ousted Over War," *New York Times,* June 30, 1967; John H. Fenton, "A Former Envoy Testifies in Peace Corps Case," *New York Times,* September 17, 1969; and Fenton, "War Foe Recalls Peace Corps Move," *New York Times,* September 21, 1969. Murray's recollections are from Schwarz, p. 107. The Peace Corps spokesman quote about Vietnam being a local issue in Chile comes from "Peace Corps Aide Ousted Over War; Volunteer in Chile Wrote Letter Scoring Bombing," *New York Times,* June 30, 1967.

The antiwar protest in El Salvador was described in a phone interview by Mark Schneider, December 16, 2008. The quotations from Secretary William Rogers's cable, Director Joseph Blatchford's letter, Richard Wilson's column, and Congressman William Scherle's statement come from the Osborn article in the *Volunteer.* The Blatchford report to Congress is cited in Ashabranner, pp. 295–98.

The seizure of a floor of the Peace Corps building is described in Peter Osnos, "Protesters Vacate Peace Corps Office," *Washington Post,* May 10, 1970; Schwarz, pp. 124–37; and Elizabeth Cobbs Hoffman, *All You Need Is Love: The Peace Corps and the Spirit of the 1960s* (Cambridge, MA: Harvard University Press, 1998), pp. 228–29. The CRV statement excerpts come from Schwarz, p. 124. Blatchford's recollections come from an interview on January 26, 2009. Thomas Roeser's recollections of the phone calls from H. R. Haldeman were reported in the John Coyne blog, April 16, 2007, at www.peacecorpsworldwide.org/babbles. Haldeman's notes can be found in White House Special Files, Haldeman, Box 41, Nixon Library, National Archives. The Ehrlichman-Blatchford phone conversation was quoted in Hoffman, p. 229.

Michael Schmicker's comment about the War Corps in Thailand comes from his privately published memoir, p. 32. Schmicker recounts his Air America escapade and his confrontation with Kevin Delany on pp. 177–93. James Jouppi's description of fraternization with GIs is on p. 618 of his privately printed memoir, *War of Hearts and Minds.*

Schmicker describes the protest meeting with the ambassador on pp. 153–58. The confrontation between Delany and Vice President Spiro Agnew's aide was described in a phone interview with Delany on December 31, 2008.

Chapter 9. The Wrath of Richard Nixon

Patrick J. Buchanan's quotes about the Peace Corps come from his memo to Richard Nixon, February 20, 1970, Box 33, Ehrlichman files, White House Special Files, Nixon Library, National Archives. Clark Mollenhoff's quotes come from his memo to Nixon, March 6, 1970, Box 33, Ehrlichman files. The Buchanan quote about changing the Peace Corps to a more altruistic outfit comes from his memo to Nixon, March 7, 1970, Box 33, Ehrlichman files.

The *Wall Street Journal* article that upset Nixon was David C. Anderson, "After Peace Corps, Some Turn Radical," March 18, 1970. Nixon's directive calling for a quiet phasing out of the Peace Corps and VISTA came in the form of a memo from John R. Brown III to Ehrlichman and Henry Kissinger, cited in *From the President: Richard Nixon's Secret Files,* Bruce Oudes, ed. (New York: Harper Perennial Library, 1990), pp. 109–10. The memo from Lamar Alexander to Bryce Harlow is dated March 26, 1970, and can be found in Box 12, White House Central Files, Nixon Library, National Archives.

Otto Passman's diatribe against the Peace Corps is in the *Congressional Record,* February 9, 1972. The memo about not doing as well as expected came from William Timmons to Ehrlichman, May 15, 1970, Box 33, Ehrlichman files. Haldeman's report that Nixon wanted to decimate the Peace Corps came from H. R. Haldeman, *The Haldeman Diaries: Inside the Nixon White House* (New York: Putnam, 1994), p. 181.

The account of the meeting in which Nixon told Blatchford to get more young men like himself is in a memo for the president's file prepared by Richard V. Allen, September 11, 1969, Box 33, Ehrlichman files. Blatchford's reports of what Nixon told him about the Peace Corps come from an interview with Blatchford on January 26, 2009, and a follow-up phone conversation on January 30, 2009.

The budget battle with Passman is described in P. David Searles, *The Peace Corps Experience: Challenge & Change, 1969–1976* (Lexington: University Press of Kentucky, 1997), pp. 171–74, and in Hoffman, pp. 231–32.

The disappointment over the removal of Vaughn and the appointment of Blatchford is described in Ashabranner, pp. 288–92. Nixon's requirement that the new director have toughness is stated in a memo from Alexander Butterfield to Harry Flemming, March 26, 1970, Box 12, White House Central Files. Lew Butler's rejection of the offer is reported in a note from Ehrlichman to Nixon, February 18, 1969, Box 33, Ehrlichman files. The Butler quote is from a January 27, 2009, e-mail.

Blatchford's New Directions are described by Searles, pp. 26–29. Blatchford's quote about the cry for skilled Volunteers comes from his undated memo to the country directors of the Peace Corps, Box 33, Ehrlichman files. Kissinger's comments on the new Blatchford approach come from his undated memo to Nixon, Box 33, Ehrlichman files.

Blatchford's memo to Alexander Haig on the recruitment of "skilled Americans of greater maturity" is dated January 7, 1970, Box 3, White House Central Files. Blatchford's memo to the Republican House members is in Ashabranner, pp. 295–99. Ronald Tschetter's quotes come from Nicholas Benequista, "World to Peace Corps: Skilled Volunteers Needed," *Christian Science Monitor,* April 25, 2008.

The request for Blatchford to look into the Micronesia problem came in a memo from Butterfield to Ehrlichman and was relayed to Blatchford on April 22, 1969, Box 33, Ehrlichman files. Blatchford's lengthy reply came in a memo to Ehrlichman, April 25, 1969, Box 33. Kissinger's reaction was relayed to Blatchford in an April 29, 1969, memo from Ehrlichman, Box 33. Blatchford's unsolicited paper, "My Observations on the Need for a New Dynamic in U.S. Policy on Latin America," was sent to Ehrlichman and Kissinger on September 9, 1969, also found in Box 33.

Blatchford described the cutting of the budget and the creation of ACTION in a January 26, 2009, interview. Nixon's admonition to put a tough guy in charge of the Peace Corps can be found in *The Haldeman Diaries*, p. 291.

The Shriver quote about ACTION can be found in Hoffman, p. 240. She describes the creation of ACTION on p. 231. It is also covered in "Merger for VISTA Cleared in Senate," *New York Times*, June 4, 1971.

Chapter 10. The Fall of the Lion of Judah
I have leaned heavily on Paulos Milkias, *Haile Selassie, Western Education, and Political Revolution in Ethiopia* (Youngstown, NY: Cambria Press, 2006), which describes in great detail the role of Western education in the revolution against the emperor.

The statistics about tenant farmers comes from my article, "Ethiopia Land Reform Hits Peasants Hardest," *Los Angeles Times*, August 29, 1968. The numbers of Americans in Ethiopia and the size of the Ethiopian military come from National Intelligence Estimate No. 75/76–70, dated May 21, 1970, and reprinted in *Foreign Relations, 1969–1976, Vol. E-5, Documents on Africa, 1969–1972* (published by the Department of State's Office of the Historian, 2005; available on www.history.state.gov).

Harris Wofford's quotes about Volunteers as Connecticut Yankees and about the radicalization of the Ethiopian Peace Corps come from an interview on March 5, 2009. The relationship between the emperor and the Volunteers is described by John Coyne on his blog www.peacecorpsworldwide.org/babbles; December 11, 2007. The Tegegne Yeteshawork quote comes from p. 1 of the Lipez-Meisler evaluation of Ethiopia in 1965.

Lipez's recollections about teaching in Ethiopia come from an e-mail message on February 8, 2009. The background on student unrest, the student quote about overthrowing His Majesty's government, and the Volunteer quote about being Americans come from my article, "Haile Selassie Challenged by Student Unrest," *Los Angeles Times*, June 1, 1969. I covered the Tilahan Gizaw killing and the bloody suppression of the student demonstrators in "Selassie Whip Has Subdued Student Revolt," *Los Angeles Times*, February 22, 1970.

Joseph Murphy's resignation and the impact of the student rebellion on the Peace Corps are covered in my "Peace Corps Caught in Political Ferment," *Los Angeles Times*, February 16, 1970. The reports of Volunteers Eleanor Shumway and Craig Johnson are quoted in the same article. The herding of students into concentration camps is described in my article, "Youths Held by Thousands in Ethiopia," *Los Angeles Times*, August 1, 1971.

The success of the student uprising, the fall of the emperor, the takeover of the revolution by the military, and the rise of Mengistu Haile Mariam are described by

Milkias in detail, chapters 9–14. The quotation of Milkias concluding that the students, not the military, powered the revolution can be found on p. xix of the same book.

The Peace Corps's difficulties in Africa were described in my *Los Angeles Times* articles, "Political Woes Hinder Peace Corps in Africa," June 30, 1969, and "Peace Corps Losing Ground with Africans," May 3, 1970. More details on Gabon came from Larry O'Brien, former Peace Corps director in Gabon, in a phone call on March 16, 2009; on Tanzania from Ron Hert, "No Room for PC in Tanzania's Policy of Self-Reliance," the *Volunteer,* September 1969; on Libya from "Libya pulls the plug on 'model' program," the *Volunteer,* December 1969. I covered the problems in Uganda in my article, "All Peace Corpsmen Pulling Out of Uganda," *Los Angeles Times,* October 6, 1972.

Chapter 11. The Militant Sam Brown
David Broder's description of Sam Brown comes from his book, *Changing of the Guard: Power and Leadership in America* (New York: Simon and Schuster, 1980), p. 140. The quote about euphoria over Brown's appointment appears in Joseph Nocera, "Sam Brown and the Peace Corps: All Talk, No ACTION," *Washington Monthly,* September 1978. Brown's background, including his work on the antiwar moratorium and his appointment to head ACTION, is covered in Francine du Plessix Gray, "A Reporter at Large: The Moratorium and the New Mobe," the *New Yorker,* January 3, 1970, and Terence Smith, "Peace Corps: Alive But Not So Well," *New York Times Magazine,* December 26, 1977. Brown explained his shift from Eugene McCarthy to Jimmy Carter in an op-ed piece, "Against McCarthy," *New York Times,* October 30, 1976.

Brown's views on changing the Peace Corps, including his quote about the Peace Corps as a remaining symbol of innocence, are described in Karen de Witt, "Peace Corps Ideas Get Badly Mired in Politics," *New York Times,* May 6, 1979. The same topic is covered in Schwarz, pp. 179–87. Brown's meeting in Tanzania is described in the Peace Corps publication, *ACTION Update,* March 1, 1978. Petty's quotes come from Schwarz, p. 183. Carolyn Payton's quote about Brown never looking at her directly comes from James M. Perry, "The Peace Corps Is Far from Peaceful under Sam Brown," *Wall Street Journal,* January 16, 1979.

The Jamaica Brigade incident is described in de Witt's May 6, 1979, *Times* article; in Warren Brown, "Efforts to Change Peace Corps Image Have Gone Nowhere," *Washington Post,* December 23, 1978 (which includes the quotes from Brown and Carter-Miller); and in the Perry article.

I have put together the story of the brouhaha in Morocco from phone interviews with Ruth Saxe and Ellen Yaffe and from the Perry article. The resignation of Payton is covered in Warren Brown, "'Political Activism' Peace Corps Goal, Ex-Director Asserts," *Washington Post,* December 8, 1978.

The Richard Celeste quotes come from a phone interview on May 21, 2009. The presidential order giving the Peace Corps autonomy is described in "President's Order Gives Peace Corps Autonomy within ACTION," *ACTION Update,* June 18, 1979. The quotes of Vice President Walter Mondale come from "Celeste Sworn In as Peace Corps Director," *ACTION Update,* July 12, 1979.

Chapter 12. Mayhem and Illness

Peace Corps Online (www.peacecorpsonline.org) lists all Peace Corps Volunteer fatalities by date, cause, and country. My account of the Bill Kinsey trial is based on Peace Corps files, obtained by John Coyne under the Freedom of Information Act. The most important document, which details all the evidence in the case and the verdict, is the text of the judgment of Judge H. G. Platt delivered in the High Court of Tanzania at Mwanza on September 19, 1966.

The Paul Sack letter to the Volunteers, dated April 1, 1966, comes from the Peace Corps files. The annoyance by Tanzanian attorney-general Mark Bomani is described in an April 2, 1966, memo by the deputy director of the Peace Corps in Tanzania, and the Peace Corps's pledge of non-interference is described in a letter from Sack to the Deputy General Counsel in Washington, July 4, 1966. The Volunteer quote to the AP appeared in Dennis Neeld, "Murder Trial Angers Peace Corps Volunteers," *Sunday Nation* (Nairobi), May 13, 1966.

The story of the Tonga murder case is reported in detail by Philip Weiss in his book *American Taboo: A Murder in the Peace Corps* (New York: Harper Perennial, 2005) and in his article, "Stalking Her Killer," *New York* magazine, May 2, 2004. The quote from the psychiatrist's testimony is on p. 259 of *American Taboo,* and the verdict and judge's recommendation is on pp. 274–75. The letters of assurance that Dennis Priven would be confined to a psychiatric hospital are on pp. 278–79.

The quote about the incidence of Peace Corps illness or death being comparable comes from "7 Peace Corpsmen die in 1969," the *Volunteer,* January–February 1970. The General Accounting Office report is "Peace Corps: Initiatives for Addressing Safety and Security Challenges, Hold Promise, but Progress Should Be Assessed," GAO-02-818, July 2002. The reply of Director Gaddi Vasquez is on pp. 47–53 of the report.

The *Dayton Daily News* series ran from October 26 to November 1, 2003: The Brian Krow case is discussed in Russell Carollo and Mei-Ling Hapgood, "Mystery Deaths: Official Records Fail to Tell Complete Story," October 29, 2003. The El Salvador gang rape case is discussed in Carollo and Hapgood, "Mission of Sacrifice: Peace Corps Volunteers Face Injury, Death in Foreign Lands," October 26, 2003. The John Hale reaction to the series ran in the *Daily News* as "Easier to Believe Myth Than Face Need for Reform," November 2, 2003. The reaction by Peggy Anderson was posted on www.peacecorpsonline.org on October 29, 2003. The Peace Corps statement on Russell Carollo of the *Dayton Daily News* is quoted on www.peacecorpsonline.org, on October 23, 2003.

The total Volunteer deaths by year from 1990 to 2007 are listed in *The Health of the Volunteer 2007* (Washington, D.C.: Peace Corps Office of Medical Services), p. 20. I compiled the totals for earlier years from *Peace Corps Online: Volunteer Fatalities by Date.* The rape statistics for 2007 are from *The Safety of the Volunteer 2007* (Washington, D.C.: Peace Corps Office of Safety and Security), p. 7. The underreporting of rape is discussed on p. 4 of the *The Safety of the Volunteer 2007* and the general feeling of safety is discussed on p. 45 of the same report. The statistics on incidence of illness come from *The Health of the Volunteer 2007,* pp. 7, 9, and 11–12. The total of medical evacuations to the United States comes from p. 25 of the same report.

Chapter 13. The Rich Lady in Her First Job for Pay
My profile of Loret Ruppe is based on the articles "Ruppe Nominated as Peace Corps Director" in *ACTION Update,* March 13, 1981; "Reagan Campaign Head To Be Peace Corps Head," *New York Times,* February 15, 1981; Kathryn Tolbert, "Winner's Way: Potomac's Loret Ruppe Bones Up to Direct the Peace Corps," *Washington Post,* March 26, 1981; a May 7, 2009, phone conversation with Deborah Harding, and a July 16, 2009, interview with Jody Olsen.

The anecdotes about the "Peach Corps" and the White House liaison can be found in Honor Moore, "The Heiress Who Saved the Peace Corps," *New York Times,* December 29, 1996. The comments about the budget being smaller than that of marching bands and filed under miscellaneous come from Loret Ruppe's speech at the thirty-fifth-anniversary celebrations, March 1, 1996, Peace Corps Online (www .peacecorpsonline.org). The anecdote about her mother at Fort Benning comes from a phone interview with Carroll Bouchard on June 10, 2009.

The quote about taking the Peace Corps out of politics comes from the anniversary speech. The Sykes letter is quoted in Francis X. Clines and Bernard Weinraub, "Briefing," *New York Times,* December 5, 1981. The controversies over Tom Pauken and Edward Curran are detailed in Mark Huber, *The Peace Corps: Out of Step with Reagan,* a Heritage Foundation report, December 5, 1984. There is more on the Pauken case in Barbara Crossette, "Peace Corps Seeks a Review of Cuts," *New York Times,* November 1, 1981, and Karen de Witt, "Peace Corps, Autonomy in Sight, Marking 20th Year," *New York Times,* June 20, 1981. There is more on the Curran case in Howard Kurtz, "Peace Corps Director Taped Talk with Her Deputy Last Summer," *Washington Post,* January 7, 1984, and in Mary Battiata, "The Curran Controversy: Reagan's Choice for NEH Chief Faces Opposition from Moderates," *Washington Post,* February 26, 1985.

The indictment of Ruppe as a thorn in President Reagan's side is on page 1 of the Heritage Foundation report. Ruppe told the story of President Reagan and the Fiji prime minister in her anniversary speech.

The Kissinger Commission recommendation on the Peace Corps can be found in *The Report of the President's National Bipartisan Commission on Central America* (New York: Macmillan, 1984), p. 84. Other significant findings about the need for both economic and military assistance to Central America and the importance of the Nicaraguan contras based in Honduras are on pp. 16–17, 48, 57, 63, 100–103, 114–15, 120–22, 125, and 138. A negative view of the report can be found in Arthur Schlesinger Jr., "Failings of the Kissinger Report," *New York Times,* January 17, 1984.

Schwarz devotes an extensive chapter to the Honduras buildup in Chapter 13 of her book, pp. 228–42. Ruppe's presentation to the Kissinger commission is included on pages 229–30. The increases in economic and military assistance to Honduras are described in the Library of Congress country study of Honduras, found at www .memory.loc.gov. The comparative sizes of the Peace Corps programs in Honduras come from the various Peace Corps annual reports.

Schwarz's quote about the smile button is on p. 229 of her book. The Dionne and Geisler quotes come from "Peace Corps: Some Ex-Volunteers Uneasy over Central American Role," *New York Times,* September 4, 1984. The Holcomb quote comes from

Schwarz, p. 238. Bill Mabie's story was recounted in an e-mail message on June 18, 2009. Carole Levin's quotes come from her June 24, 2009, e-mail. Steve Lenzo related his story in a June 16, 2009, e-mail. Olsen's quotes come from the July 16, 2009, interview.

Chapter 14. 200,000 Stories
The three memoirs reviewed in this chapter are Mike Tidwell, *The Ponds of Kalambayi: An African Sojourn* (New York: Lyons & Burford, 1990); Ellen Urbani Hiltebrand, *When I Was Elena* (Sag Harbor, NY: Permanent Press, 2006); and Barbara E. Joe, *Triumph & Hope: Golden Years with the Peace Corps in Honduras* (self-published, 2008).

Chapter 15. A New Name and a New World
Paul Coverdell's quote about not hiding the name of the United States and Alan Cranston's quotes about sending the wrong message come from Bill McAllister, "Peace Corps Flap: What's in a Name?" *Washington Post*, April 27, 1990. Jody Olsen's story of telling aides that Coverdell's mind was made up about the name was related in an interview on July 16, 2009. David Lamb's description of Coverdell came in an e-mail on August 4, 2009.

President George H. W. Bush's June 15, 1990, remarks to the Volunteers en route to Eastern Europe come from the Bush Library and were reprinted by Peace Corps Online (www.peacecorpsonline.org). The former Soviet bloc countries receiving Volunteers by 1995 are listed in the Peace Corps Congressional Budget Presentation, FY 1997. The GAO analysis can be found in its report, GAO/NSIAD-95–6, *Peace Corps: New Programs in Former Eastern Bloc Counties Should Be Strengthened* (December 1994). Ellen Yaffe's quote comes from an August 18, 2009, phone interview.

The doubling of the program in Poland by Philadelphia industrialist Edward Piszek was described by Tim Carroll in a phone interview on September 15, 2009. The story was repeated in more detail in "The Peace Corps in Poland: They Came, Did Their Work, and Are Moving On," in *The World of English*, April 18, 2003, reprinted at Peace Corps Online (www.peacecorpsonline.org).

Carroll's remark about standing in a line for a latrine in the Ukraine comes from an e-mail, August 23, 2009. The description of Meg Small's business trips and the need for suits and business cards in the Ukraine was reported by James Rupert, "In E. Europe, the Peace Corps Means Business," *Washington Post*, December 29, 1994. Claire St. Amant's quote about the age of her colleagues in the Ukraine was published in her article, "Not Your Father's Peace Corps," *Wall Street Journal*, August 21, 2009. Amy Utzinger's descriptions of Peace Corps life in Poland come from an e-mail on August 21, 2009. Mark Gearan's quotes come from a telephone interview on October 6, 2009. Inspector-General Gerard Roy's report was quoted by Joel Thurtell, "As Peace Corps Turns 30, Vets Fear Political Agenda," *Detroit Free Press*, undated.

Al Kamen's article on Coverdell's trips was published as "Director's Domestic Trips Favor His Home Town," *Washington Post*, January 2, 1991. Colman McCarthy's quotes appeared in his column, "Playing Politics with the Peace Corps," *Washington Post*, January 19, 1991. David Broder's comments on Coverdell and the quote from Senator Snowe are in his column, "Sen. Coverdell: A Peacemaker Admired, Cherished," *Washington Post,* July 30, 2000. Barbara Ferris's plea against naming the Peace Corps building in honor of Coverdell came in a message to former Volunteers, carried at Peace Corps Online (www.peacecorpsonline.org), July 14, 2001. Senator Dodd's plea to the Senate is in the Congressional Record for February 15, 2001, pp. S1530–32.

Chapter 16. The Expansive Mood of the Clinton Years

The profile of Carol Bellamy is based on a September 24, 2009, phone interview with Bellamy, an August 18, 2009, phone interview with Ellen Yaffe; Malcolm Gladwell, "From New York Political Wars to Ranking Idealist," *Washington Post,* September 29, 1993; Donnie Radcliffe, "Faithful to the Corps: Carol Bellamy Returns to Head the Agency She Served as a Young Volunteer," *Washington Post,* March 2, 1994; Karen De Witt, "Washington at Work: Chief and Agency Both at Crossroads as Bellamy Takes Peace Corps Helm," *New York Times,* October 15, 1995; Barbara Crossette, "Carol Bellamy—From City Hall to the World's Stage," *New York Times,* April 22, 2002; and the blog John Coyne Babbles, May 18, 2009, at www.peacecorpsworldwide.org/babbles.

The quotes of Dambaugh and Coyne about Bellamy are in Karen De Witt, "New Yorker in Line to Direct the Peace Corps," *New York Times,* June 11, 1993. Coyne reassessed her in e-mails, September 14 and 16, 2009. The politicking behind the UNICEF appointment is described by me in "Carol Bellamy: Affirmative Action: From the Peace Corps to UNICEF," *Los Angeles Times,* May 10, 1995. Her quotes about being a Volunteer and the director come from the same interview.

Shriver's quotes are from his November 29, 1990, oral history interview, LBJ Library. Shalala's 1995 remarks on Gearan were carried at Peace Corps Online (peacecorps online.org) on February 4, 2002. The quotes of Chairman Gilman, Senators Dodd and Coverdell, the five former Volunteers serving in the House, and Shalala come from "The Peace Corps: 10,000 Volunteers by the Year 2000," the transcript of the March 18, 1998, hearing of the House Committee on International Relations, which can be found at http://commdocs.house.gov/committees/intlrel.

Gearan's quote about the political appropriations saga comes from a phone interview on October 6, 2009; Schneider's quote about the lack of a constituency comes from an interview on September 8, 2009; and Bellamy's quote comes from a phone interview on September 24, 2009.

Chapter 17. The Quiet Bush Years

The Christiane Amanpour incident is recounted on the blog John Coyne Babbles (www.peacecorpsworldwide.org/babbles), March 18, 2008. Background to the Orange County case and the quote about Vasquez's career coming to an end can be found in Mark Platte, Rene Lynch, and Eric Bailey, "Gaddi Vasquez to Resign as Orange County Supervisor," *Los Angeles Times,* August 8, 1995. Background about Vasquez and his speech to the Republican convention is discussed in Frank del Olmo, "The GOP Loses its Great Latino Hope," *Los Angeles Times,* August 14, 1995.

Judy Mann's attack on the nomination is in her column, "Peace Corps Deserves Better than GOP Deadwood," *Washington Post,"* November 9, 2001. Joan Borsten and Roni Love's comments can be found on "What Returned Volunteers say about

Gaddi Vasquez," at Peace Corps Online (www.peacecorpsonline.org), August 1 and September 2, 2001. Vaughn's views on Vasquez were expressed in an article in the *Tucson Citizen,* September 10, 2001, and in his testimony to the Senate Foreign Relations Committee, November 14, 2001, found at www.peacecorpsonline.org. Vasquez was opposed in the *New York Times* editorial, "An Uninspiring Peace Corps Nominee," August 24, 2001, and in the *Los Angeles Times* editorial, "Not the One for Peace Corps," August 20, 2001. The confirmation of Vasquez is covered in "Peace Corps Online Exclusive: Senate Foreign Relations Committee Approves Vasquez 14 Votes to 4 Votes," www.peacecorpsonline.org, December 12, 2001, and in Associated Press, "U.S. Senate Confirms Gaddi Vasquez as Peace Corps Director," www.peacecorpsonline.org, January 26, 2002.

President Bush's plans for the Peace Corps are described in Elisabeth Bumiller, "A Nation Challenged: Volunteers," *New York Times,* February 16, 2002. Vasquez's remarks to Orange County officials are quoted in Dena Bunis, "Gaddi Vasquez at Peace in New Role," *Orange County Register,* September 16, 2002. The on-again, off-again resignation of Vasquez is covered in the Vasquez statement of resignation, October 23, 2003, www.peacecorpsonline.org; Al Kamen, "Peace Corps Chief Does About-Face," *Washington Post,* December 3, 2003; Patrick McGreevy, "Inside Politics: Routine Council Salute Brings Scolding from China," *Los Angeles Times,* December 8, 2003; and the Vasquez announcement that he was not resigning was released on December 18, 2003, www.peacecorpsonline.org.

The controversy over the political briefings of the Peace Corps staff is covered in Paul Kane, "Diplomats Received Political Briefings," *Washington Post,* July 24, 2007, Ralph Mayrell, "Peace Corps Politicization and Bureaucracy Criticized," Voice of America (www.voanews.com), August 2, 2007, and Matthew Blake, "All Politics is International," the *Nation,* July 25, 2007.

The story of the anti–Iraq war protest in the Dominican Republic is based on phone interviews with Aaron Kauffman (December 1, 2009), Aaron Drendel (November 24, 2009, plus several e-mail messages), and Jody Olsen (November 18, 2009) and on Sasha Polakow-Suransky, "Pre-empting Protest," the *Nation,* May 16, 1993.

The Robert Strauss articles were "Too Many Innocents Abroad," *New York Times,* January 9, 2008, and "Think Again: The Peace Corps," *Foreign Policy,* April 2008. Peace Corps director Ronald Tschetter's letter of reply was published in the July/August issue of *Foreign Policy.* The comments of Blair Reeves and Emily Armitage were published on the magazine's Web site, http:/blog.foreignpolicy.com/peacecorps. Senator Dodd's comments came in a letter to the *New York Times,* published January 14, 2008, replying to the piece by Strauss.

Chapter 18. Diplomatic Troubles

The story about the expulsion of the Peace Corps director from Tanzania is based on a November 10, 2009, interview with Christine Djondo and several of her subsequent e-mail messages; a December 2, 2009, phone interview with Ambassador Michael Retzer; a November 18, 2009, phone interview with Jody Olsen; an April 30, 2007, cable from Peace Corps director Tschetter to Ambassador Retzer; a June 28, 2007, letter from Assistant Secretary of State Jeffrey T. Bergner to Djondo; Tschetter's May 10, 2007, "Message to the Peace Corps Staff and Volunteers of Tanzania"; the Peace Corps's undated "Background and General Talking Points" on the issue; Retzer's annual campaign contributions from watchdog.net; a listing of Republican "rangers" by Public Citizen on www.whitehouseforsale.org; the official Peace Corps statement from press director Amanda Host, June 14, 2007, on Peace Corps Online (www.peacecorpsonline .org); numerous statements of support for Djondo from Volunteers on www .peacecorpsonline.org; and Ellyn Ferguson, "Dodd Puts Hold on Mark Green's Nomination for U.S. Ambassador to Tanzania, *Green Bay Press-Gazette,* June 27, 2007.

The exchange between Shriver and G. Mennen Williams is covered in the notes on an undated meeting between Peace Corps and State Department officials, Box 1, Subject File of the Office of the Director, 1961–66, National Archives. Ambassador Leland Barrows's complaints about peanut butter and Peace Corps housing is covered in my January 13, 1966, evaluation report on Cameroon, National Archives. The ambassador's later comments on the Peace Corps come from his oral history interview on February 4, 1971, by the JFK Library, obtainable online (www.jfklibrary.org/ Historical-Resources/archives).

The contrasting instructions to ambassadors can be found in a cable from Secretary of State Condoleezza Rice, marked "From the Secretary to all chiefs of mission," Subject: "Peace Corps State Department Relations," Ref: 04 State 258893; and "President George W. Bush's Letter of Instruction to Chiefs of Mission," dated July 30, 2003. Olsen's comments come from the November 18, 2009, phone interview. The quotes from the Peace Corps Act can be found in Section 2503. Brent Ashabranner's discussion of a foundation-run Peace Corps can be found in his memoir, p. 284.

Shriver's CIA policy and Kennedy's instruction to call Helms are covered in Stossel, pp. 270–72. The Grogan quote comes from Rice, p. 133, and the Dodd-Castro conversation is covered in Rice, p. 135.

Deutch's testimony was covered by Peace Corps Online under "Testimony of Coverdell," June 23, 2001. The relations with the CIA in Tanzania were described by Paul Sack and Eugene Mihaly in phone interviews December 8, 2009, and November 30, 2009, respectively.

My account of the controversy in Bolivia is based on Jean Friedman-Rudovsky and Brian Ross, "Peace Corps, Fulbright Scholar Asked to 'Spy' on Cubans, Venzuelans," ABC News, February 8, 2008; Alvaro Zuazo. "Morales Accuses U.S. Official of Spying," Associated Press, February 11, 2008; Andrew Whalen, "Ex-Volunteers Are Angry at Peace Corps Bolivia Pullout," Associated Press, October 11, 2008; and Joshua Partlow, "Policy and Passions Collide in Bolivia," *Washington Post,* October 23, 2008.

The story of Edward Lee Howard is covered in David Wise, "The Spy Who Got Away," *New York Times Magazine,* November 2, 1986, and in John Coyne, "The Spy Who Was a PCV," www.peacecorpswriters.org.

Chapter 19. Obama and the Future
Barack Obama's Cornell College speech can be found on www.barackobama.org. The story of the battle to increase the Peace Corps appropriation and the work of Rajeev

Goyal and More Peace Corps is based on Laurence Leamer, "Obama's First Betrayal," on Huffington Post, January 18, 2009; Laurence Leamer, "The Peace Corps Crisis," Huffington Post, May 14, 2009; interview with Rajeev Goyal, September 22, 2009 (and subsequent e-mail messages); Rajeev Goyal, "What Happened to Obama's Promise of 16,000 Peace Corps Volunteers by 2011?" Peace Corps Online (www.peacecorpsonline .org), December 3, 2009; and Rajeev Goyal, "Congratulations! Senate Approves Highest Single-Year Increase in Peace Corps History," an e-mail broadcast to many on December 14, 2009.

The rumor about James Arena-DeRosa as a candidate for director is covered in Al Kamen, "No Peace at the Corps," a segment of his "In the Loop" column, *Washington Post,* May 11, 2009, and David Searles, "A Worrisome Possibility: The Candidacy of James Arena-DeRosa," posted on the John Coyne Babbles blog on www.peacecorpsworldwide.org, May 15, 2009.

My biographical profile of Aaron Williams is based on a January 26, 2010, interview with Williams; phone interviews of Kate Raftery and William Reese on January 4, 2010; the official Peace Corps biography on www.peacecorps.gov; the biography on the White House press release announcing the appointment, July 14, 2009, www .whitehouse.gov/the_press_office; and the transcript of Tavis Smiley's interview of Williams on October 12, 2009, www.pbs.org.

The comments of Hugh Pickens about the confirmation hearings were posted as "Senate Confirmation Hearings for Aaron Williams to Become the 18th Director of the Peace Corps" on www.peacecorpsonline.org on July 20, 2009. David Gauvey Herbert's interview of Aaron Williams, "As the Peace Corps Turns 50, What Now?" ran as an "Insider Interview" in the *National Journal,* September 17, 2009. Williams's remarks clarifying what he meant were made in our January 26, 2010, interview.

Afterword: Does the Peace Corps Do Any Good?

The story of Peruvian president Alejandro Toledo and the Peace Corps Volunteers is based on Tyler Bridges, "The Peace Corps President," *Tucson Weekly,* September 8, 2005; Nancy and Joel Meister, "Making a Difference: One Life At a Time," *Peace Corps Writers,* July 2002; Tyler Bridges, "The Professor and the President," *Palo Alto Weekly,* July 21, 2004; and Tyler Bridges, "The Contender," *Stanford Magazine,* March 1, 2001. Toledo's remarks to the Peace Corps were reprinted in "Toledo Thanks Peace Corps," posted at Peace Corps Online (www.peacecorpsonline.org), March 12, 2006.

The 2008 annual report can be found on www.peacecorpsonlinelorg. The quote of Debbie Erickson can be found in Terence Smith, "Peace Corps: Alive But Not So Well," *New York Times Magazine,* December 36, 1977. Judy Guskin's quote can be found in Milton Viorst, ed., *Making a Difference: The Peace Corps at Twenty-Five* (New York: Weidenfeld & Nicolson, 1986), p. 177. Hapgood and Bennett reprinted excerpts from Leslie Hanscom's evaluation of Afghanistan on pp. 120–22.

Details about the Wisconsin calendar can be found at www.rpcv.calendar.org, about the work of the Peace Corps Alumni Foundation for Philippine Development at www.rpcvphilippines.org, about the work of the Returned Peace Corps Volunteers of South Florida at www.rpcvsf.org, and about the Marafiki wa Tanzania at www .fotanzania.org.

Matt Marek's story was told as "Former NPCA Staffer on the Ground in Haiti for Red Cross," Peace Corps Polyglot, blog of the National Peace Corps Association, www.peacecorpsconnect.org, January 14, 2010, and as "People Who Make a Difference—Matthew Marek," on the Red Cross Web site, www.redcross.org, January 13, 2010. The Alice O'Grady story comes from the Accra Academy Alumni Web site, www .accraacaalumni.com, and from a July 31, 2008, e-mail sent by Laura Damon to all members of Ghana I.

The names of noted alumni come almost entirely from the Peace Corps Web site, www.peacecorps.gov. Jack Vaughn told me the story about Ambassador Robert Gelbard in a phone conversation on March 27, 2009.